.

PSYCHOPATHY, PERVERSION, AND LUST HOMICIDE

PSYCHOPATHY, PERVERSION, AND LUST HOMICIDE

Recognizing the Mental Disorders That Power Serial Killers

Duane L. Dobbert

Forensic Psychology

PRAEGER

An Imprint of ABC-CLIO, LLC

A B C CLIO

Santa Barbara, California • Denver, Colorado • Oxford, England

Library of Congress Cataloging-in-Publication Data

Dobbert, Duane L.
   Psychopathy, perversion, and lust homicide : recognizing the mental disorders that power serial killers / Duane L. Dobbert.
      p. cm.
   Includes index.
   ISBN 978-0-313-36621-5 (hard copy : alk. paper) — ISBN 978-0-313-36622-2 (ebook)
   1. Sex crimes—United States. 2. Serial murderers—United States—Biography. 3. Sex offenders—United States. 4. Serial murders—United States—Case studies. 5. Psychosexual disorders. I. Title.
   HV6592.D64 2009
   364.152'32092273—dc22   2009014079

13   12   11   10   09   1   2   3   4   5

This book is also available on the World Wide Web as an eBook.
Visit www.abc-clio.com for details.

ABC-CLIO, LLC
130 Cremona Drive, P.O. Box 1911
Santa Barbara, California 93116-1911

This book is printed on acid-free paper. ∞
Manufactured in the United States of America

This book is dedicated to Joyce Elaine Dobbert,
my wife and partner in all things important.
Without her personal sacrifice and unconditional
support, this book would not have been published.

Contents

Preface

The U.S. public has a love affair with mystery and crime. Mystery has long been a staple in popular reading, while the publicization of criminal forensics in high-profile crimes and trials, and the evolution of a seemingly endless stream of movies and television series, has precipitated a quantum leap in interest in the justice disciplines. Forensic professionals thank Hannibal Lecter and *CSI: Crime Scene Investigation* for bringing their profession from the Hollywood backlot to the front stage. However, this interest and notoriety expose the public to forensic capabilities without complete accuracy. Hollywood portrays DNA analysis, for example, as a scientific activity that can be completed within the hour-long weekly segment of a forensic series, while in reality the laboratory process takes much longer, and the volume of requests for analysis has produced backups that exceed six months.

On the other hand, this exposure has precipitated a public demand for knowledge regarding the realities of criminal activity. Forensic professionals are now responding not only to the requests of the criminal justice system, but also to a demanding and knowledgeable media spurred on by the need to scoop the story and meet the demands of the knowledge-thirsty public. Forensic professionals can no longer rely on esoteric jargon to explain their findings, but rather must find language that meets the average reader's ability to understand. Juries no longer accept the testimony of forensics experts at face value, but rather expect to understand the findings and rule on their relevance to a particular case.

Forensic professionals are popular invitees to cocktail and dinner parties. Previously excused as "science/math types," they are now the evening's entertainment. With the exception of the television talking heads, forensic professionals are beginning to camouflage their career activities to avoid the paparazzi-like attention. Meanwhile, novelists with no forensic credentials and university professors with no practitioner experience exacerbate the proliferation of inaccurate forensic information. Consequently, academically prepared and field-experienced forensic practitioners have been required to take off their lab coats, shake off their need for privacy, and exit the "forensic closet." The public demands, and has a reasonable expectation of understanding, information about the reality of criminal activity and forensic science. Forensic professionals must provide accurate and answers to the public understandable to the layperson. Failure to do so results in a continuous stream of inaccurate information supplied by the forensic "wannabes."

Serial murder tops the list of the criminal activities that most interest the general public, which is infatuated with the intellectual chess game of "Who done it and why?" The public has difficulty understanding that information regarding an ongoing investigation is withheld. The answer, "because it's an ongoing investigation," is no longer acceptable. The media demand information because their readers and listeners need it to continue their intellectual chess game—their real-life version of "Clue." Media demands and subsequent airing of vital information commonly contaminate ongoing investigations and increase the difficulty of investigating the crime.

The other obvious reason why criminal investigators and forensic professionals try to keep their findings from public exposure is that the information is incomplete in relationship to the investigation. Investigation of a crime with an unknown suspect requires comparison of forensic data from similar crimes from the past. This process was hampered throughout most of the history of criminal investigation by the absence of a criminal history depository. It was not until 1985 that the U.S. Federal Bureau of Investigation (FBI) implemented the Violent Criminal Apprehension Program (VICAP). The goal of VICAP was to become a central depository for data on violent crimes throughout the United States. While the objective was worthy, it was also lofty. The FBI does not have the authority to demand the reporting of crime by law enforcement officials through VICAP. It can request reporting, and the federal government can tie monetary rewards to compliance, but it cannot require adherence. Law enforcement is overburdened with reporting functions. Law enforcement jurisdictions are notorious for their unwillingness to share information on unsolved crimes. They are not interested in having another jurisdiction create the illusion that they are better because they solved the crime. The prima donna approach of the FBI has done little to change this attitude. Law enforcement agencies are not willing to share in the "collar." This mentality, in which "To Protect and Serve" is germane only to specific jurisdictions where a crime has occurred, is a significant hurdle to solving crimes committed by persons who move about committing crimes in different locations—as is commonly the case with serial killers.

Consequently, serial killers have been and continue to be successful in eluding detection and apprehension. The public outcry is "how could this person commit so many murders over such a long period of time without being caught?" The inquiry is valid. The answer is an embarrassment for the criminal justice system. It is a systemic failure to share information and look beyond the individual murder that is committed in a specific jurisdiction. If one considers the number of individual jurisdictions throughout the United States, then in the absence of shared information, a serial killer may never be recognized because he is always a "first offender" in every individual jurisdiction.

The concept of investigating individual crimes is also a hurdle. Unless a particular crime is particularly heinous or the victim has celebrity status, the case becomes one of many being investigated by a jurisdiction. In large urban areas, murders are commonplace and homicide units are attempting to investigate numerous cases at the same time. Detectives find themselves "putting out fires," running from one lead to another, perhaps on multiple cases. It is difficult to visualize patterns of behavior when the workload is demanding.

While VICAP's goal is admirable, the continuation of serial murder is a demonstration of its limited effectiveness. The U.S. Constitution establishes the right of individual states to govern their constituents, and consequently the federal government, via the FBI, cannot intrude in an individual state beyond their designated jurisdiction without invitation from the state. Therefore, it behooves individual jurisdictions to assimilate new knowledge.

To answer the "Who are they?" and "Why?" inquiries requires analysis of convicted serial killers. It has long been the assumption that serial killers have little in common with each other and, consequently, cannot be recognized. This book demonstrates the opposite. It examines the social and criminal histories, psychological profiles, and behavior patterns of 22 infamous serial killers. As the reader proceeds from case to case, he or she will recognize similarities in behavioral patterns as suggested by the author.

The author presents the following hypothesis: Is it not logical to assume that if we can identify similarities in the behavioral patterns of serial killers, then we may be able to recognize these patterns in an individual crime? Is it then possible to delineate a suspect group according to the behavior demonstrated in the crime? Is it also possible to identify precursor behaviors and utilize these as a variable in plea bargaining and sentencing?

The author not only suggests this possibility, but also demonstrates it.

Acknowledgments

I am pleased to acknowledge the research assistance provided by the following undergraduate and graduate students in the Criminal Forensic Studies Program of the College of Professional Studies at Florida Gulf Coast University.

RESEARCH ASSOCIATES

Patrick Atwell
Andrea Benscoter
Kaylynn Berrios
Merilee Bingham
Ashley Bryant
Holly Cholvin
Kim Detscher
Carrie Ernst
Sarah Hetzler
Sandi Kraft
Amanda McNall
Nicole Negron
Courtney Rhoden
Jennifer Rogers
Valerie Ziajka

1

Definition and Description of Lust Homicide

The Merriam-Webster Dictionary defines homicide as "a killing of one human being by another," and defines murder as "the crime of unlawfully killing a person especially with malice aforethought." As the subject of this book is the premeditated killing of numerous persons, the term "murder" is more appropriate for our discussion.

Merriam-Webster defines lust as "intense or unbridled sexual desire." Thus the combined definition of lust murder is the premeditated unlawful killing of a person motivated by intense and unbridled sexual desire.

Such is the case with the examples provided in the Preface. Jeffrey Dahmer, Ted Bundy, John Wayne Gacy, Kenneth Bianchi, Ed Gein, Richard Ramírez, and Henry Lee Lucas are serial killers who unlawfully and with premeditation killed hundreds of persons in meeting their intense and unbridled sexual desires. While many persons kill others unlawfully and with premeditation, their act is not typically motivated by intense sexual desire.

The act of homicide may or may not be premeditated or intentional. A drunk driver whose erratic driving results in the death of another is not guilty of premeditation or intent, but rather is guilty of killing another person by driving while impaired by alcohol. In a state of sobriety, the driver has no intention of killing another person. Likewise, an armed robber may have no intention of killing a store clerk until the store clerk resists and confronts him with a handgun. The ensuing death was not premeditated. The armed robbery was premeditated. Current criminal codes define the death of a person during the commission of a felony as felony murder, and the defendant faces the same penalties as a person who kills with premeditation.

A death resulting from a bar fight is usually not premeditated and intentional. The dead person may have initiated the fight resulting in his or her own death. Regardless, an unlawful death of a person has taken place. In the absence of a weapon, the person committing the crime would more than likely be charged with a lesser offense—second degree or nonpremeditated murder—resulting in a significantly reduced sentence.

Consequently, one must carefully contemplate the circumstances leading up to and resulting in the death of a person. In order for a definition of "lust homicide/murder" to be established, two conditions must be met:

1. Is the death of the person unlawful, intentional, and premeditated?
2. Is the death the result of the motivation of intense sexual desire?

In the absence of one of these prerequisites, a different definition must be prescribed.

It is significant to examine the concept of "unlawful" in relationship to conduct that fits the second criterion: intense sexual desire. It is not uncommon for persons to die during sexual activity. What if the death occurs during a behavior statutorily designated as a criminal sexual conduct? For example, if a man is engaged in sexual intercourse with a prostitute and dies during this engagement, is the prostitute guilty of lust homicide/murder? The act of prostitution is considered criminal sexual conduct in 49 of the 50 states, the exception being Nevada; therefore the act of prostitution is unlawful. The act of prostitution is also premeditated. However, the prostitute has no intention of killing her customer. Consequently, she would not be charged with premeditated lust homicide/murder.

In contrast is the case of serial killer Aileen Wournos. Wournos was convicted of the murders of six strangers, committed during 1989 and 1990 while working as a prostitute. Interestingly, while she did commit these murders with intent and premeditation and during acts of criminal sexual conduct, she did not commit them with the motivation of intense sexual desire. Her motivations for the murders were robbery and retribution to those men from her past who abused her. Further, "dead men cannot identify and testify." However, in this day of DNA sequencing, dead men *can* identify and testify, and they tell no tales. Aileen Wournos was a deeply disturbed woman whose life, from a very early age, was characterized by abuse. She did not commit her murders because of intense sexual drive and consequently, is excluded from the definition of a lust homicide/murder serial killer and this study.

Other circumstances also muddy the water. Statistics indicate that 60 percent of women who die annually from wrongful causes die at the hands of current or previous lovers. These deaths are attributed to cases of domestic violence and violence by former intimate partners. Should these cases be defined as lust homicide/murder? At first blush, it appears that the criteria established in the definition have been met; however, further scrutiny indicates otherwise.

Women who die at the hands of current or former intimate partners are particularly apt to be victims of wrongful death precipitated by anger, rage, jealousy, and retribution. The motivation for these deaths is not intense sexual drive. These men kill their girlfriend, ex-girlfriend, spouse, or ex-spouse because they are angry. The anger may be direct or displaced. Men kill this group of women because they are angry with them or are displacing their aggression upon them. A husband who spent his paycheck at the tavern takes his aggression out directly on his wife when she confronts him about his irresponsible drunken behavior. A man who is reprimanded by his supervisor cannot take out his aggression directly on the supervisor for fear of losing his job, and therefore he beats his wife or girlfriend to release his rage. Such direct or displaced anger results in thousands of wrongful deaths each year.

Similarly, women die at the hands of ex-boyfriends and ex-husbands who cannot accept rejection or are jealous of their former partner's new suitor. While displacing their anger on the new suitor may be more appropriate and cathartic for such men, the potential of being the recipient of a beating is a deterrent. Consequently, the weaker woman becomes the recipient of the beating.

In both situations, the motivation influencing the behavior is not intense sexual desire. In some of these cases, the victim may also be sexually assaulted; however, it is not intense sexual desire that precipitates the sexual assault, but rather a desire to inflict retribution and humiliation. Finally, the rage is uncontrollable and the death is accidental rather than premeditated. The physical and sexual assault may have been premeditated, but the death was not.

For the purposes of this study, then, the sample of murderers to be considered is governed by the following criteria:

1. They must have committed multiple murders over a course of time, in contrast to a mass murderer, who kills many persons at one time,
2. The deaths must be premeditated and intentional;
3. The murders must be motivated by intense sexual desire.

Bibliography and Suggested Readings

American Psychiatric Association. (2000). *Diagnostic and Statistical Manual of Mental Disorders* (Rev. 4th ed.). Arlington, VA: Author.

Andrews, D., & Bonta, J. (1994). *The Psychology of Criminal Conduct.* Cincinnati, OH: Anderson.

Brussel, J. (1968). *Casebook of a Crime Psychiatrist.* New York: Geis.

Dobbert, D. L. (2004). *Halting the Sexual Predators among Us.* Westport, CT: Praeger.

Dobbert, D. L. (2007). *Understanding Personality Disorders.* Westport, CT: Praeger.

Eller, J. (2006). *Violence and Culture.* Belmont, CA: Thomson.

Fox, J., & Levin, J. (2001). *The Will to Kill.* Needham Heights, MA: Allyn & Bacon.

Hankin, B., & Abela, J. (2005). *Development of Psychopathology.* Thousand Oaks, CA: Sage.

Holmes, R., & Holmes, S. (2002). *Profiling Violent Crimes.* Thousand Oaks, CA: Sage.

Pervin, L. (1990). *Handbook of Personality.* New York: Guilford.

Prothrow-Stith, D., & Spivak, H. (2004). *Murder Is No Accident.* San Francisco, CA: Jossey-Bass.

Toch, H. (1992). *Violent Men.* Washington, DC: American Psychological Association.

Weiner, N., & Wolfgang, M. (1989). *Pathways to Criminal Violence.* Newberry Park, CA: Sage.

Yarris, R. (1991). *Homicide: Causative Factors and Roots.* Lexington, MA: Lexington.

Yudofsky, S. (2005). *Fatal Flaws.* Arlington, VA: American Psychiatric Association.

Zahn, M., Brownstein, H., & Jackson, S. (2004). *Violence: From Theory to Research.* Southington, CT: Anderson.

2

Clinical Definition and Description of Psychopathy

The term "psychopathy" defies a clear definition. The origin of the term is from the first two editions of the *Diagnostic and Statistical Manual of Mental Disorders, DSM-I* (1952) and *DSM-II* (1968), authored and published by the American Psychiatric Association. In the third edition, *DSM-III* (1981), the American Psychiatric Association attempted to clarify the diagnostic classification by changing the term to "antisocial personality disorder." Controversy continued and the criterion for this classification was modified in the *DSM-III-R* (revised, 1987), the *DSM-IV* (1994), and the *DSM-IV-TR* (text revision, 2000).

Despite continuing efforts to bring consensus to the classification, the controversy was exacerbated. Clinicians cannot agree on a definition that covers the full range of symptoms, etiologies, and behaviors of this classification. The matter is further convoluted by the addition of the terms "sociopath," "sociopathic personality disorder," and "sociopathy." This author chooses not to identify different terms for a similar set of symptoms and behaviors. Rather, I suggest that psychopathy, sociopathy, and antisocial personality disorder represent the same set of symptoms and behaviors, but sit on a continuum from less to more severe. I contend that attempting to differentiate the three is a fruitless debate and confusing to this audience.

It is simply more convenient to utilize the current American Psychiatric Association definition of "antisocial personality disorder" and acknowledge that persons afflicted with this disorder experience it at different levels of severity, resulting in differing behavioral manifestations from mild to extreme. This approach is also appropriate because clinicians offering current diagnoses and testimony must follow the established professional criteria set forth by the American Psychiatric Association in the *DSM-IV-TR* (2000). As it is common for "lay" persons to recognize the term "psychopathy," this term will be utilized throughout this study.

The American Psychiatric Association's current definition of antisocial personality disorder is as follows:

DSM-IV-TR Diagnostic Criteria for Antisocial Personality Disorder (301.7)
    A. There is a pervasive pattern of disregard for and violation of the rights of others occurring since age 15 years, as indicated by three (or more) of the following:

1. failure to conform to social norms with respect to lawful behaviors as indicated by repeatedly performing acts that are grounds for arrest
2. deceitfulness, as indicated by repeated lying, use of aliases, or conning others for personal profit or pleasure
3. impulsivity or failure to plan ahead
4. irritability and aggressiveness, as indicated by repeated physical fights or assaults
5. reckless disregard for safety of self or others
6. consistent irresponsibility, as indicated by repeated failure to sustain consistent work behavior or honor financial obligations
7. lack of remorse, as indicated by being indifferent to or rationalizing having hurt, mistreated, or stolen from another.

    B. The individual is at least age 18 years.
    C. There is evidence of conduct disorder with onset before age 15 years.
    D. The occurrence of antisocial behavior is not exclusively during the course of schizophrenia or a manic episode. [Dobbert, 2004, p.79]

While the above definition is designated for the classification of antisocial personality disorder, this definition will be also utilized for the term "psychopathy" utilized throughout this book.

In acknowledgement that the three terms previously discussed (psychopathy, sociopathy, and antisocial personality disorder) are differentiated by the severity of the symptoms and behaviors, a discussion of the parameters will assist in the understanding these differences while placed on the same continuum.

A. A PERVASIVE PATTERN OF DISREGARD FOR THE RIGHTS OF OTHERS

The first of the four primary criteria listed above (A–D) suggests that there is room for differentiation in severity: "There is a pervasive pattern of disregard for and violation of the rights of others occurring since age 15 years, as indicated by three (or more) of the following. . . ." A person thus cannot be diagnosed with antisocial personality disorder unless they demonstrate at least three of the second-level criteria listed under this primary criterion; however, the American Psychiatric Association identifies seven such criteria (1–7), suggesting that a person who demonstrates more than three is more severely afflicted. I will consider each of the seven second-level criteria in turn.

1. Failure to conform to social norms with respect to lawful behaviors as indicated by repeatedly performing acts that are grounds for arrest

Criterion (1) is sufficiently vague to suggest that there are great variations in the violations of social norms that are grounds for arrest. Obviously, one must inquire as to the minimum number of incidents after which such acts are considered to have been performed "repeatedly." Further, one must inquire as to the severity of the unlawful behavior. Unlawful behavior has numerous possible definitions. On the least severe end of the behavioral continuum are those behaviors that are defined as "status offenses." The Juvenile Code of every state prescribes behaviors that, if performed by a minor child, are subject to the jurisdiction of the juvenile court. These same behaviors, if performed by a person not defined as a "minor child," are not violations of law. Examples of these "status offenses" include running away from home, skipping school, smoking, and incorrigibility or not obeying the lawful commands of one's parents or guardian. Should a youth reside in a state where a 15-year-old is considered a minor child (as is the case in virtually all states), then the commission of these behaviors is a violation of law and the child is subject to the jurisdiction of the juvenile court, which may impose punishments including incarceration. This youth also meets criterion (1) for the diagnosis of antisocial personality disorder.

On the opposite end of the criterion (1) behavioral continuum will be considerably more severe behavior, up to and including multiple murders. However, the criterion fulfilled by these behaviors remains the same, although the severity of the behaviors has significantly increased. Consequently, the type and severity of the violations of law are strong indicators of the severity of the disorder. While multiple murders are very obvious indicators of disorder, one must evaluate other behaviors and their degrees of severity. This examination and judgment is in the hands of the clinician and perhaps the courts. Due to the significant level of vagueness in the American Psychiatric Association's definition, interpretations are subject to the values of the person in judgment as well as the social norms of the specific geographic location.

A 15-year-old or older youth who resides in a small rural community and repeatedly smokes marijuana may be considered a serious law violator, while the same youth repeatedly smoking marijuana in an urban community may be considered to be merely conforming to the expectations of his peer group. Likewise, a person who repeatedly shoplifts is a concern in a small rural community, while the same person residing in a major urban community is, so to speak, "small potatoes." The law enforcement agencies in urban communities have much more severe crimes to investigate and the courts would be absolutely overwhelmed if every shoplifter was arrested and prosecuted.

In closing this discussion of criterion (1), it should be noted that numerous variables intervene in producing behaviors, and consequently a clear and just definition of psychopathy is not readily formulable.

2. Deceitfulness, as indicated by repeated lying, use of aliases, or conning others for personal profit and pleasure

Again in criterion (2), there is a very wide range of behaviors that may qualify one for a diagnosis of psychopathy. Recognizing that the age of 15 clearly falls into the adolescent age group, the behavior of deceitfulness or lying is an expected behavior. The caveat of "for personal profit and pleasure" does not exclude typical adolescent behavior. Adolescents lie to avoid the consequences of their behavior, which, when reversed, is the attainment of pleasure.

In contrast, a person who adopts a new identity for purposes of theft is displaying a much more serious behavior. The person who creates elaborate plans to "con" others out of their personal possessions is also demonstrating behavior closer to the severe end of the continuum. Where then does one draw the line for meeting this criterion? The criterion lacks quantitative, time frame, and descriptive variables to assist in the judgment of the behavior, and thus loses the quality of objectivity. Again, the judgment is in the "eye of the beholder" and subject to geographical differences in norms, values, and mores.

3. Impulsivity or failure to plan ahead

Criterion (3) is a definition of adolescence. All adolescents demonstrate differing levels of impulsivity. It is inherent to the developmental stage. Failure to recognize the consequences of one's behavior, the inability to defer gratification, and the attitude of "if it feels good, do it" are foundation expectations for the developmental stage of adolescence. Few youths are blessed with the discipline to evaluate all of the consequences of their actions or avoid pleasurable activities. This criterion is further complicated by physiological variables. Youths afflicted with attention deficit and/or hyperactivity disorders have even less capacity to plan ahead and avoid impulsivity.

Normal adolescence expires with time and is replaced by responsible, rational behavior. In contrast, the adult who does not plan ahead and evaluate the consequences of his impulsive actions is at risk of achieving this criterion. An adult's impulsive behavior that subjects him and others to harm is of concern, and the seriousness of his behaviors positions him on the continuum for this criterion. This criterion is less subject to variations in judgment influenced by individual and geographical norms. Irresponsible impulsive behavior is readily determined in mature adults.

4. Irritability and aggressiveness, as indicated by physical fights or assaults

Numerous clinicians have suggested that the trait or behavior of "irritability" be removed from criterion (4). Irritable behavior has numerous etiologies in chronic or acute states that may be precipitated by physical, emotional, and situational variables and are not as obvious or relevant as the "aggressiveness, as indicated by physical fights or assaults" criterion. This latter aspect of the criterion requires examination and judgment.

Fighting and assaultive behaviors also fall on a continuum of less to more severity. Many youths grow up in an environment where aggressive and fighting behavior is normative. The young man who grows up wrestling, boxing, and playing football and hockey, grows up "rough and tough." The behavior is usually modeled and reinforced by fathers and brothers. It is not these behaviors that are wrong, but rather, how they are manifested. The youth and adult who is an aggressive hockey player commonly finds himself "throwing his gloves on the ice" and fighting a player from an opposing team. The football linebacker who is not filling the holes and hitting hard finds himself sitting on the bench. These activities often continue long into adulthood, and do not meet criterion (4).

Behaviors that do meet criterion (4) are manifested on the street, in the tavern, and in the workplace. These behaviors are obvious because the afflicted person is "looking" for a fight and initiates one. Further, and most significantly, he has intent of causing pain and injury. He does not stop his assault when it is obvious he has won the fight. He continues to pummel the other party into absolute submission. He will also commonly use a weapon. These behaviors are the serious end of the criterion (4) continuum.

This criterion also must take into consideration forcing another into non-consensual sexual activity. Rape and other forms of nonconsensual sex are at the very end of the continuum and must be viewed as having much greater significance than the previous criterion, (3).

5. Reckless disregard for safety of self or others

This criterion is also influenced by adolescence. Adolescents are notorious for their involvement in extreme and dangerous activities. Immaturity and the failure to consider the consequences of one's actions are typical adolescent characteristics. Consequently, one must contemplate whether participation in a dangerous activity is characteristic of the age and maturity of the individual. Adolescents often believe that they are invincible, and that the fact that someone else was injured doing a given activity does not mean they will be. Adolescents are adventurous, full of life, and easily influenced by their peers. Adults forget how many times their mothers inquired, "If John jumps off the end of cliff, does that mean you have to do likewise?" Of course, all adolescents respond, "Of course not," but are secret jumpers. If John survived the jump and found it thrilling, you know others will follow his lead.

This criterion requires examination not only of age and maturity, but also of the degree of disregard for the safety of others. A youth may ride his motorcycle too fast, but may choose to slow down if his girlfriend is sitting on the back and asks him to do so because she is frightened. Failure to slow down when asked demonstrates not only immaturity and disregard for his own safety, but also disregard for the safety of his girlfriend, and in essence disrespects her. Chronic disregard for the safety of others is the major concern of this criterion, and it plays out along a continuum.

The occasional disregard for others' safety because of a lack of sensitivity sits at one end of the continuum; the continuous disregard for the safety of others is at the opposite end. This continuous disregard for the safety of others is symptomatic of a level of egocentricity in which an individual takes others are considerably less significant than him- or herself. If a person continues his dangerous activity even in light of the danger to others, he is selfish and finds the other's safety insignificant and secondary to his own pleasure. These behaviors are also distinguished by levels of severity. The father who is more interested in watching his favorite sport on television while babysitting his infant demonstrates a level of disregard and egocentricity. The situation becomes increasingly severe if he is watching his sporting event in the family room and his toddler is playing outside by the pool. This is a direct disregard for the safety of others, but seriously dangerous.

A father who rides his motorcycle after drinking and without his helmet is foolish and disregards the well-being of his family should he crash. This is an indirect form of disregard for the safety of others. A father who drinks and rides his motorcycle without wearing his helmet *and* takes his young child along for the ride, also without a helmet, is directly disregarding the safety of others.

As with the other criteria, one must carefully examine age, maturity, and frequency of behaviors before criterion (5) is counted in a diagnosis of psychopathy.

6. Consistent irresponsibility, as indicated by repeated failure to sustain consistent work behavior or honor financial obligations

This criterion on its own is precipitated by numerous variables. One does not have to be diagnosed with psychopathy to be financially irresponsible or unable to maintain gainful employment. In contemporary society, and particularly in the era of subprime mortgage rates, financial irresponsibility is commonplace and precipitates financial disaster for normally responsible persons. Foreclosures are at a historic high, and while greed and financial irresponsibility may be the causes in many cases, the more normal desire to have one's own home is also a precipitating variable.

The concept of maintaining gainful employment must also be carefully examined. There is a population within the United States that will not work. This large group of people are so numerous that they are statistically significant and are excluded from the assessment of the unemployment figure. These people are content to stay at home and not even look for work. They may fake illnesses and disabilities to qualify for social security unemployment benefits, choose to live with others who will financially take care of them, and procrastinate in looking for work.

This criterion is fulfilled by, for example, a person who commits himself to a contract and then does not fulfill it, a man who buys a home never intending to make a payment and force eviction, or a person who can never maintain employment. Such a person seeks out and gains employment only to demonstrate work habits that force the employer to terminate him. It is also common for such an individual to work at a job long enough to become a union member or to be eligible for unemployment compensation should he be released. This latter person manipulates the workplace for his own egocentric agenda.

7. Lack of remorse, as indicated by being indifferent to or rationalizing having hurt, mistreated, or stolen from another

This criterion is very significant, and is one that this author contends needs to be requisite for a diagnosis of psychopathy. Sigmund Freud would have referred to the behavior described in this criterion as "superego deficient." The person who demonstrates this criterion possesses a deficiency in conscience. It is because of this deficiency in conscience that he can hurt, mistreat, or steal from others and experience no guilt or remorse.

This criterion is very difficult for the majority of people to understand. If one possesses a conscience, it is extremely difficult to comprehend or believe someone who does not. However, when one intellectually accepts the possibility of existence without a conscience, the behaviors that can be performed by a conscience-deficient person are readily observable. The person who is conscience-deficient experiences no guilt for his behaviors, and consequently does what he pleases without concern for others. It is the extreme of egocentricity. The only things that are important are those that meet his needs. Others' needs are irrelevant.

When a person of conscience commits a behavior that wrongs another, he experiences guilt. If his act goes undetected, he experiences anxiety that it will become detected and he will be identified as the perpetrator. Conscience is a broad concept, but this moral compass controls our behavior. The guilt and anxiety reflect not merely the fear of being caught for the behavior, but rather an awareness that the behavior is inherently wrong. In the absence of the intrinsic feeling of right versus wrong, no anxiety or guilt is experienced in performing socially determined "wrong" behavior.

This leads to the interesting discussion regarding the origin of the conscience. How does an individual develop a conscience and thus the knowledge of what is right and what is wrong? Even Darwin would conclude that the conscience is developed though nurture and not a genetically created psychological foundation. Parenting and guidance from others, good and bad, shapes the development or lack of development of the conscience. Lawrence Kohlberg, an American developmental psychologist, postulated (1958) that morals develop through stages. Children learn their early morals and values from their parents or other parental figures. They do not cognitively process situations regarding value or moral decisions at an early age, instead responding to situations based upon what they have learned from their parental figures. It is not until they begin to mature that they cognitively process situations independently.

Parents or parental figures typically instruct their children with prescribed behaviors, reinforce them through rewards, and attempt to extinguish wrong behaviors through punishment. These persons in the guidance role have significant direct influence upon the development of the conscience. The system of reinforcement and punishments establishes a set of appropriate behaviors and, consequently, inappropriate behaviors. The consistent application of rewards and punishment ingrain a set of behaviors that are deemed right or wrong. When a child performs a wrong behavior, one that hurts another, he or she begins to feel remorse. The child may feel truly sorry for the injury he has caused another, or he may feel sorry that he has been caught doing the wrong behavior and expect punishment. True conscience demonstrates remorse for the injury caused, rather than only a fear of punishment.

Albert Bandura, a developmental psychologist, posits in his social learning theory that behavior does not have to be experienced in order to be learned. This theoretical perspective suggests that children learn from observing others. The child who observes his brother punished for a specific behavior learns that the behavior is "wrong" and should be avoided. On the other hand, when he observes his father strike his mother over a disagreement and sees that there is no consequence, he learns that striking others is an acceptable behavior—or at least that striking his mother, or striking girls and women, is acceptable. Thus the development of conscience is influenced.

Two additional etiological perspectives include the "overly pampered" child and the "abused and neglected" child. An overly pampered child is both directly and indirectly informed that he is special and better than others. A child who is always praised and informed that he is the brightest, most attractive, and so on learns that he is different from others, in fact, that they are better than others. If there are no consequences, or inconsistent application of consequences, for inappropriate behavior, a child learns that "anything is okay"—that there are no "wrong" behaviors for him, and he is special and better than others. This pampered child usually finds out something is amiss when he attends school and his "special" status is not acknowledged by the teacher and his peer group. His inappropriate behaviors are incongruent with the classroom rules and the social mores of the playground. His behavior changes to meet the norm, unless his parents vehemently support him.

If the parent intervenes and prevents this natural adjustment of the child's behavior, the child's egocentric perception continues to develop. If parents hire an attorney to defend their child after the child is expelled for smoking marijuana in school, the child learns that rules, regulations, and laws are for others, not for him. This child develops no conscience for injury to others, because others are insignificant. His needs, wants, and desires are paramount. He is entitled to do as he pleases.

Children who are severely abused and neglected often learn that they cannot trust their parent or parental figure for a safe environment. They also learn that this supposedly close person is the source of their pain and suffering. These children learn they can only trust themselves and develop an egocentricity to look out for themselves and themselves only. As a result, they develop a deficient conscience. They do not experience anxiety, guilt, or remorse for their behaviors that are injurious to others. Their motto becomes "Do unto others, before they do unto you."

The range of behaviors that fall on the criterion (7) continuum are many and diverse in severity. The most serious behaviors at the severe end of the continuum, such as serial rape, lust homicide, and serial murder, are obvious. At the less serious end of the continuum, one finds behaviors that injure others that may not be unlawful, but for which the individual concerned demonstrates an obvious and unusual lack of remorse. A husband who has many mistresses may not be in violation of the law; however, his behavior is harmful to his wife, his children, and the women of his affairs. He feels no guilt for these behaviors and no remorse for the pain that others have experienced. A corporate executive who, in competition for the next promotion, spreads an unsubstantiated rumor that his competitor is having an affair with his secretary, and experiences no remorse for the ensuing fallout, also displays behavior falling under this criterion.

C. THERE IS EVIDENCE OF CONDUCT DISORDER WITH ONSET BEFORE AGE 15 YEARS

This author has chosen to discuss this primary criterion because the diagnostic criteria for conduct disorder correlate very closely with adult psychopathy, the topic of this study, and the discussion suggests that some conduct disorder behavior may, if fact, be predictive of the most severe behaviors of psychopathy.

The American Psychiatric Association indicates that an adult cannot be diagnosed with antisocial personality disorder unless diagnosed with conduct disorder as a child or adolescent. The criteria for a conduct disorder diagnosis fall into general categories including aggressive and violent behavior, destruction of property, pathological lying, theft, and incorrigibility. As in the case of antisocial personality disorder, the severity of conduct disorder includes a significant continuum from least to most severe behaviors in each of the above-mentioned categories, which we will now examine.

As a caveat, it is critically important that the reader carefully consider the following behaviors in light of behaviors that are common and expected with adolescents, as well as differences associated with cultural variation and urban versus rural residency. The reader must also examine his or her personal frame of reference and definitions of appropriate versus inappropriate behavior in order to objectively evaluate this discussion. The values and rules that govern our individual lives and daily choices and activities are vastly diverse. Cultural mores, religion, socioeconomics, and age influence our opinions and, consequently, our judgments. An open mind will benefit the reader as these behaviors are examined.

Aggression and Violent Behavior
Aggressive behavior is widely accepted and many forms of violence are not merely acceptable, but reinforced through rewards. Varsity letters for high

school football are presented as an award for violent aggressive behavior. The adolescent who cannot "take" or "give" violent tackles rides the bench, does not see playing time, and is not rewarded with the Varsity letter. This practice is played out in every high school, junior high school, and "Pop Warner" age-group football team in the United States. Replays of the most violent "hits" from the past weekend's college and pro football games are played over and over on prime-time television. Professional wrestling, boxing, and extreme fighting have an enormous fan base. U.S. society rewards violent aggressive behavior in the sporting arena.

It is not necessary for a youth to participate in a physically aggressive sport in order to adopt an attitude that aggressive violent behavior is acceptable. There are few high school adolescents that do not covet the "varsity jacket." It is the badge of success and is recognized and applauded by adults as well as those youths awaiting their opportunity to demonstrate their violent prowess in athletics. Adolescent females "drool" over the varsity athletes and this is observed by those youths awaiting their chance. Consequently, despite efforts to deter youths from fighting, the rewards for violent encounters outweigh the consequences. A three-day school suspension for fighting is insignificant to a youth who is not openly revered as a "tough" guy who fears little. While parents openly discipline their son for the fighting suspension, many fathers secretly praise their son for "standing his ground." A youth who comes home from school with a black eye and has not defended himself against the school bully is directly and indirectly ridiculed by his family and peers. In other words, it is better to have fought the good fight and lost than to shy away with cowardice.

Consequently, while the American Psychiatric Association may consider fighting a criterion for a diagnosis for conduct disorder, society glamorizes the behavior. Thus, violent aggressive behavior must be carefully examined. While fighting may not be a definitive example of the behavior described by the "aggressive and violent behavior" criterion, the bullying of weaker, smaller, and younger children is an accurate illustrative case. The use of a weapon, when a weapon is not necessary, is another accurate example. The conduct-disordered youth or adolescent delights in causing injury. He is not merely interested in defeating his opponent; he wishes to cause him painful harm.

Theft as been identified as a criterion for a diagnosis of conduct disorder; however, there are few youths and adolescents that have not shoplifted. The aggressive form of theft demonstrated by the conduct-disordered youth or adolescent is strong-arm robbery. Interestingly, while these youths may covet another's money or possession, it is the fear they instill through their violent behavior that thrills them. The "rush" of the encounter and the ensuing pain they deliver is more psychologically rewarding than the physical reward of the money or possession.

Conduct-disordered adolescents also engage in nonconsensual sexual activity. While perhaps stopping short of rape, they will fondle their girl-friend beyond her willingness to participate. Adolescent hormones are expected to run uncontrolled, yet most adolescents will stop at their girl-friend's insistence. Conduct-disordered adolescents do not, as they feel enti-tled and want their sexual desires met without consideration of their date. These youths will also demonstrate their lack of concern for the young woman by bragging about their encounter with their peers.

Another significant expression of violent aggressive behavior is cruelty to animals. This is a common behavior exhibited by conduct-disordered youths and adolescents, and it is a perfect demonstration of a lack of remorse and empathy. The behavior usually starts out with minor cruel activities of kicking cats and dogs, and progresses to the point of killing animals for enjoyment.

Malicious Destruction of Property

It is not uncommon for youths and adolescents to participate in minor instances of malicious destruction of property. Pumpkins are smashed on people's porches, eggs and snowballs are thrown at passing vehicles, and stop signs are stolen. These activities are "rites of passage" for adolescents. It may be inappropriate and unlawful behavior, but is commonplace and not a cri-terion for a diagnosis of conduct-disorder.

Intentional destructive behaviors that cause the victim financial suffering fit the criteria for conduct disorder. The slashing of a teacher's car tires because the teacher "fronted" a youth is an excellent example. The late night smashing of the storefront window of a proprietor who prohibited a youth from coming in his store is another example of a premeditated act of retribution. Arson for the joy of watching the destruction of a building, or in retribution, is a behavior consistent with conduct disorder. All of these behaviors demonstrate a lack of empathy for the victim. Such minimal concern for others is exemplified by the behavior of throwing large rocks off of highway overpasses at passing vehicles.

Incorrigibility

All adolescents demonstrate incorrigibility. It is an expected behavior. This author is more concerned with adolescents that follow all of the parental and school-imposed rules without question or dissent. The developmental stage of adolescence is a time of self-discovery. It is a time to challenge the values imposed by parents and legitimate institutions. It is a time to challenge authority and a time to experiment. Consequently, adolescents smoke tobacco and marijuana, and drink alcohol—behaviors that are inconsistent with their parents', and society's, expectations and laws. The mere fact that the greatest majority of all adolescents engage in some of these activities demonstrates that they are normal expected behaviors and not indicative of conduct disorder.

The American Psychiatric Association and most states consider skipping school, failure to obey reasonable parental commands, and violation of curfew as illegal and indicative of conduct disorder. This author suggests that these behaviors are normal and expected and merely indicative of healthy adolescence. Law prohibits minor children from "running away from home." Juvenile justice professionals recognize that these laws are ludicrous, as adolescents commonly run away from home to escape conditions within the home that include domestic violence, abuse, neglect, and family sexual assault. Securely detaining an adolescent for running away from a neglectful abusive environment is unethical and victimizes the youth a second time. As mentioned above, these behaviors are classified as "status offenses." The youth or adolescent is in violation of the law merely because of his or her status as a "minor child." Interestingly, states differ in their determination of the age of a "minor child". A youth residing in one state is considered a "minor child" until his or her 17th birthday, while in the adjacent state the age may be 15. Consequently, "running away from home" is legal in one state and illegal in the other because of the difference in this definition.

The most serious problem associated with "status offenses" is that a youth who is charged and convicted with one of these behaviors may very well end up detained in a secure residential facility with true conduct-disordered adolescents who have been judged guilty of serious felonious conduct. The negative labeling of being forced into confinement with felonious delinquents has devastating negative implications of the non-conduct-disordered adolescent who was exhibiting expected, normal adolescent behaviors. Society has now labeled this "status offense" youth as a delinquent, and his or her activities and peer group may change. Coaches prohibit these inaccurately defined delinquents from athletic participation, and school principals place them in special education classes. Unfortunately these special education classes are designated for youths or adolescents with severe behavioral problems.

Society's naive response to these "status offense" youth precipitates the development of emotional impairment and subsequent criminal activity.

THE RELATIONSHIP BETWEEN CONDUCT DISORDER AND ANTISOCIAL PERSONALITY DISORDER

Conduct disorder and antisocial personality disorder do correlate. The American Psychiatric Association, through its criteria for antisocial personality disorder, requires that the afflicted individual be previously diagnosed with conduct disorder. However, not all youths or adolescents diagnosed with conduct disorder are subsequently diagnosed with antisocial personality disorder. In summary, all antisocial personality disorder–diagnosed adults were previously conduct disordered youths or adolescents, but not all conduct-disordered youths or adolescents display antisocial personality disorder as adults.

Who then *do* become the adults with antisocial personality disorder? Two variables explain the relationship. The earlier that a youth demonstrates conduct disorder behaviors, the higher the likelihood of developing the adult disorder. Further, the more severe the behaviors on the conduct disorder continuum, the higher the probability of developing the adult disorder. In reality, serious and chronic conduct disorder behavior is predictive of psychopathy.

Bibliography and Suggested Readings

American Psychiatric Association. (2000). *Diagnostic and Statistical Manual of Mental Disorders* (Rev. 4th ed.). Arlington, VA: Author.

Black, D., & Larson, L. (2000). *Bad Boys, Bad Men: Confronting Antisocial Personality Disorder*. New York: Oxford University Press.

Cleckley, H. (1988). *The Mask of Sanity* (5th ed.). Previous editions 1941, 1950, 1955, 1964, 1976. St. Louis: Mosby Co.

Dobbert, D. L. (2004). *Halting the Sexual Predators among Us*. Westport, CT: Praeger.

Dobbert, D. L. (2007). *Understanding Personality Disorders*. Westport, CT: Praeger.

Giannangelo, S. (1996). *The Psychopathology of Serial Murder*. Westport, CT: Praeger.

Hare, R. (1991). *The Hare Psychopathy Checklist—Revised*. Toronto: Multi-Health Systems.

Hare, R. (1996). Psychopathy: A clinical construct whose time has come. *Criminal Justice and Behavior 23*, 25–54.

Hare, R. (1999). *Without Conscience: The Disturbing World of the Psychopaths among Us*. New York: Guilford Press.

Jenkins, R. (1960). The psychopath or antisocial personality. *Journal of Nervous and Mental Disease 131*, 318–34.

Lykken, D. (1995). *The Antisocial Personalities*. Hillsdale: Erlbaum.

McCord, W., & McCord, J. (1964). *The Psychopath: An Essay on the Criminal Mind*. Princeton: Van Nostrand.

Meloy, J. R. (1995). *The Psychopathic Mind: Origins, Dynamics, and Treatment*. New York: Jason Aronson.

Millon, T., Simonsen, E., Birket-Smith, M., & Davis, R. (1998). *Psychopathy: Antisocial, Criminal, and Violent Behavior*. New York: Guilford Press.

Owen, D. (2004). *Criminal Minds: The Science and Psychology of Profiling*. New York: Barnes & Noble.

Petherick, W. (2005). *The Science of Criminal Profiling*. New York: Barnes & Noble Books.

Reid, W., Walker, J., & Dorr, D. (Eds.). (1986). *Unmasking the Psychopath: Antisocial Personality and Related Syndromes*. New York: Norton.

Samenow, S. (2002). *Straight Talk about Criminals: Understanding and Treating Antisocial Behavior*. New York: Jason Aronson.

Samenow, S. (2004). *Inside the Criminal Mind*. New York: Random House.

Sher, K., & Trull, T. (1994). Personality and disinhibitory psychopathology: Alcoholism and antisocial personality disorder. *Journal of Abnormal Psychology 103*, 92–102.

Stout, M. (2005). *The Sociopath Next Door*. New York: Broadway.

Toch, H., & Adams, K. (1994). *The Disturbed Violent Offender*. Washington: American Psychological Association.

Wolman, B. (1999). *Antisocial Behavior: Personality Disorders from Hostility to Homicide*. New York: Prometheus Books.

3

Clinical Definition and Description of the Sexual Paraphilias and Disorders

The American Psychiatric Association, in the *Diagnostic and Statistical Manual of Disorders* (*DSM-IV-TR,* 2000), identifies a set of sexual disorders under the diagnostic classification of paraphilias. Included in this grouping are exhibitionism, fetishism, frotteurism, pedophilia, sexual masochism, sexual sadism, transvestic fetishism, and voyeurism. This list is by no means exclusive. Numerous other paraphilias have been identified and discussed by clinicians. Dobbert, in *Halting the Sexual Predators among Us* (2004), discusses the paraphilias of telephone scatologia, necrophilia, partialism, zoophilia, coprophilia, urophilia, and klismaphilia. The goal of this study is to demonstrate that the motivating variables supporting lust homicide are the sexual paraphilias. Consequently, it is critical to examine these paraphilias in order for the reader to develop a level of familiarity with the general diagnostic category, the specific paraphilias, and the behaviors that are typically manifested.

REQUISITE CRITERIA

In order for a person to be diagnosed with one or more of the sexual paraphilias, a specific criterion must be met. A person who is afflicted with a paraphilia is recurrently and intensely sexually aroused by a specific type of stimulus. Further, it is very significant that these persons generally cannot be sexually aroused in the absence of the specific stimulus. In recognition of this requisite criterion for diagnoses, an evaluation of the specific paraphilias focuses on the stimuli and the behavioral manifestations. The paraphilias will be examined in alphabetical order. This order does not suggest a taxonomy of paraphilias based on the seriousness of their behavioral manifestations. As with the personality disorders, the behavioral manifestations for each of the paraphilias are positioned on a continuum from least to most serious.

GENERAL CHARACTERISTICS

The American Psychiatric Association has determined that the paraphilias, with the exception of sexual masochism, are male-exclusive disorders. This is not to say that no women are afflicted with a paraphilia, but rather that the number of afflicted women is so few compared to the number of afflicted men that they are not statistically significant.

Persons accurately diagnosed with a paraphilia are not exhibiting the behavior because they are mentally ill. Persons afflicted with paraphilias are completely cognizant of their behavior, as well as of the legal status of their conduct. They are also fully aware of the legal sanctions for performing those paraphiliac behaviors that are in violation of the law. They are demonstrating these behaviors because of uncontrollable urges to perform them. These behaviors provide sexual arousal and subsequent sexual gratification. Afflicted persons are fulfilling their intrinsic psychological needs by performing the behavior. Consequently, a plea of insanity is not applicable and will not excuse their unlawful behavior.

Persons may exhibit behaviors of more than one paraphilia. It is critical to carefully examine these behaviors to determine whether a diagnosis of multiple paraphilias is accurate, or whether a primary paraphilia produces behavioral manifestations that may fit the diagnostic criteria for another paraphilia. Such is often the case, as will be examined in the discussion of pedophilia.

COPROPHILIA

Coprophilia is a relatively uncommon paraphilia and unfortunately for the discussion of paraphilias is alphabetically first. Persons afflicted with coprophilia experience recurrent, intense sexual arousal over human feces. The behavioral activities include being in close proximity to, handling, and eating feces. It is rare that a person is diagnosed with this paraphilia, because its definition suggests randomness. It is more common for a person to find sexual arousal from the human waste of a specific person who is of sexual interest. One must then contemplate whether the diagnosis is accurate, or whether the recurrent, intense sexual arousal is instead elicited by the person of sexual attraction and interest. Regardless, this paraphilia suggests significant emotional impairment.

EXHIBITIONISM

A person afflicted with exhibitionism is recurrently, intensely sexually aroused by displaying their genitalia to an unsuspecting stranger. It is important to stress the significance of two aspects of this diagnostic criterion: sexual arousal, and the involvement of an unsuspecting stranger. The element of sexual arousal eliminates an exotic dancer from this diagnosis. The exotic dancer is not sexually aroused while displaying his or her genitalia to customers, but rather is acknowledging that men and women alike will pay him/her to remove clothing. Exotic dance clubs and private party strippers often make a handsome tax-free living by taking off their clothing in the presence of others. The element of an unsuspecting stranger also excludes the exotic dancer from this paraphilia. The audience may be comprised of strangers; however, they have paid an entrance fee because of the expectation that they will watch dancers remove their clothing.

The person accurately diagnosed with this paraphilia displays his genitalia to random persons. The random nature of his victims demonstrates that it is the act of displaying his genitalia that is the arousing stimulus. If a man only displays his genitalia to a specific group, such as elementary-age girls, it is likely that the stimulus is the victim group, and not the act of displaying his genitals. This man is recurrently, intensely sexually aroused by elementary-age girls, and the act of displaying his genitals aims to entice the little girl. He is sexually aroused and subsequently sexually gratified by displaying his genitals to little girls.

Mental illness is another consideration here. The American Psychiatric Association recognizes the behaviors of displaying one's genitals and public masturbation as behavioral manifestations of schizophrenia. Consequently, it is imperative that the person be carefully examined for other diagnostic criteria of schizophrenia.

FETISHISM

A person afflicted with fetishism is recurrently, intensely sexually aroused by a specific inanimate object, the fetish. This paraphilia is generally reserved for men who are sexually aroused by women's undergarments. These men are sexually aroused by the touch and feel of women's underpants, and, in severe cases, they are unable to achieve sexual arousal in the absence of the fetish stimulus. It is relatively common for these afflicted men to wear the underwear themselves, or to require their sex partner to wear them. There are three exclusions that must be acknowledged.

A diagnosis of fetishism is inappropriate if a person is sexually aroused in wearing objects of clothing for purposes of cross-dressing to engage in gay or lesbian sexual activity. The person is not sexually aroused by the wearing of the clothing, but rather is sexually aroused by the sexual activity with a same-gender partner.

A second exclusion pertains to an analysis of the fetish garment. A sexually aroused adult man in possession of the underwear of a prepubescent boy or girl is not sexually aroused by the item of clothing, but rather by the fantasy thought of child who would be wearing the clothing. It is extremely common to find pedophiles in possession of clothing that are age- and gender-relevant to their fantasy love group.

The final exclusion is sex toys. A person is not sexually aroused by the possession of a sex toy, but rather utilizes the sex toy to initiate and enhance sexual arousal and pleasure. Persons who utilize sex toys for self-arousal or as part of a couple's sex play are not afflicted with the fetishism paraphilia. A sex toy is not a fetish, unless a person cannot achieve sexual arousal in its absence.

FROTTEURISM

A person afflicted with the paraphilia frotteurism is recurrently, intensely sexually aroused by the behavior of either fondling or rubbing his genitals on nonconsenting strangers.

The *DSM-IV-TR* discusses behavior that is typical for a consideration of frotteurism. Individuals diagnosed with this paraphilia have the recurring habit of rubbing their genitals against an unknowing and non-consenting person in crowded locations such as subways, buses, and crowded streets. Some may use their hands to fondle the breasts, buttocks, and genitals of non-consenting persons. While performing the behavior, they fantasize that the victim is aroused and enjoying the caress. This behavior intensifies their sexual arousal. (Dobbert, 2004, p. 20)

In comparison with the previous paraphilias, these behaviors are more significant and serious. This man is touching his victim. The behavior is criminal assault and battery. There is one exclusion that may be considered for a diagnosis of frotteurism. Adolescent males in particular are intensely sexually aroused at the opportunity to engage in whatever form of sexual activity they can achieve with their girlfriends. The young man who fails to stop fondling a girlfriend who repeatedly has told him to stop is probably not afflicted with frotteurism, but rather with raging hormones.

Victimology is important to consider with frotteurism. The adolescent or adult male who fondles a prepubescent child is sexually aroused by the fantasy love victim and not the specific fondling behavior. He is more likely afflicted with pedophilia.

Victims of frotteurism who fail to provide a consequence to the offending perpetrator are endangering themselves. It is probable that an offending person chooses to fondle or rub his genitals against a person that he is attracted to. If the behavior is random with women of various ages, then a diagnosis of frotteurism is appropriate; however, if the behavior is restricted to a certain age-group, then one may conclude that the victim is a member of the perpetrator's fantasy love group. If the victim fails to scream or slap the offender, she risks two implications: the offender's behavior is reinforced, and worse, he may believe that the victim truly enjoyed the caress. The potential for reoccurrence of the behavior with the same victim increases significantly. The offender may very well begin a pattern of stalking behavior to identify the victim's workplace, residence, and commonly traveled routes. His behavior becomes more brazen because of the failure to provide a consequence for the fondling. A slap or a scream will inform him that the victim does not consent to his behavior. A criminal charge, and perhaps court-ordered therapy, may deter him from further nonconsenting fondling.

KLISMAPHILIA

Similar to coprophilia, klismaphilia has a focus on human wastes. A person afflicted with klismaphilia is recurrently, intensely sexually aroused over receiving an enema. While this paraphilia is exotic and unusual, it is mentioned here because of its close relationship to sexual masochism and sexual sadism, both of which are discussed later in this chapter. Klismaphilia may be a behavioral manifestation of these paraphilias.

NECROPHILIA

One of the more bizarre sexual paraphilias is necrophilia. The focus of necrophilia is corpses. An individual afflicted with necrophilia has recurrent, intense sexual arousal involving corpses. The severity of the paraphilia is identifiable by the behavior of the paraphiliac. Some individuals are sexually aroused merely by the sight or image of a corpse. On the opposite end of the continuum are the individuals who engage in sexual activity with a corpse. Regardless, the behavior and subsequent intense sexual arousal are aberrant. (Dobbert, 2004, p. 37)

There is significant relevance in including necrophilia in this discussion of the paraphilias. As is demonstrated in the case studies in the second section of this book, many serial killers exhibit behavioral manifestations diagnostically consistent with necrophilia. Jeffrey Dahmer, John Wayne Gacy, and Ed Gein were sexually aroused by activities with corpses.

PARTIALISM

Partialism is a paraphilia that has a wide range of behavioral manifestations. Individuals afflicted with partialism are recurrently, intensely sexually aroused over specific body parts that are not sex organs. This is more common than some of the more exotic paraphilias. On the least serious end of the partialism continuum would be a person who is recurrently, intensely sexually aroused by women's feet. A person so afflicted might find employment in a high-end women's shoe store. Women are delighted to find attentive shoe clerks that admire and compliment them on their feet. The paraphiliac has found the perfect "legal" activity in which to fulfill his sexually aberrant behavior. The attentive shoe clerk sits on a stool in front of the female customer, carefully removes her shoes, and gently massages her feet, much to the delight of the customer. The clerk is sexually aroused by placing her foot in his crotch. His erection goes unnoticed.

On the opposite end of the continuum, the more serious behavioral manifestations include the surgical removal and saving of the desired body part. Jeffrey Dahmer removed and saved body parts from his victims, but these were primarily sex organs. He was not sexually aroused by these body parts in particular, but rather by the memories of his sexual encounters with the victim. Other serial killers have saved body parts not as "trophies" but rather because they produced sexual arousal, and the subsequent fondling produced sexual gratification.

PEDOPHILIA

Persons afflicted with pedophilia are recurrently, intensely sexually aroused by urges for, fantasies of, and the attainment of sexual activity with children. The American Psychiatric Association in their definition specifically indicate "prepubescent" children; however, society is not familiar with that distinction and, consequently, groups all child sex offenders in this diagnostic category. There is a significant and "real" difference between those persons who are sexually aroused by prepubescent children and those sexually aroused by older children, specifically children who have come to puberty. This differentiation must be carefully examined.

Sexual activity with "minor" children is prohibited in every state. There is no such thing as a minor child consenting to sexual relationships. It is prohibited by the criminal codes of every state and the penalties are severe. These penalties include lengthy prison sentences and, commonly, lifelong registration of residence. The younger the assaulted child, the more severe the penalty.

To reiterate, the pedophile is recurrently, intensely sexually aroused by pre-pubescent children. The pedophile will always have a gender and age prefer-ence. It is uncommon for a pedophile to be aroused by both girls and boys. Further, sexual arousal is extremely uncommon with preschool children. Children of elementary school age are the typical fantasy love group. Just as the pedophile will have a gender preference, he will also have an age-group preference within the general category of prepubescents. One may prefer lit-tle girls between the ages of 8–10 years, while another's fantasy love group may be 10- to 12-year-old boys. The gender and age-group preference is unique to the individual pedophile.

Pedophilia is considered to be chronic and lifelong. Pedophiles' thoughts of sexual activity are overwhelming and commonly monopolize all thought processes. The etiology of pedophilia is frequently associated with early child-hood sexual encounters. It is common that a pedophile was raised in an envi-ronment where he was emotionally neglected and/or abused by a trusted person: father, mother, grandparent, uncle, older sibling. The child is emo-tionally neglected, abused, and generally ignored until "bathing," during which the abusive, neglectful individual fondles the child. The trusted per-son demonstrates love and affection and the young child begins to define such sexual contact as the appropriate method of demonstrating love and affection.

The behavioral symptoms of pedophilia begin to manifest at the time of puberty. When the sexually abused adolescent wishes to show love and affec-tion, he does so with sexual behaviors. Adolescents who come to the atten-tion of the authorities for these behaviors commonly receive a therapeutic intervention. As the adolescent is still malleable, the rate of successful reha-bilitation is relatively high. Unfortunately, in the absence of a therapeutic intervention, pedophilia becomes ingrained during psychosexual develop-ment and the rate of successful rehabilitation drops off rapidly. Most clini-cians consider adult pedophiles untreatable, and thus criminal codes provide safety to the community through stiff penalties, including long periods of incarceration.

Pedophiles do not believe their behaviors are wrong or immoral. They believe that loving a child is a normal and appropriate behavior. Pedophiles possess the delusion that the child will love them equally in return. Conse-quently, it is never their intention to kill the child. They love the child. The child dies because he or she begins to cry and scream. The pedophile attempts to silence the screams by putting his hand on the mouth and, inad-vertently, the nose of the child while holding the child down with his body. The adult body weight pressing upon the child, and the clamping shut of the nose and mouth by the man's hand, results in the child's death. Other children die from strangulation, blows to the head, and inhaled chemicals used to silence the child's crying and screaming. Some children die as the result of having the capacity of identifying the perpetrator.

A child abducted by a pedophile stranger rarely lives longer than 24 hours, but while the death is a "wrongful death," it is not premeditated but rather accidental. However, it cannot be considered an accident, because the death happens during the commission of kidnapping. Thus the death is legally considered felony murder, and due to the sexual nature of the abduction it is classified as a "lust homicide" and the subject of this study.

Will the pedophile abduct another child if he has previously murdered a child? The pedophile will experience great remorse and grieve over the death of his fantasy lover. However, the overwhelming pedophiliac sexual desire will return and he will abduct another child. Because it is anomaly for a child abducted by a stranger to live longer than 24 hours, it is highly probable that a pedophile may murder more than one child, qualifying him as a serial killer; and because the motivation driving the abduction is sexual, this behavior is serial lust homicide.

Persons who are recurrently, intensely sexually aroused by children that have reached puberty are referred to as "hebephiles." The prefix "hebe" is derived from "Hebe," the daughter of Hara and Zeus, the Greek goddess of youth, and reflects the concepts of "flowering," sexual maturity, virginity, and purity. Hebephiles, like pedophiles, are sexually aroused by a specific gender and age-group that meets their intrinsic psychosexual needs. They are not sexually aroused by younger children or by older adolescents and adults. They are attracted to the purity of the "virgin" concept, maintaining the delusion that this youth will fall in love with them following their sexual encounter and remain with them as their lover forever. However, this is a false belief and it is very uncommon for a pubescent youth abducted by a stranger to live through the encounter. The hebephile's delusion disappears when the youth fights back and the hebephile realizes that this child will not be his lover forever. The potential for serial lust homicide is again high due to the overwhelming sexual drive. John Wayne Gacy murdered 33 pubescent boys, 27 of whom he buried in his Chicago suburban crawl space.

Some hebephiles have access to pubescent children through marriage. In Vladimir Nabokov's 1955 novel *Lolita,* an adult male marries Lolita's mother to gain access to Lolita. In director Adrian Lyne's 1998 Trimark film production of *Lolita,* actor Jeremy Irons brilliantly demonstrates the overwhelming obsessive nature of hebephilia in marrying Melanie Griffith's character to obtain access to her daughter.

The etiology of hebephilia is similar to pedophilia. While the American Psychiatric Association indicates that pedophilia (and, consequently, hebephilia) is an exclusively male disorder, the number of adult women who engage in sexual activity with adolescent boys appears to be increasing. The recent spate of female teachers being charged with criminal sexual conduct for their sexual activity with adolescent males students suggests that perhaps women are statistically significant in this diagnosis. The question is whether there are an increasing number of women who are afflicted with hebephilia, or whether it is becoming more popular for the victims to come forth with the information. Prior to the first media reports of female teachers involved in sexual conduct with their male adolescent students, the victims were reluctant to come forward. Young men would not have this discussion with their parents and would not engage in "locker room" conversation about the behavior. Further, I suspect that these young male victims did not want the activity to cease. It was a pleasurable experience that they did not want terminated by idle talk.

There is an additional etiology to hebephilia. Nabokov's novel presents the etiology of the main character's hebephilia as posttraumatic stress disorder. The hebephile in the novel falls in love as an adolescent and has intercourse with his adolescent girlfriend; the girlfriend tragically dies and he is devastated by the loss. As he proceeds through adolescence to adulthood, he experiences rejection as he attempts age-appropriate sexual relationships. These rejections force him back in time to a place of acceptance and comfort: his relationship with his adolescent girlfriend. He does not experience frustration or anxiety in the presence of pubescent girls, and in fact finds himself sexually aroused. This gender- and age-group becomes his sexual comfort zone, and he develops a delusional belief that Lolita will love him forever after their sexual encounter.

Law enforcement utilizes this recognition of the age and gender preference of the hebephile in delineating the suspect group. A hebephile may solicit sex from a prostitute who is young and who overtly displays her youthfulness by dressing in a parochial school girl uniform. This delineated group become suspects in the investigation of a murder of a pubescent girl.

Clinicians contemplate the posttraumatic stress disorder etiology of hebephilia from additional traumatic experiences. A youth who loses a parent to death, divorce, or separation may also find a sense of well-being in reliving the pleasurable, nurturing, nonsexual experiences of the past. Pedophiles and hebephiles are similar in that they experience anxiety in the absence of their fantasy love group. When experiencing environmental stressors, they revert back to a time of love and comfort and this is the "love" of their fantasy love group. Age- and gender-relevant pornography, clothing, toys, photos, and advertisements fuel their fantasy, stimulate their sexual arousal, and allow for sexual gratification and a reduction in the anxiety caused by environmental stressors. When this cache of stimuli no longer produces the required sexual arousal, pedophiles and hebephiles seek out "flesh." They leave the confines of their homes and seek out their fantasy love group in their normal haunts.

Pedophiles "stalk" elementary schools, playgrounds, and Little League athletic practices and games. Hebephiles "stalk" junior high schools, cheerleading practices, shopping malls, and beaches. Both pedophiles and hebephiles modify their hobbies and interests in order to be closer to their fantasy love group. They volunteer to be Cub and Boy Scout leaders, soccer coaches, and band and choir directors, and they gain employment as recreation and recess supervisors, day care center employees, and mall security guards.

SEXUAL MASOCHISM AND SEXUAL SADISM

Sexual masochism is the one paraphilia that the American Psychiatric Association indicates is not male-exclusive. Persons afflicted with sexual masochism are recurrently, intensely sexually aroused by being the recipient of real and imagined pain, humiliation, and degradation. They can not achieve sexual arousal in the absence of these stimuli. Here lies the severity of this paraphilia. While some self-inflicted pain may achieve sexual arousal and subsequent gratification, it is short-lived, and the masochist must rely on another person to provide the pain and humiliation needed to achieve arousal. The sexual sadist is quick to assume his rightful role and deliver the requisite pain, humiliation, and degradation.

The sexual sadist is recurrently, intensely sexually aroused by delivering pain, humiliation, and degradation to another. He can not achieve sexual arousal unless he is delivering the requisite pain, humiliation, and degradation. All major communities in the United States have S/M clubs and taverns that cater to straight, gay, lesbian, and bisexual sexual sadists and sexual masochists. While this appears to be the solution to the problem of persons afflicted with these paraphilias, that is not quite accurate. Sexual sadists have an ever-increasing need for heightened stimulation. Similar to a heroin addict who requires larger and larger doses of heroin to fend off withdrawal, the sexual sadist requires higher levels of stimulation to achieve sexual arousal. In contrast, the sexual masochist has limits established by pain threshold. At some point in time the pain becomes more intense that they can endure, and they refuse to participate any further. The sadist has three choices:

1. Agree to limit the amount of pain delivered, but with the expense of reduced sexual arousal;
2. Find another sexual masochist with a higher pain threshold; or
3. Force nonconsensual activity on his partner, also known as rape.

The sexual masochist is never involved in lust homicides, unless as an unwilling accomplice fearful of losing his or her relationship with the sexual sadist, or his or her own life. Persons who commit serial lust homicide are commonly sexual sadists. This will be demonstrated repeatedly in the case study section of this book.

TELEPHONE SCATOLOGIA

Persons afflicted with telephone scatologoia are recurrently, intensely sexually aroused by the making of obscene phone calls. Interestingly, this paraphilia has been modified to include persons who are sexually aroused by placing phone calls or making internet connections for the purpose of receiving sexually explicit conversations. The internet has empowered persons who lack the social skills to develop intimate relationships to achieve autoerotic sexual arousal and sexual gratification by purchasing a seductive phone call or watching a stranger engage in erotic behavior. This practice has produced serious financial problems for those men who are "internet-addicted" to the practice.

Society questions whether this activity produces sexual predators. This author suggests that the economic implications of this behavior are much greater than its potential for "producing" more sexual paraphiliacs. A person predisposed to autoerotic behavior is more apt to remain at home and sexually gratify himself than to take his paraphilia to the streets of our communities. Such persons are already socially inept, and this media activity will probably continue to meet their autoerotic needs.

TRANSVESTIC FETISHISM

The object of the recurrent, intense sexual arousal for a person afflicted with transvestic fetishism is cross-dressing. The American Psychiatric Association indicates that this paraphilia is exclusive to heterosexual males. Following that diagnostic exclusion, one can infer that fetishistic cross-dressing is not undertaken for purposes of attracting gay sex partners; rather, the cross-dressing in itself produces sexual arousal, and, consequently, autoerotic behavior and sexual gratification.

Transvestic fetishism is not an easy paraphilia to completely understand because there are additional psychological impairments that may also be influencing the sexual arousal. A heterosexual male diagnosed with gender identity disorder despises his male genitalia. As a child, a boy with gender identity disorder may refuse to urinate while standing and may choose to dress in girls' clothing. This disorder is relatively common in boys raised in a totally female-dominated environment, particularly if they are teased and ridiculed by their female siblings and companions. This boy finds his penis repugnant and may indicate a desire to "rid" himself of it.

Adult males who cross-dress may do so for different reasons. Some may choose to dress as a woman because they are gay and wish to attract a gay companion who prefers his partner to "look" the part of a woman. Others may do so because of gender identity disorder, and may even attempt transgender surgery. However, as the American Psychiatric Association excludes homosexual males from this diagnosis, one must conclude it is the act and appearance of being dressed as a woman that is sexually arousing for transvestic fetishists. The paraphilia is further characterized by dressing as a woman in full garment, accessories, and makeup. This is in contrast to a person who is afflicted with the fetishism paraphilia: the person afflicted with fetishism is recurrently, intensely sexually aroused over a specific type of garment, and may be either heterosexual or gay.

UROPHILIA

The person afflicted with urophilia is recurrently, intensely sexually aroused by human urine. This is manifested in his response to the sight, smell, and taste of urine and to the rubbing of urine on himself. This paraphilia is difficult to diagnose because of the potential of other intervening variables. The man may be sexually aroused over fantasies of the genitals of a person rather than that person's urine.

It is also possible that the man is afflicted with sexual masochism, and one of the manifestations of this is the "golden shower." A "golden shower" is one person urinating on another. The question becomes: is the man sexually aroused by the humiliating act of being urinated upon, as he would be in sexual masochism; sexually aroused by the partner's genitalia; or sexually aroused by the urine itself?

VOYEURISM

The person afflicted with the paraphilia voyeurism is recurrently, intensely sexually aroused over watching nonconsenting persons in the act of changing clothes, bathing, or engaging in sexual activity. "Peeping Tom" is the nonclinical terminology utilized to characterize the voyeur.

It is significant to carefully examine victimology in order to make an accurate diagnosis. The act of nonconsensual watching must have random victims, rather than victims that are age- and gender-specific. If a man is engaged in the nonconsensual observation of prepubescent girls in the act of bathing, the paraphilia is likely pedophilia and the fantasy love group is pre-pubescent girls. If, on the other hand, the man is "peeping" into residential bathrooms and bedrooms randomly, it is the act of nonconsensual observing that is sexually arousing, thus the diagnosis of voyeurism.

ZOOPHILIA

The final paraphilia to be discussed is zoophilia. A person who is accurately diagnosed with zoophilia is recurrently, intensely sexually aroused by sexual activity with animals. This is an exotic paraphilia, and persons accurately diagnosed with it are extremely rare. The American Psychiatric Association requires that the sexually arousing stimulus be sexual activity with an animal, excluding other variables.

Variables that influence this diagnosis include sexual activity with animals that is part of the sexual conduct between human partners. Numerous mammals and reptiles have been utilized as "sex toys" by heterosexual, gay, and lesbian couples. Small mammals and reptiles have been inserted into the vaginas of women and the anuses of both men and women. There are numerous accounts of trauma center interventions necessary when the mammal or the reptile cannot be retrieved.

The "true" zoophiliac must be sexually aroused over sexual activity with an animal to the exclusion of other sexual stimuli. Adolescent males may experiment with intercourse with animals, but rarely does this become a paraphiliac behavior.

Bibliography and Suggested Readings

American Psychiatric Association. (2000). *Diagnostic and Statistical Manual of Mental Disorders* (Rev. 4th ed.). Arlington, VA: Author.

Bandura, A. (1977). *Social Learning Theory.* Englewood Cliffs, NJ: Prentice Hall.

Bartol, C. R. (2002). *Criminal Behavior: A Psychosocial Approach* (6th ed.). Upper Saddle River, NJ: Prentice Hall.

Belknap, J. (1996). *The Invisible Woman.* Belmont, CA: Wadsworth.

Blinder, M. (1985). *Lovers, Killers, Husbands and Wives.* New York: St. Martin's Press.

Burgess, A. W. (Ed.). (1985). *Rape and Sexual Assault.* New York: Garland.

Colt, G. H. (1998). Were you born that way? *Life 21*(4), 38–42.

Crowell, N. A., & Burgess, A. W. (Eds.). (1996). *Understanding Violence against Women.* Washington, DC: National Academy Press.

Deary, I. A., Peter, A., & Austin, E. (1998). Personality traits and personality disorders. *The British Journal of Psychology 89*(4), 647–661.

Dobbert, D. L. (2004). *Halting the Sexual Predators among Us.* Westport, CT: Praeger.

Dobbert, D. L. (1981, January). *Profiling and Predicting the Violent Offender*. Paper presented at the meeting of the National Conference on Serious and Violent Offenders, Detroit, MI.

Douglas, J. E., Burgess, A. W., Burgess, A. G., & Ressler, R. K. (1992). *Crime Classification Manual*. San Francisco, CA: Jossey-Bass.

Douglas, J., & Olshaker, M. (1997). *Journey into Darkness*. New York: Simon and Schuster.

Eysenck, H. J. (1977). *Crime and Personality*. London, UK: Routledge.

Eysenck, M. W., & Keane, M. T. (1995). *Cognitive Psychology* (3rd ed.). East Sussex, UK: Psychology Press.

Flora, R. (2001). *How to Work with Sex Offenders: A Handbook for Criminal Justice, Human Service, and Mental Health Professions*. Binghamton, NY: Hayworth.

Goody, E. (1977). *Deviant Behavior* (5th ed.). Upper Saddle River, NJ: Prentice Hall.

Groth, N., Burgess, A., & Holmstead, L. (1977). Rape, power, anger, and sexuality. *American Journal of Psychiatry 134*, 1239–1243.

Hasslet, V. B., & Hersen, M. (1999). *Handbook of Psychological Approaches with Violent Offenders: Contemporary Strategies and Issues*. New York: Kluwer.

Hazelwood, R. R., & Warren, J. (1989). The serial rapist. *FBI Law Enforcement Bulletin*, 49–63.

Hodgson, J. F., & Kelley, D. S. (2001). *Sexual Violence: Policies, Practices, and Challenges in the United States and Canada*. Westport, CT: Praeger.

Holmes, R. M., & Holmes, S. T. (2002). *Profiling Violent Crimes* (3rd ed.). Thousand Oaks, CA: Sage.

Horney, K. (1950). *Neurosis and Human Growth*. New York: Norton.

Keeney, B. T., & Heide, K. M. (1994). Gender differences in serial murderers. *Journal of Interpersonal Violence 9*(3), 383–398.

Knight, R. A., & Prentky, R. A. (1987). The developmental antecedents and adult adaptations of rapist subtypes. *Criminal Justice and Behavior 14*, 403–426.

Lane, B., & Gregg, W. (1992). *The Encyclopedia of Serial Killers* (Rev. ed.). New York: Berkeley.

Masters, W. H., & Johnson, V. E. (1966). *Human Sexual Response*. Boston, MA: Little and Brown.

Medows, R. J. (2001). *Understanding Violence and Victimization* (2nd ed.). Upper Saddle River, NJ: Prentice Hall.

Nathanson, D. L. (1992). *Shame and Pride*. New York, NY: W. W. Norton.

National Center for the Analysis of Violent Crime. (1992). *Investigator's Guide to Allegations of "Ritual" Child Abuse* (brochure). Quantico, VA: Author.

Olsen, J. (1974). *The Man with the Candy*. New York: Simon and Schuster.

Piaget, J. (1967). *Six Psychological Studies*. New York: Random House.

Rolling, D., & London, S. (1996). *The Making of a Serial Killer*. Portland, OR: Feral House.

Rowe, D. C. (2002). *Biology and Crime*. Los Angeles, CA: Roxbury.

Sadler, A. E. (1996). *Family Violence*. San Diego, CA: Greenhaven Press.

Schwartz, M. D. (Ed.). (1997). *Researching Sexual Violence against Women.* Thousand Oaks, CA: Sage.

Sgarzi, J. M., & McDevitt, J. (2003). *Victimology.* Upper Saddle River, NJ: Prentice Hall.

VanderZanden, J. W. (1997). *Human Development* (6th ed.). New York: McGraw Hill.

Warren, J., Reboussin, R., Hazelwood, R. R., & Wright, J. A. (1991). Prediction of rapist type and violence from verbal, physical, and sexual scales. *Journal of Interpersonal Violence* 6(1), 55–67.

4

Herman Mudgett, a.k.a. H. H. Holmes (1860–1896)

Herman Mudgett, more commonly known as H. H. Holmes, was an obscure character from U.S. history who became a household name following the publication of the bestselling nonfiction book, *The Devil in the White City*, in 2003. While the book reads like a fiction novel, it is an extraordinary story about the construction of the Chicago World's Fair in 1893. The story of serial killer H.H. Holmes parallels the World's Fair. During this same period of time H. H. Holmes committed heinous murders. He confessed to 27 murders, though some estimates implicate him in nearly 200 deaths.

Holmes was born Herman Webster Mudgett on May 16, 1860, in New Hampshire to Levi and Theodate Mudgett. Levi and Theodate were strict disciplinarians and Mudgett was subject to physical and emotional abuse and neglect. It was reported that following his complaining of a toothache, Levi took Mudgett to the shed where he extracted the tooth with pliers. Mudgett was small in stature and subject to harassment by his peers. At an early age, Mudgett developed a fascination for the mutilation of animals. Mudgett would capture stray animals and perform surgical experiments upon them. Mudgett was 11 years old when he committed his first murder, killing his friend and companion, and disguising the incident to appear as a tragic accident in an abandoned house.

While in his undergraduate studies, Mudgett married Clara Lovering. He used her money to pay his tuition. He enrolled in the University of Michigan Medical School in 1879, and his desire for an expensive lifestyle required fraudulent activities to keep him satisfied. During his studies at the University, Mudgett devised a plan to steal corpses, conduct medical experiments upon them, and then utilize these bodies in an insurance fraud. He would create false names and take out insurance policies identifying himself as the beneficiary. He would later steal a corpse, mutilate the body to camouflage its true identity, and file a life insurance claim. Mudgett recognized that continuing with this activity would eventually draw scrutiny. He enlisted the assistance of a fellow student in the insurance fraud scheme, and upon collecting money from an insurance company he murdered his accomplice rather than splitting the beneficiary award.

Mudgett also engaged in the activity of stealing corpses from morgues and selling these bodies to medical schools for use as teaching cadavers. Further, he established schemes to steal money from other students. Mudgett was an engaging and handsome man who exploited beautiful young female students. Following courtship, Mudgett would "blackmail" them out of their savings and allowances reserved for tuition and living expenses. He neglected Clara and his son Theodore, and following his most successful life insurance fraud, collecting $12,500, he abandoned them.

Mudgett created numerous aliases, which he used to exploit others. As Franklin Pratt, he worked in collections for the Dearborn Company. Following the collection of $2,300 from Dearborn debtors, he disappeared without turning the money in to the company. Mudgett disappeared for a period of six years, then reappeared and married Myrta Belknap in 1887 under the alias H. H. Holmes. Holmes worked at a pharmacy in the Chicago area owned by Dr. and Mrs. E. Holton. Dr. Holton was suffering from cancer, and following his death, Mrs. Holton sold the store to Holmes. Mrs. Holton mysteriously disappeared after the sale of the store, and Holmes would tell others that she moved to the West Coast.

Holmes then ran the pharmacy under the name of Dr. H. H. Holmes. His engaging personality encouraged a growth in clientele, many of whom were attractive single women. Two years after purchasing the pharmacy from Mrs. Holton, Holmes purchased a large lot across the street with the intent of building a hotel to provide accommodations for the Chicago World's Fair of 1983, known as the Columbian Exposition.

Holmes designed the hotel himself and carefully supervised its construction. Holmes would repeatedly change construction crews in order that no one single crew would have specific knowledge regarding the finished product. This three-story structure was comprised of hotel rooms, shops, and offices. The exterior of the building was elegant with roman columns and gilded signs, and it hid the true nature of the building.

Behind the doors of this grand hotel were rooms without windows, doors that locked from the outside, hidden passages, and a chute that led to the basement. The basement was equipped with surgical tables, restraint devices, and a crematorium furnace where bodies were burned. Holmes installed devices to blow gas into the rooms and asphyxiate his victims.

Holmes advertised the hotel as a location close to the vast employment opportunities at the Exposition, and hundreds of people flocked to it in hopes of employment. During the period of the Exposition Holmes would attract young women to his hotel with the promise of work. In residence at the hotel, these young women would meet their demise. Holmes would murder some in the gas filled rooms or asphyxiate them in a large bank vault installed in the basement. Holmes would remove their organs and flesh from their bodies, selling the organs and skeletons to medical schools through his previous connections. Remaining parts of the bodies were disposed of in large vats filled with acid and in the crematorium furnace. It is believed that Holmes also performed illegal abortions and most of the victims died from the procedure.

Holmes advertised his hotel and the availability of employment through small newspapers in the Midwest. The promise of work brought a flood of visitors, predominately young women, to Chicago and to Holmes's murder castle. Holmes would offer employment to the young women, which included life insurance policies. Holmes paid the premiums but also designated himself as the beneficiary. Holmes would torture the young women until they gave him their valuables. After they no longer served a purpose, Holmes would murder them and process their bodies for their organs and skeletons. The exact count of the number of victims at the murder castle is unknown, with speculation in excess of 100.

Holmes refused to pay his bills to the contractors who built the hotel under the excuse of poor workmanship. This indebtedness and his need for a flamboyant lifestyle brought creditors to the door, and he fled Chicago for Texas. In Texas, he proposed marriage to one of two heiress sisters. He murdered these sisters and set their house on fire, hoping to collect the $60,000 in life insurance from their relatives. Holmes intended on using the money to initiate another hotel project in Texas; however, law enforcement officials were suspicious of his actions.

Prior to the completion of the Chicago murder castle, Holmes had hired Benjamin Pitezel as an assistant. Pitezel was thoroughly enamored with Holmes and his lifestyle. He was the only person who was suspected to have knowledge of Holmes's activity in the hotel. Pitezal was soon to find a similar fate as Holmes's other victims. Pitezal agreed to take out a life insurance policy with his wife and Holmes identified as the beneficiaries; he was to fake his death in a laboratory fire. Holmes was to find a cadaver to disfigure and utilize as Pitezel's body. Holmes murdered Pitezel and told Pitezel's wife that he was hiding in South America while the life insurance claim was being processed. Holmes also persuaded Pitezel's wife to allow three of her five children to stay in his custody while they separately moved about the United States and Canada attempting to avoid investigation of Pitezel's death.

A Philadelphia detective investigating Pitezel's death tracked Holmes to Toronto, Ontario, where the bodies of two of Pitezel's daughters were discovered. Holmes had moved to Indianapolis where he rented a home later to be located by the Philadelphia detective. Bones and teeth from Pitezel's son were found in the fireplace of the home where Holmes had burned the remains of the body. Law enforcement ended Holmes's reign of terror when they arrested him in Philadelphia. Holding Holmes on an outstanding warrant for horse theft in Texas, detectives began the gruesome chore of investigating the Chicago murder castle. Skeletons, bones, and human remains were found in the basement and the furnace of the hotel.

Holmes was convicted of the death of Benjamin Pitezel and three of his children. It wasn't until later that he would confess to the murders in the Chicago hotel. He informed his attorney that he had committed 133 murders. Holmes was executed by hanging on May 7, 1896, in Philadelphia.

EVALUATION

Despite the absence of a psychiatric evaluation, Holmes's pathological lying, absolute absence of remorse or empathy for his victims, and calm poised nature convince this author that he was afflicted with psychopathic personality disorder. There is little evidence to demonstrate that he was recurrently, intensely sexually aroused by his activities, and consequently he may not have been afflicted with the sexual sadism paraphilia. However, one can readily recognize his sadistic cruelty, which obviously met his intrinsic psychological needs. He derived pleasure in the torture and murder of his victims. Regardless of whether he was sexually aroused, his actions pleased him or he would never have continued with his gruesome behavior.

Obviously, one must contemplate what psychological and/or sociological variables may have precipitated the development of Holmes's psychopathy. Children who are severely abused and neglected often develop extraordinary egocentricity. Unable to rely upon their parents for love, affection, and safety, they learn that they can only rely on themselves. This extreme level of egocentricity allows them not only to have no feeling for the plight of others, but also to exacerbate the condition of others with no remorse. Holmes's early behavior of cruelty to animals suggests an early interest in sadistic behavior.

Further, Holmes was not particularly discriminating in the selection of his victims. While the majority of his victims were young women, Holmes also murdered men and children without hesitation. It appears that women were a pleasant and probably sexual activity, but that the delivering of pain and suffering to anyone was the most pleasurable activity for Holmes. This suggests that Holmes did not have a particular fantasy love group that produced recurrent, intense sexual arousal, but that, rather, the sadism itself was psychologically fulfilling.

Bibliography and Suggested Readings

Borowski, J. (Producer/Director). (2004). *H. H. Holmes: America's First Serial Killer* [Documentary]. Chicago: Waterfront.

Eckert, A. (1985). *The Scarlet Mansion.* New York : Little, Brown.

Filippelli, C. (2000). *H. H. Holmes: Dr. Death, America's First Serial Killer.* Retrieved from http://www.crimelibrary.com/serial6/holmes/bibliography.htm.

Franke, D. (1975). *The Torture Doctor.* New York: Avon.

Larson, E. (2003). *The Devil and the White City.* New York: First Vintage.

Schechter, H. (1994). *Depraved: The Shocking True Story of America's First Serial Killer.* New York: Pocket Books.

5

Peter Kürten (1883–1931)

The German serial killer Peter Kürten was dubbed "the monster of Düsseldorf" because of the string of heinous crimes, sexual assaults, and murders he committed. Kürten was convicted and sentenced to death, and was executed by guillotine on July 2, 1931, at the Klingelputz Prison in Cologne. His case study reflects his comorbid diagnoses, psychopathy and sexual sadism.

Kürten was born on May 26, 1883, in Köln-Mülheim to an alcoholic, sexually assaultive father and a victimized mother. The family of 13 lived in a one-bedroom apartment. The father would sexually assault Kürten's mother and sisters in the presence of him and his siblings. Kürten's father was convicted of molesting his 13-year-old daughter and sentenced to prison.

During Kürten's youth he associated with a dogcatcher who lived in the same building as his family. This dogcatcher would allow Kürten to work with him and demonstrated torture on the animals; he encouraged Kürten to masturbate while torturing and killing the animals. During adolescence, the height of psychosexual development, Kürten visited local farms and stables and committed acts of bestiality on the farm animals. Incorporating torture with the bestiality, Kürten found an increased sense of sexual gratification. He became sexually aroused by the delivery of pain and suffering to the animal and the sight of the animal's blood. Kürten also found watching fires to be sexually arousing, and began to commit arson in order to achieve sexual arousal and gratification.

During his youth he engaged in a variety of minor criminal activities that resulted in convictions and jail sentences. Kürten received 27 prison sentences. While he sexually assaulted many women, his first acknowledged murder occurred on May 25, 1913. Kürten had been supporting himself by committing burglaries of inns and hotels. On this date, while burglarizing an inn in Mulheim, he found a 13-year-old girl sleeping. He strangled, sexually assaulted, and then cut the throat of this girl.

Following the Mulheim murder, Kürten engaged in numerous assaults and burglaries that resulted in his conviction and imprisonment of eight years. He was released from prison in 1921, and he moved to Altenburg, where he would meet and marry his wife. He was able to avoid prosecution and conviction on allegations of the rape of two servants. In 1925, Kürten moved back to Düsseldorf, where his sexually assaultive behavior peaked. During the next four years, it is believed that he committed numerous sexual assaults, arsons, and murders.

On February 8, 1929, Kürten assaulted a woman, stabbing her 24 times and leaving her for dead. On February 13, he murdered a mechanic, stabbing him 20 times. The sadism must have driven this behavior, as his murder of a man is an anomaly. In August 1929, Kürten began a murder spree. He murdered two girls, ages 5 and 14, who were attending a fair. He strangled both girls, then cut one's throat and decapitated the other. He then attempted to rape a woman, stabbing her repeatedly with sufficient force to break the point of his dagger in her back.

His killing spree continued. In September, Kürten raped a servant girl and bludgeoned her to death with a hammer. In October, he attacked two servant girls with the hammer, and in November, he stabbed a five-year-old girl 36 times. Kürten relished reading about the murders in the press, and after murdering this five-year-old, he sent a map to the Düsseldorf police indicating the location of the grave of the child.

Following a brief hiatus, Kürten resumed his attacks in February 1929. While he committed numerous assaults in the next four months, all of the victims survived. On May 23, 1929, he raped a young woman, but did not murder her as she offered no resistance. The young woman was able to describe Kürten and led the authorities to his residence. Kürten was arrested on May 24, 1929.

Peter Kürten entered a plea of not guilty on grounds of insanity; however, he eventually confessed to 79 charges of assault and murder. Kürten was convicted of nine murders and seven counts of attempted murder. He was sentenced to death, and on July 2, he was executed via the guillotine.

EVALUATION

Peter Kürten's behavior provides evidence of the pathology that led to his heinous murders. Further, his comments to his psychiatrist following his conviction provide insight into the disorders that provided the motivation.

Kürten was capable of committing these tortuous assaults and brutal murders because he lacked empathy for his victims and remorse for his own behavior. Put briefly, he was conscience-deficient. In the absence of conscience, Kürten was free to meet his own intrinsic needs without the barrier of feeling guilt for the injury he caused others. His needs were of greater importance to him than those of his victims. In fact, he viewed his victims as a means of pleasuring himself. He regarded his victims as at the same level as the animals utilized in his bestiality: merely objects used to sexually gratify himself.

Kürten was afflicted with sexual sadism, and this was evident throughout his life. He derived recurrent, intense sexual arousal over the delivery of "real," not imagined, pain and humiliation. One can easily trace his sexual sadism through the behavioral manifestations demonstrated in his assaultive conduct. Kürten would experience greater sexual gratification through the combination of sexual intercourse with and sadistic behavior to his victim than he would experience through the intercourse alone. He indicated that observing the blood of his victims was sexually arousing and gratifying. He was known to "taste" the blood of his animal and human victims, and due to this behavior was also referred to as the "vampire of Düsseldorf."

The etiology of Kürten's psychopathy and sexual sadism is relatively transparent. He was raised in an environment where his father demonstrated his own psychopathy by sexually assaulting his mother and sexually molesting his daughters. Kürten's father modeled behavior in which the father's sexual gratification was treated as an imperative superior to the needs and interests of his family. His father's failure to recognize his mother's and sister's interests also demonstrated women's lack of value, and indicated that women were placed on this earth to meet the needs of the dominant male.

Kürten's sexual sadism was initiated through his relationship with the dog-catcher neighbor. The neighbor modeled and demonstrated bestiality, torture, and animal mutilation. No negative value was associated with this behavior. Consequently, when Kürten was taught to masturbate while inflicting torture and mutilation on the animal, he experienced the pleasure of sexual gratification without negative moral judgment. This modeling continued the loss of conscience.

In a word, Peter Kürten was taught that life other than his own was not sacred but, rather, insignificant. Kürten learned that anything that was pleasurable to him, regardless of its effect on others, was not only acceptable, but desirable. Animal and human victims possessed little if any value beyond meeting Kürten's need for sexual exploitation and gratification.

Bibliography and Suggested Readings

American Psychiatric Association. (2000). *Diagnostic and Statistical Manual of Mental Disorders* (Rev. 4th ed.). Arlington, VA: Author.

Cameron, D., & Frazer, E. (1987). *The Lust to Kill.* New York: New York University Press.

Dobbert, D. L. (2004). *Halting the Sexual Predators among Us.* Westport, CT: Praeger.

Dobbert, D. L. (2007). *Understanding Personality Disorders.* Westport, CT: Praeger.

Ellis, A., & Gallo, J. (1971). *Murder and Assassination.* New York: Lyle Stuart.

Gilbert, A. (1999). *Peter Kürten: The Vampire of Dusseldorf.* Retrieved from http://www.trutv.com/library/crime/serial_killers/history/Kürten/index_1.html.

Kerr, P. (1990). *The Pale Criminal.* London: Viking.

Kohn, G. (1986). *Dictionary of Culprits and Criminals.* Lanham, MD: Rowan & Littlefield.

McDonald, J. (1986). *The Murderer and his Victim.* Springfield, IL: Thomas.

Nasy, J. (1986). *Almanac of World Crime.* New York: Bonanza.

6

Earle Leonard Nelson (1897–1928)

Cesare Lombroso (1835–1909) has often been referred to as the "father of criminological theory," yet his theoretical perspective that criminals were "born" as such—rather than being the product of society's ills—has generally been rejected in contemporary criminological thought. Lombroso contended that criminal behavior was an inherited trait, but most interestingly suggested that criminals could be identified by their physical traits. He posited that one could identify criminals by the physical traits of a low sloping forehead, a long lower jaw, high cheekbones, a large chin, and long arms. While this theoretical perspective lacked research credibility and has been described as a case of hysterical, rather than historical, criminological theory, Earle Nelson meets Lombroso's diagnostic criteria. Nicknamed "the Gorilla Killer," Nelson displayed the appropriate physical traits, included a receding forehead, protruding lips, and huge hands.

Earle Leonard Nelson was born in 1897 and was executed in Winnipeg, Manitoba, in Canada on January 13, 1928. He was found guilty of and executed for the murder of Emily Patterson; however, it is believed that he murdered a minimum of 24 women and one child.

Nelson's mother, Frances, died seven months after Earle's birth from syphilis that she had contracted from his father, James. The syphilis would take James's life seven months later. Following James's death, Earle was placed with his grandparents, Lars and Jennie Nelson, and his aunt Lillian. Lillian was an extremely religious woman who preached to Earle that sex was dirty and had claimed his mother's life. Her puritanical views and rigid parenting of Earle contributed to his emotional impairments. At the age of 10, Earle was riding his bicycle and was struck by a streetcar, resulting in serious head trauma. Although he survived the injuries, he was physically scarred and subject to frequent headaches. However, it is doubtful that this trauma was a precipitating variable in Nelson's homicidal behavior. Rather, it was the rigid, strictly imposed religious views of his adopted family that initiated his career of murder.

Earle Nelson's first manifestation of his sexual urges occurred just prior to his 21st birthday. He attempted to rape a 12-year-old neighborhood girl. The girl's scream alerted her parents, and he terminated his assault and fled. He was arrested the next day and due to his erratic behavior was placed in the Napa State Hospital with a provisional diagnosis of psychopathy. Even as early as 1918, mental health practitioners recognized that psychopathy was an untreatable condition; however, they chose to leave him in residence. Nelson escaped several times and was returned to the facility, but finally, during one of these episodes of truancy, the hospital released him rather than accepting him back if he was found.

While on truant status and using a false name, he married Mary Martin in San Francisco, Cailifornia. The marriage was short-lived as Nelson could not find work and was demonstrating erratic and dangerous behaviors, including threats to kill his wife. At her request for assistance, the San Francisco court remanded him again to the Napa State Hospital. Once again, Nelson walked away from the facility, and he was discharged on March 10, 1925, without any interest in locating him. His trail of murder was to soon begin.

On October 18, 1925, the strangled body of Olla McCoy was found in Philadelphia. On November 6, May Murray was found strangled to death, and on November 9, Lillian Weiner was found murdered in the same manner. The three homicides had similarities to suggest that their murders were committed by the same person. Each of the women was displaying a "Room for Rent" sign at her home, and each had been strangled and sexually assaulted postmortem. Further, each woman was bound with strips of cloth in a specific and complicated knot. Finally, in each case, items were stolen from the residences and ended up in local pawn shops. The pawn shop broker was able to provide a description of the suspect; however, he was never identified nor apprehended.

Murders with similar characteristics began to appear in San Francisco, California, in February 1926. On February 20, a landlady named Clara Newman was found strangled and sexually assaulted. The number of murdered landladies began to grow rapidly. The murders occurred over a wide geographic range, and thus the job of locating the murderer was more difficult. Additional murders attributed to Earle Leonard Nelson include:

- Laura Beal, San Jose, CA, March 2, 1926
- Lillian St. Mary, San Francisco, CA, June 10, 1926

- Anna Russell, Santa Barbara, CA, June 24, 1926
- Mary Nesbit, Oakland, CA, August 16, 1926
- Beata Withers, Portland, OR, October 19, 1926
- Mabel Fluke, Portland, OR, October 20, 1926
- Virginia Grant, Portland, OR, October 21, 1926
- Wilhelmina Edmunds, San Francisco, CA, November 18, 1926
- Florence Monks, Seattle, WA, November 23, 1926
- Blanche Meyers, Portland, OR, November 29, 1926
- Elizabeth Beard, Council Bluffs, IA, December 23, 1926
- Bonnie Pace, Kansas City, KS, December 28, 1926
- Germainia Harpin and her eight-month-old daughter, Kansas City, KS, December 28, 1926
- Mary McConnell, Philadelphia, PA, April 27, 1927
- Jeannie Randolph, Buffalo, NY, May 30, 1927
- Minnie May, Detroit, MI, June 1, 1927
- Maureen Atworthy, Detroit, MI, June 1, 1927
- Mary Sietsma, Chicago, IL, June 2, 1927
- Lola Cowan, Winnipeg, Manitoba, Canada, June 9, 1927
- Emily Patterson, Winnipeg, Manitoba, Canada, June 10, 1927

Police work in the 1920s was seriously compromised by the lack of ability to share information across jurisdictional lines. While law enforcement agencies historically are reluctant to share their information and consequently the glory of the collar, in Nelson's case this was not an attitudinal failure to communicate, but a technological problem. Nelson was not only moving about within a given state, but also traveling to states all over the nation, and the final two murders occurred in Canada. However, the Los Angeles police, in the investigation of the murder in Santa Barbara, California, reached across jurisdictional lines and identified similarities in the murders committed in San Jose and San Francisco. It became apparent that the jurisdictions were all seeking the same probable suspect. On July 1, 1926, the Los Angeles police department placed a "wanted" bulletin in the *Daily Police Bulletin*, describing the murders and giving brief descriptions of the suspect. Unfortunately, the state of communication hindered the department's ability to communicate nationally, and Earle Nelson was able to commit 17 additional murders before his apprehension in Canada.

Nelson was apprehended because of the murders he committed in Canada. He hitchhiked to Winnipeg, Manitoba on June 8, 1927, and it is here that he changed his pattern of behavior. Earle was moving about the United States staying at rooming houses. While at the rooming house he would murder the landlady, sexually assault the corpse, and stuff the dead body under the bed. He would then rob money and clothing from the residence. He would take the clothing to a secondhand store and exchange it for other clothing and cash, thus changing his appearance should he have been observed by a witness. The stolen money would provide him food while he was traveling. However, in Winnipeg, he changed his pattern and did not murder the landlady. Lola Cowan, age 14, was going door to door selling artificial flowers. Nelson was sitting on the porch of the boarding house where he had just rented a room. He informed Lola that he had money upstairs in his room. Lola followed him to his upstairs bedroom where he proceeded to strangle her and repeatedly raped her lifeless body. He stuffed her body under a bed in a spare room. The next morning he packed up Lola's belongings and left the boarding house. What Nelson left behind was not only Lola's dead body, but also a live landlady who could provide the police with an excellent description.

However, despite his repeated raping of Lola's dead body, Nelson dropped in at the house of William and Emily Patterson, who were displaying a "Room for Rent" sign in their window. He informed Emily that he did not have any money but was willing to do home repair jobs in return for his stay. Emily agreed, and shortly thereafter Nelson attacked her in the kitchen. A vicious struggle ensued, but Nelson's massive hands were successful in strangling Emily. Following his rape of her dead body, he shoved her under the bed and then proceeded to search the house. He stole one of William Patterson's suits and discovered $70 in cash hidden in a suitcase. Following his normal pattern, Nelson took the ill-fitting suit to the secondhand store and exchanged it for different clothing. He then proceeded to leave Winnipeg and travel to Regina, Saskatchewan. In the interim, the bodies of Lola Cowan and Emily Patterson had been discovered and witnesses who had observed Nelson fixing a screen door at the Patterson home came forth with a description. The Winnipeg chief of detectives recognized the similarities of these murders to those of the "Strangler" being sought for numerous murders in the United States. Bulletins were place in the daily newspapers of Winnipeg, Brandon, Regina, Saskatoon, and Calgary.

On June 13, Nelson read the newspaper in Regina, Saskatchewan and realized that he had been accurately described. As was his practice, he stopped at a secondhand clothing store to exchange his clothing, where the clerk, who had read the morning newspaper, was alerted by the Winnipeg labels on the clothing and the matching description of the suspect. After Nelson left the store, the clerk called the police and a massive manhunt began. Nelson hitchhiked to Wakopa, a small town just north of the U.S.-Canadian border. He stopped into a store to purchase food and the store manager, sensing that this was the subject of the massive manhunt, contacted the Manitoba Provincial Police. Only a single constable was assigned to this small town, but he was able to arrest Nelson without incident. The constable detained Nelson in the minuscule jail cell and then proceeded to contact the chief of detectives in Winnipeg. The chief of detectives loaded a train with officers and proceeded to take custody of the "Strangler." In the interim, Nelson found a rusty nail in the jail cell and successfully picked the lock and freed himself. The constable sounded the alarm when he discovered Nelson's escape. Nelson was captured shortly thereafter as he attempted to "jump" a train headed for the border.

The Winnipeg police photographed and fingerprinted Nelson and sent the photos and prints to the U.S. law enforcement departments investigating the "Strangler" murders in their jurisdictions. They also set up lineups for witnesses to identify the stranger observed at the two boarding houses. Fingerprints delivered by the San Francisco police department confirmed that Nelson, although using an alias, was in fact the "Strangler" murderer they were attempting to identify. The Provincial Court felt that they had sufficient evidence to proceed with a trial for the murder of Emily Patterson. On November 4, 1927, the jury deliberated for 48 minutes and found Nelson guilty of the murder of Emily Patterson. On Friday, January 13, Nelson was taken to the gallows and hanged.

EVALUATION

As indicated in the preface paragraph to this case study, Earle Leonard Nelson was able to murder at least 24 women and one child because of the ineffectiveness of law enforcement. However, it must be stressed that this ineffectiveness was not due to malfeasance, but rather the lack of technology. It is reasonable to assume that Nelson's murderous spree would have been shortened significantly with contemporary technology and law enforcement's commitment to sharing information.

The forces that motivated and enabled Nelson to commit this lengthy list of homicides is obvious. Nelson was not mentally ill, although nonclinicians would say someone would have to be "crazy" to engage in the behaviors he did. Nelson is easily diagnosed with psychopathic personality disorder and it was this psychopathy that enabled him to continue with his murders. He was conscience-deficient and felt no guilt or remorse for his behavior, nor empathy for his victims. His overwhelming egocentricity precluded him from recognizing the value of human life other than his own. His needs, wants, and desires were of superior importance to the needs, wants, and desires of others. Consequently, he took what he wanted when he wanted it.

Nelson was also afflicted with the paraphilias of sexual sadism and necrophilia. He experienced uncontrollable, recurrent, intense sexual arousal in delivering pain, humiliation, and death to his victims. He did not utilize weapons to murder his victims. He used his powerful hands to strangle them. He was sexually aroused by the terror he observed when looking into the eyes of the women he was strangling. It is obvious that Nelson was driven by sadism; otherwise he would have utilized a weapon to kill his victims.

Nelson's sexual arousal may also have been associated with the sexual assault of his dead victims. He repeatedly raped the lifeless bodies of his victims. While this may be attributed to a desire to inflict the most extreme form of humiliation on his victims, it could also be attributed to necrophilia. Nelson's execution made accurate diagnosis impossible.

The obvious question regarding Nelson's paraphilias pertains to etiology. Unfortunately, his execution prohibited any exploration of the variables that may have precipitated his pathology. This author, relying on four decades of forensic behavioral analysis, suggests that the overwhelming pattern of emotional abuse presented by Nelson's grandparents and aunt is the culprit. A child who loses both parents to syphilis as an infant does not identify indiscriminate, unprotected sexual activity as the variable that precipitated his parents' demise; rather, it is the puritanical ranting of relatives that characterizes sexual activity as "dirty" and immoral. At some point in Nelson's psychosexual development, he was "educated" to believe that women who have a "Room for Rent" are loose, easy women who carry the disease that killed his mother and father, and that these women must be eliminated.

The comorbidity of psychopathy, sexual sadism, necrophilia, and sustained emotional abuse regarding the immorality of sex produced Earle Leonard Nelson, "The Gorilla Murderer," the "Strangler" who took the lives of at least 24 women and one child.

Bibliography and Suggested Readings

American Psychiatric Association. (2000). *Diagnostic and Statistical Manual of Mental Disorders* (Rev. 4th ed.). Arlington, VA: Author.

Anderson, F. (1974). *The Dark Strangler: A Study in Strange Behavior*. Calgary: Frontier.

Dobbert, D. L. (2004). *Halting the Sexual Predators among Us*. Westport, CT: Praeger.

Dobbert, D. L. (2007). *Understanding Personality Disorders*. Westport, CT: Praeger.

Douglas, J., & Olshaker, M. (2000). *The Anatomy of Motive: The FBI's Legendary Mindhunter Explores the Key to Understanding and Catching Violent Criminals*. New York: Simon and Schuster.

Musson, H., & Alldoff, F. (1938). *Strangler of Twenty Women: The Amazing Career of America's Murdering Monster*. Washington, DC: MacFadden.

Schechter, H. (1998). *Bestial: The Savage Trail of a True American Monster*. New York: Pocket.

7

Ed Gein (1906–1984)

Ed Gein (pronounced "geen") was a serial killer who demonstrated a plethora of bizarre behavior over the course of his life. His behavior was so bizarre that contemporary movie characters such as the son from the movie *Psycho* and Buffalo Bill from *The Silence of the Lambs* were patterned after him.

Edward Theodore Gein was born in 1906 to George and Augusta Gein in Lacrosse, Wisconsin. He was the second child in the family. His brother Henry was seven years older than him. Ed's father George was a blacksmith by trade, and his mother Augusta was the proprietor of a small grocery store. The combined income allowed the Geins to enjoy a reasonably comfortable living. However, it was Augusta's plan to save enough money to move the family to a much smaller rural community. Augusta was a deeply religious woman who obsessed over her perception of the immorality and sinfulness of the Lacrosse community. Augusta was also an extremely dominant and overpowering woman who was persistent and dogmatic in her beliefs. She ran the household with an iron fist and forced her views of the world upon the family.

In 1914, Augusta had saved sufficient money for the family to purchase a 170-acre farm in Plainfield, Wisconsin. The farm was secluded in the rural wilderness and Augusta relished in the absence of "sinners." Her forced isolation of the family precipitated social and emotional issues for the children. Preoccupied with the world of sinners, Augusta would force-feed the Bible to the boys and bicker with George. George, finally tiring of her constant bickering, became a serious alcoholic and physically abused Augusta. This fueled her obsession with the sins associated with the consumption of alcohol. Her preoccupation with sin and damnation extended to her beliefs about women of ill repute. Augusta would lecture the boys regarding the sins of the flesh associated with women and premarital sex, and discouraged their association with girls. Recognizing that other boys would talk of sinful things to her sons, she stressed the importance of staying away from these boys at school.

The tiny class of a dozen or so students would ridicule Ed and eventually shunned him. Ed was effeminate in stature, unattractive, and terribly shy, thus increasing the ridicule from his classmates. When he did attempt to establish friendships with classmates, Augusta would scold him and prohibit him from seeing the other children. When confronted by others he would not defend himself and would cry. Ed did have reasonable reading skills, and he would escape in storybooks. He looked upon his mother as the protector of good and the preventer of evil, and he did not question her dogmatic beliefs. He followed her regimen of sin-free behavior to the best of his ability.

The rural residence was surrounded by woods that Ed and his brother would explore. With no other playmates they spent all of their time together, working on farm chores or hunting in the nearby woods. Fearful of idle hands doing the devil's work, Augusta stayed in complete control over the boys. She feared that they would grow up to be worthless drunks like their father. Her daily Bible readings and morality lectures to the boys continued well into their teens. Despite her efforts to keep the boys pure of sexual thought, she would catch Ed gratifying himself in the bathtub while looking at the pleasurable photographs in a geographical magazine. As he attempted to hide himself below the water's surface, Augusta would rant and rave about his sinfulness and eventual eternal damnation. However, Augusta could not prevent the onset of adolescence and puberty, and her outrageous tirades pushed the boys into curiosity about the female anatomy. Ed would hear the boys at school comment on girls' anatomical features and talk of their sexual encounters. He began to fantasize about kissing a girl and perhaps even having a date, but the guilt instilled in him by his mother prohibited him from developing appropriate psychosexual health.

The boys would spend whatever free time they could find exploring the woods and hunting. The one location on the farm that they were prohibited from viewing was a shed. Terrified of being caught by his mother, Ed one day peeked through the crack in the door of the prohibited shed and watched in fascination as his parents butchered a hog, and he became sexually aroused.

George Gein finally succumbed to the ravages of his alcohol abuse and died of pneumonia in 1940. Ed, age 34, and Henry, age 41, continued to live at home with Augusta and worked the farm. Augusta's lectures on immorality and womanizing decreased following the death of George. Henry would attempt to persuade Ed to patronize the local taverns, but Ed remained steadfast in his devotion to his mother and in his adherence to her rules and expectations. Henry became increasingly concerned about Ed's dependent attachment to his mother, and openly criticized both of them.

In 1944, Henry died a suspicious death. A particularly dry spring left the farm fields arid and ripe for brushfires. While working in the fields, Henry and Ed became trapped by a brushfire that raged out of control. Ed escaped the fire, but Henry did not. Ed summoned the local sheriff and remarkably led the search party directly to Henry's body. Law enforcement officials found Henry's body untouched by the flames but with a bruised head and minor burns. His death was ruled accidental by reason of asphyxiation. There was insufficient evidence to suggest a wrongful death. Henry's death was a severe blow to Augusta, but Ed comforted her by telling her it was God's will and that he could take care of the two of them.

Ed increased his activity around the farm as well as doing odd jobs for neighbors. While Augusta continued to direct commands to Ed, he never waivered in his belief that she was the consummate wonderful mother and that he was the perfect son and provider. Augusta became concerned that Ed was developing strange thoughts, and noted that he would spend endless hours in his room reading books on women's anatomy and on tribal cannibalism. What Augusta believed to be filth, Ed considered educational. He would frequent secondhand bookstores looking for exotic reading material.

Later in 1944, Augusta suffered from a stroke, the first of a series that eventually took her life in 1945. Augusta's death left Ed Gein alone for the first time in his life. He stayed on at the farm and took on additional odd jobs to make ends meet. He would visit his mother's grave regularly to ease his loneliness and grief. It was reported that he would "command" her to rise from her grave. Gein also became less of a recluse and spent more time in town talking with people at the stores and even at the tavern. He was even capable of reducing his fear of women, and initiated conversations with them.

Gein read an article in the newspaper reporting the death and internment of a local woman. This began Gein's journey into grave robbing. He was not interested in stealing valuables from the deceased women, but rather in looking at their dead bodies. He began to steal the corpses or just specific body parts he desired. He would bury the coffin and then take the body or parts back to the farmhouse. As Gein was continuing on with his grave robbing he was also frequenting the Pine Grove Tavern, which was managed by Mary Hogan, a 54-year-old divorcee. Gein would converse with Hogan and listen to her talk with other customers in a flirtatious manner. Hogan was also kind to Gein, and these behaviors were inconsistent to him. Augusta had educated Gein about the virtues of women and indicated that there were only two types: god-fearing saintly women such as his mother, and all other women who were evil and would lead a man to his eternal damnation. Gein could not understand how Hogan was so wonderful to him yet also flirted with other customers. She did not fit his mother's characterization of a monogamous woman; therefore he imagined she must be evil, and thus that she had to be punished.

On December 4, 1954, Mary Hogan went missing. The only evidence was a blood trail inside the tavern. The police were unable to solve the crime. However, several days following her disappearance, Gein was assisting a friend with farm chores when they began discussing the Mary Hogan disappearance. Gein indicated that the police really didn't know what they were doing because she was probably dead and buried in the woods somewhere. The neighbor rebuked Gein for making light of her disappearance, and Gein laughed and said that she was not really missing, but rather was hanging around his farmhouse somewhere. The neighbor dismissed Gein's comments as absurd and inappropriate.

With the Pine Grove Tavern closed, Gein found himself lonely again. He decided to sell the farm and farmhouse as he didn't need that much space for himself. Unable to sell the farm and house, he closed off the upper floor and part of the first floor.

Gein made regular trips into town to shop at the local hardware store owned by a 58-year-old widow named Bernice Worden. On November 16, 1957, he drove his truck to town to purchase antifreeze at the hardware store. Gein purchased the antifreeze and then shot Worden with a .22 caliber rifle. He took Worden's body and the cash register. That evening Worden's son, a deputy sheriff, stopped by the hardware store but found it locked up for the day. Assuming his mother was at home, he stopped by her house only to find it empty. Worden's son called the sheriff and both returned to the store and broke their way inside. They found a pool of blood and the fired .22 caliber rifle. They also found that the cash register was missing. Checking the store's registry, they found the last entry was the purchase of antifreeze by Ed Gein.

Bernice Worden's son and the sheriff proceeded to Ed Gein's home. Finding him not at home, they walked around the farmhouse and saw the shed with the door unlocked. As they entered the dark shed, they bumped into a carcass hanging from the rafters. Assuming that it was a deer killed during the current hunting season, they held open the door to brighten the carcass. The carcass had been neatly gutted and split; however, it did not appear to be the carcass of a deer. They realized that they were looking at a decapitated woman. The woman was hung from the rafters on steel hooks through her ankles, in much the same manner as one would butcher a deer. They assumed it was the body of Bernice Worden, but identification was impossible at that time due to the absence of the head.

Ed Gein was visiting a neighbor down the road and when the sheriff entered the home, Gein greeted him warmly. The sheriff asked Gein to get his hat and coat and come with him. Gein asked where they were going, and the sheriff informed him they were going to the county jail. Gein demonstrated no emotion and did not offer any confession. Once secured in the patrol car, the sheriff radioed for his other deputies to enter Gein's home and called the state crime laboratory for assistance in processing the crime scene.

On November 17, officers from several jurisdictions assisted in the processing of the farmhouse, which they nicknamed the murder factory. The contents of the home challenged even the most experienced law enforcement officers. The investigators found Bernice Worden's head in a burlap bag and her intestines wrapped in newspaper. Bernice's heart was found in a pan on the stove and the refrigerator was stacked with human organs. This initiated a presumption of cannibalism.

As the officers proceeded to search the farmhouse the list of human remains increased. Authorities found two human skulls on Gein's bedposts, a number of shrunken heads, a lampshade covered with human skin, four chairs upholstered with human skin, a shoebox containing nine salted vulvas, a belt constructed from human nipples, four human noses, ten female heads with the skullcaps removed, nine facial masks of human skin, and a bowl made from an inverted skull. A full woman's body suit was located, sewn with human skin, a mask, and a breast. It was suggested that Gein would wear the body suit and walk around his home and yard. Gein admitted during the investigation that on moonlit nights he would wear the body suit and declared that his mother would now approve of him.

During his psychiatric evaluation Gein admitted to stealing body parts from 40 graves. Defense counsel was appointed for Gein and the attorney immediately entered a plea of not guilty by reason of insanity. Gein was remanded to the Central State Hospital for the Criminally Insane for evaluation. Following several psychiatric evaluations, it was determined that Gein was incompetent and could not assist in his defense, and consequently he was remanded to the State Hospital. Ten years later, in 1968, it was determined that Gein was competent to stand trail for the murder of Bernice Worden. Gein was found guilty, but insane. He was returned to the State Hospital, where he remained until his death in 1984 at the age of 78.

EVALUATION

It is obvious from his psychiatric evaluations that Ed Gein was mentally ill, and it was this mental illness that precipitated his criminal behavior. It is significant to examine those variables that may have led to the development of the mental illness.

During one of the psychiatric evaluations, Gein indicated that he had always had trouble with girls and sex. He indicated that he felt that his mother would have preferred that he was a girl rather than a boy. He wondered if he could have a transsexual operation to change his gender. Most of his reading material dealt with the subject of the female anatomy. Variables in the development of Gein's gender identity disorder included not only his mother's dominance, but also established standards of conduct for women. Gein felt he would receive his mother's approval not simply if he was a woman, but specifically if he was a good, god-fearing woman.

The suggestion of cannibalism is within reason, as Ed Gein's mental illness created the incredible delusion that he could transform himself into a woman. The body suit would provide the outward appearance, and he probably believed that by ingesting women's body parts he would develop a woman's body chemistry, organs, and genitals.

Bibliography and Suggested Readings

American Psychiatric Association. (2000). *Diagnostic and Statistical Manual of Mental Disorders* (Rev. 4th ed.). Arlington, VA: Author.

Dobbert, D. L. (2004). *Halting the Sexual Predators among Us.* Westport, CT: Praeger.

Dobbert, D. L. (2007). *Understanding Personality Disorders.* Westport, CT: Praeger.

Newton, M. (1999). *The Encyclopedia of Serial Killers.* New York: Checkmark.

Schechter, H. (1997). *The A to Z Encyclopedia of Serial Killers.* New York: Pocket.

Woods, P. (1995). *Ed Gein—Psycho!* New York: St. Martin's.

8

Henry Lee Lucas (1936–2001)

Henry Lee Lucas was born on August 23, 1936, in Montgomery County, Virginia. While he resided with his parents, the majority of his siblings were living with relatives or in foster care. Henry lived with his brother and his parents in a dirt-floor log cabin with four rooms. Henry's mother, Viola, was an alcoholic prostitute who entertained her customers in the presence of her husband and two boys. Henry's father, Anderson, was also an alcoholic, and had lost his legs when, in a drunken stupor, he fell under the wheels of a slow moving train. Subsequently nicknamed "No Legs," Anderson would spend his days skinning mink and selling pencils. On one occasion, rather than watch Viola have sex with a customer, Anderson stayed outside in the snow of winter drinking. He subsequently caught pneumonia and died.

Viola was a vicious woman who would regularly beat Henry and force him to watch her have sex with her customers. Henry and his brother were forced to steal food from neighbors or to eat from garbage cans in order to survive. Viola beat Henry so severely on one occasion that he was in a coma for 36 hours. Viola would tell Henry it was good for him and he would grow up strong. Viola also dressed Henry in girls' clothing, curled his hair into ringlets, and sent him off to school dressed in this manner. At an early age, Henry received an accidental knife wound to his eye, inflicted by his brother. The lack of medical attention resulted in the loss of the eye, and he was given a glass prosthesis.

Henry became obsessed with sex at about the age of 13. He and his brother would have sex and would practice bestiality with animals they had killed. Henry indicated to authorities that he committed his first murder in

1952 at the age of 14 while attempting to rape a girl. In 1952 Henry was convicted of breaking and entering, and was committed to the Beaumont Training School for Boys in Virginia. During his one year in residence Henry had sex with another incarcerated boy and attempted to escape on numerous occasions. Henry confessed to raping his 12-year-old niece the day after he was released from Beaumont.

In 1954, Henry was convicted of several counts of breaking and entering and burglary, and he was sentenced as an adult to four years in the Virginia State Penitentiary. In 1956, Henry and another inmate escaped while on a work detail. He remained at large for two months, and upon apprehension he was returned to the Virginia State Penitentiary, where he would remain until he was paroled in September 1959. Following his parole, he moved to Tecumseh, Michigan, to live with his half-sister Opal. While he was in hiding from his prison escape, Henry had met a woman named Stella. Now living with Opal, Henry proposed to Stella, and she agreed to marry him and moved to Tecumseh.

Henry's mother, Viola, decided to visit Opal and Henry. Viola was interested in Henry returning to Virginia to take care of the cabin. Upon her arrival in Tecumseh, she found Henry and Stella celebrating their engagement. Viola became infuriated and told Henry that he could not marry Stella. Stella, in great turmoil, left Opal's home, provoking Henry's wrath for Viola. Viola hit Henry over the head with a broom and Henry slapped her in retaliation. However, Henry (allegedly unknowingly) had a knife in his hand, and Viola was subsequently found lying on the floor, dead. In 1960, Henry Lee Lucas was charged with and convicted of the second-degree murder of his mother and sentenced to 20 to 40 years of imprisonment with the Michigan Department of Corrections.

Lucas was committed to the state prison of Southern Michigan, a maximum security prison in Jackson, Michigan. During his stay at Southern Michigan Penitentiary, Lucas attempted suicide on two occasions and complained of hearing voices in his head. He was transferred to the prison and psychiatric institution at Ionia, Michigan. He remained at Ionia for four and one-half years, during which time he received drug and electroshock treatments. Following his release from Ionia, Lucas was returned to the Southern Michigan Penitentiary until he was released in 1970, due to prison overcrowding conditions. At the time of his release he allegedly told corrections officers that he was not ready to be released, as he "would kill again." Lucas, although never charged, claimed that he killed two women within sight of the prison shortly after his release. He indicated that he did not kill for sex, but rather for revenge, to demonstrate to the prison officials that he was not ready for release.

Lucas was arrested in 1971 for the attempted kidnapping of a teenage girl at gunpoint. Having violated his parole, he was returned to Southern Michigan Penitentiary, where he served another four years. Lucas was released from prison in late August, 1975. Following his release he traveled to Maryland to visit his half-sister Almeda and her daughter Aomia. While staying with Almeda and Aomia, he met and began dating Betty Crawford. On December 5, 1975, Lucas and Crawford were married and the couple, with Crawford's three children, traveled from state to state as Lucas attempted to find steady work. In July 1977, Crawford accused Lucas of molesting her daughters. Lucas denied the accusations and headed to Florida.

While living in Florida, Lucas met a transvestite named Ottis Toole. (While a complete case study of Ottis Toole is not given in this book, a brief discussion of him follows this Henry Lee Lucas case study.) The two developed a homosexual relationship and moved into Toole's mother's home. Among others, Toole's eleven-year-old niece, Becky Toole, resided in the home. On November 5, 1978, Lucas and Toole murdered a teenage married couple. They shot the young man and kidnapped the young woman. Toole became infuriated with Lucas's repeated raping of the young woman and ordered her out of the car, at which time he emptied his revolver into her. Lucas and Toole continued on a robbery, rape, and murder spree, killing gas station owners, vagrants, and persons with broken-down vehicles. In October 1979, Toole and Lucas stopped to assist a young woman whose car was broken down on the side of an interstate highway. Five days later her body was found nude and with 35 stab wounds in the upper chest, neck, arms, and back. Her nipples had been cut off.

On October 31, 1979, Lucas murdered a young woman who was later nicknamed "orange socks" and became significant in his criminal conviction and sentencing. This young woman was hitchhiking and she and Lucas had sex. Later when Lucas wanted to have sex with her again, she refused, and Lucas strangled her and left her dead alongside the highway wearing only her "orange socks." Lucas and Toole continued on their murder spree, which they designated as the work of the "hand of death." The designation "hand of death" referred to a satanic cult that Lucas had joined in 1979. It is believed that Lucas was paid to commit murder and kidnapped babies to sell on the black market.

Lucas and Toole returned to Florida. Lucas moved in with Toole's niece, Becky Powell, and they lived as man and wife. Following the death of Toole's mother, Lucas and Powell left Florida to journey to California. Lucas committed numerous robberies on their journey. After arriving in California, Lucas and Powell traveled to Oregon and Washington, where Lucas was later alleged to have committed numerous rapes and murders. Throughout their hitchhiking journey through the West, the pair were befriended by persons, many of whom allowed them to stay at their homes in exchange for chores and caring for family members. Lucas would later confess to committing several murders while staying at these persons' homes. At one particular home in Texas, the elderly woman Becky Powell was caring for discussed Christian values. Powell decided that she wanted to return to Florida, confess her sins, and begin a new sin-free life. Lucas and Powell argued and Powell struck Lucas in the head. Instinctively, Lucas stabbed Powell in the chest. He had sex with her corpse and later indicated that it was the first time he felt remorse for his actions. In order to establish a cover for his murder of Powell, he returned to the woman who had befriended Powell. Lucas informed the woman that Powell had left with a truck driver. The woman was suspicious and interrogated Lucas about Powell's disappearance. Lucas raped and murdered the woman. He was a prime suspect in the murder, but there was insufficient evidence to issue a warrant for his arrest.

Lucas left Texas and traveled through the Midwest, leaving scores of raped and murdered victims. He then returned to Texas in hopes of finding work in exchange for housing and food, and went back to the same town where he had murdered the elderly woman. The town sheriff had an outstanding warrant for his arrest on a charge of auto theft. Lucas was arrested and placed in jail. While in jail, he attempted suicide several times and began to hallucinate. He indicated that he saw light in his jail cell and that he was talking with "God," who was encouraging him to confess his sins. Lucas began to confess to the murders of 40 persons; when corrections officers failed to believe him, he began drawing pictures of the victims' faces and provided explicit details regarding the murders. Lucas was arraigned in a Texas courthouse. The judge was careful to be sure that Lucas was fully aware of his Miranda Rights, and of the fact that as a result of confessing to these murders, he would probably spend the rest of his life in prison. Lucas acknowledged that he was aware of his rights, and continued to confess.

In the fall of 1983, Lucas was convicted of the murders of both the elderly woman and Becky Powell. Lucas was subsequently charged and convicted of the 1979 "orange socks" murder and sentenced to death. He was also sentenced to life in prison for the murder of Becky Powell, 75 years' imprisonment for the murder of the elderly woman, and life sentences for 7 other murders.

While Lucas was in jail, law enforcement officers from numerous states arrived to interrogate him regarding unsolved homicides in their respective states. At one point in time, Lucas confessed to 600 murders. Many of the cases could not be substantiated; however, many were confessed through Lucas providing information as to the location of the bodies. An execution date for the "orange socks" murder sentence was set, but was delayed in order for Lucas to appear before a Florida Grand Jury on several capital murder cases. While Lucas was sitting on death row, Texas governor George Bush commuted the death sentence as conflicting evidence created doubt regarding Lucas's culpability in the "orange socks" murder. Lucas died in a Texas prison of heart failure on March 13, 2001.

EVALUATION

Henry Lee Lucas was the subject of numerous psychological and psychiatric evaluations. His numerous convictions for heinous behaviors, suicide attempts, and manifestations of mental illness led clinical personnel from all over the United States to examine him. Lucas's diagnoses run the gamut from borderline mental retardation to schizophrenia. However, the majority of the clinical examiners have diagnosed him with psychopathic personality disorder accompanied by compulsive sexual sadism. Examining just the murders for which Lucas was convicted demonstrates these two diagnoses. If one takes into consideration the case studies, it can also be concluded that Henry Lee Lucas was afflicted with the paraphilia necrophilia.

Henry Lee Lucas demonstrated no remorse for behavior or empathy for his victims, with the exception of Becky Powell. His absolute lack of conscience allowed him to be guilt-free and to commit more murders than any other serial killer in the United States. His cruelty to and torture of his victims is an additional manifestation of his psychopathy. While some clinicians diagnosed Lucas as seriously emotionally impaired and/or schizophrenic, the symptoms supporting these diagnoses can also be explained as Lucas's manipulation of the clinicians, and such manipulation is a classic characteristic of psychopathy. Lucas's suicide attempt successfully prompted his transfer from the Southern Michigan Penitentiary in Jackson, Michigan, to the Riverside Prison in Ionia, Michigan. At the time of Lucas's imprisonment at Southern Michigan Penitentiary, this prison was the largest walled maximum security prison in the United States, with nearly 5,000 inmates. It was an extremely dangerous prison. Riverside, on the other hand, was a small prison designated for mentally ill inmates and those inmates that required protective custody. It was a very safe prison in comparison to other Michigan State prisons. Lucas's auditory and visual hallucinations began at the same time as he began to confess to the murders. The alleged hallucinations were a convenient manipulative attempt to reduce his culpability in the murders of Becky Powell and the elderly Texas woman. Lucas's statements of seeing light in his cell and talking with God would provide his attorney with the defense that Lucas was not guilty by reason of insanity. If Lucas could successfully demonstrate that schizophrenia was at work in one of the murders, the same defense could be utilized on all subsequent charges. Further, the heinous torturous activity associated with the murders would provide for reasonable doubt of Lucas's sanity in the minds of the jurors.

In light of this manipulative skill, one must also question the accuracy of a diagnosis of borderline mental retardation. While one may certainly conclude that Lucas's actions were impulsive, his malingering behavior to produce diagnoses of suicide and schizophrenia is not indicative of someone of intellectual deficiency.

The behaviors Lucas demonstrated during his rapes and murders are certainly consistent with the paraphilia of sexual sadism. Lucas derived intrinsic psychological pleasure from the aggravated nature of his assaults. He was recurrently, intensely sexually aroused through the delivery of pain to his victims. This is readily assessed given the excessive nature of the method of murder. Lucas stabbed more often than required, mutilated the bodies, and used more force than necessary to control his victims. Further, one must conclude the act of homicide fulfilled a final irresistible urge and was sexually gratifying. Lucas left no living victims, not because he was maintaining his anonymity, but rather because he derived pleasure in the lust-filled homicide. While Lucas did have sexual activity with corpses, he probably was not afflicted with necrophilia. Although his behaviors are demonstrations of necrophilia, there are no indications that he had sexual intercourse with victims other than the ones he murdered. Consequently, one may conclude that his intense sexual arousal over the sadistic behavior manifested in the act of homicide carried over to the victim after she died.

The etiology of Lucas's psychopathy is rather straightforward. While some clinicians have attributed his psychopathy to physiological disorders, the personality disorder and paraphilia were shaped by his life experiences. Viola's violent, cruel behavior toward Lucas, his brother, and his father produced a hatred of women. Lucas's early experiences of sexual sadism with animals and observation of his mother's sexual conduct in prostitution fueled his pathological obsession with sex. His mother's lack of conscience and morality pertaining to sex, as well as her cruelty without remorse toward Lucas, became a hurdle in the development of Lucas's morality and conscience. The adage "if it feels good, do it" became a foundation of Lucas's psychosexual development.

Further, Lucas could rely on no one to protect him from his mother's wrath. His father, Anderson, was a worthless alcoholic who could not protect himself from Viola, much less protect his sons. He could not stop Viola's promiscuous behavior or even force her to throw her boyfriend/pimp out of the same house. Anderson escaped through alcohol, and then finally through suicide by falling asleep in the snow. While he did not die that night, he did contract pneumonia, resulting in his death. Lucas could only rely on himself. He developed a level of total egocentricity that consequently prohibited him from acknowledging the wants, needs, and desires of others. While Lucas did express remorse over the death of Becky Powell, he was exhibiting grief not over her death, but rather over his loss of a readily available and fully consensual sexual partner.

Henry Lee Lucas's psychopathy and sexual sadism were precipitated by systematic abuse and acts of perversion.

OTTIS TOOLE

Lucas's accomplice in several of his murders was Ottis Toole. Toole was born on March 5, 1947, in Jacksonville Florida. It is reported that he was intellectually deficient and was severely abused emotionally and physically as a child. Toole was allegedly molested by a friend of his father's at the age of six. Toole was homosexual, visited gay bars, and was a gay prostitute as an adolescent. He traveled throughout the United States with Lucas, and while he, like Lucas, admitted to hundreds of murders, only a half a dozen have been directly attributed to him. Toole was convicted of murdering 64-year-old George Sonnenburg and of the 1983 murder of 19-year-old Ada Johnson of Jacksonville, Florida. He was sentenced to death. While in prison, he confessed to four additional murders, each of which brought an additional life sentence.

Toole died in prison on September 15, 1996, and made a deathbed confession to his niece that he had murdered and decapitated Adam Walsh on July 27, 1981. However, it was not until December 16, 2008, that the niece informed authorities. Adam Walsh—the son of John Walsh, founder of the Center for Missing and Exploited Children—was abducted on July 27, 1981, from a Sears Department store in Hollywood, Florida. Adam's decapitated head was retrieved from a canal in Vero Beach, Florida, on August 10, 1981.

On July 27, 2006, President George Bush signed the Adam Walsh Child Protection and Safety Act. This act creates a national database for convicted sex offenders and child abusers, and specifies increased penalties for persons committing criminal sexual acts against children.

Bibliography and Suggested Reading

American Psychiatric Association. (2000). *Diagnostic and Statistical Manual of Mental Disorders*, (Rev. 4th ed.). Arlington, VA: Author.
Associated Press. (1993, August 23). Drifter Sits on Death Row.

Call, M. (1985). *Hand of Death: The Henry Lee Lucas Story.* Maryville: Prescott.

Cox, M. (1992). *The Confessions of Henry Lee Lucas.* Warner Publishing.

Dobbert, D. L. (2004). *Halting the Sexual Predators among Us.* Westport, CT: Praeger.

Dobbert, D. L. (2007). *Understanding Personality Disorders.* Westport, CT: Praeger.

Frasier, D. K. (1996). Henry Lee Lucas. In *Murder Cases of the Twentieth Century.* Jefferson: McFarland.

Grimm, F. (1983, October 17). Killer's Confessions Lead Investigators on Trail of Murder. *Miami Herald.*

Nash, J. R. (1990). *Encyclopedia of Word Crime, 2001.* Wilmette: Crime Books.

Nelson, T. (1983, August 28). Possibly 100 Bodies Mark Lucas' Troubled Past. *Houston Chronicle.*

Norris, J. (1988). *Serial Killers: The Growing Menace.* New York: Doubleday.

Norris, J. (1991). *Henry Lee Lucas: The Shocking True Story of America's Most Notorious Serial Killer.* New York: Kensington.

Ressler, R., & Shachtman, T. (1992). *Whoever Fights Monsters.* New York: St. Martin's Press.

Schechter, H., & Everitt, D. (1996). Henry Lee Lucas. In *The A–Z Encyclopedia of Serial Killers.* New York: Simon & Schuster.

9

Andrei Chikatilo (1936–1994)

Andrei Chikatilo was born on October 16, 1936, in a small Ukrainian village outside of Soviet Russia. Chikatilo's early life was characterized by the terror and impoverishment of World War II. Extreme cold, poverty, and starvation were characteristics of this era. Stalin forced small farmers to give their crops to the government to support the war effort and feed all of the people of the Soviet Union. The terror of the nearby Nazi occupation and of bombing was psychologically damaging. It has been reported, with some question as to accuracy, that Chikatilo's mother told him that his older brother had been captured and cannibalized. Chikatilo's terror increased as his father was drafted into military service. His father was captured and held captive, and upon his release from the prison camp was ridiculed as a traitor for surrendering to the Germans, rather than being received as a war hero. These wartime events caused emotional impairments in Chikatilo that were manifested in rage, social ineptness, and impotence. The heinous manifestation of his pathology would later result in the murder of 53 women and children, and the dubious distinction of being the world's most prolific killer. Typical of the Soviet Union, the specifics of Chikatilo's 12-year criminal career of lust homicides were hidden from the public, as Soviet officials vehemently insisted that serial killers did not exist in the Soviet Union and were only a Western phenomenon.

Chikatilo completed mandatory military service in 1960 and found work as an engineer in Rodionovo. He married in 1963, and, following the completion of a teaching degree in Russian Literature, received a job as a teacher. His career in education was short-lived following several complaints that he had molested students.

In 1978, Chikatilo commited his first documented murder. The body of a 9-year-old girl was found in the Grusheva River in the Rostov Oblast province. The crime scene analysts determined that the culprit apparently attempted to rape the child, but experienced premature ejaculation, as semen was found on her clothing. He then stabbed her to death. Although Chikatilo was a suspect in the crime, another man, Alexander Kravchenko—a previously convicted rapist—was arrested and confessed to the murder during torture. Chikatilo was released and Kravchenko was executed. During Chikatilo's murder trial in 1992, the presiding judge found him guilty of this murder and recognized the wrongful execution of Kravchenko.

In continuing due form, the Soviet Union does not identify another murder committed by Chikatilo until 1982, four years later. It is more than likely that he committed numerous other murders during this period of time, but that the bodies were not found, the murders were not aggressively investigated, and they were not attributed to Chikatilo. During 1982 Chikatilo would commit several more murders. The victimology was similar, forcing the authorities to suggest that a single person had committed the murders. Chikatilo would approach vagrants and runaways at rail and bus stations, lure them into the forest, and murder them. His pattern changed in 1983, and he began to approach women as well as children. The women were prostitutes or homeless and he would offer them money for sex. His impotence would manifest in rage, and this would be expressed through his mutilation of the bodies. At this juncture one must contemplate whether Chikatilo was sexually aroused by the sexual activity resulting in his premature ejaculation, or whether the sadistic mutilation produced the sexual arousal. His pattern also varied, as his child victims were both boys and girls. This suggests that it was the sexual sadism of his crimes that stimulated Chikatilo's recurrent, intense sexual arousal, rather than the age and gender of his victims.

By 1983, six bodies had been discovered, and Moscow established a task force mandated with the responsibility of identifying and arresting the killer. The task force began its investigation of the murders with the interrogation and torture-like techniques used on known sex offenders, homosexuals, and mentally retarded men. Hundreds of men were held for prolonged periods of time, and some young men confessed to the crimes due to torture, fear, and mental deficiencies. One young homosexual male committed suicide during his prolonged captivity. Chikatilo was interrogated, yet due to an incorrect blood test was determined not to be a suspect and released. By 1984, despite the extensive efforts of the task force, another 15 murders took place.

The police began utilizing decoys at the bus and train stations in hopes of having the killer approach one of them. In 1984, Chikatilo was arrested for suspicious behavior at a bus station. During his interrogation, it was determined that he was wanted on a charge of theft from a previous employer. He was convicted of the theft and sentenced to a year in prison. He was released after three months of incarceration, and relocated to Novocherkassk. While the task force indicated that no new murders were coming forth, Chikatilo's incarceration and subsequent relocation would explain the apparent stop in murders. Despite the authorities' contention that the murders had stopped, Chikatilo murdered two women in Novocherkassk in 1985, a young boy in Revda in 1987, and two others in Zapopozhye and Leningrad. It is difficult to determine whether the failure to identify these additional murders as being related to the earlier murders resulted from ineffective communication and the lack of a central depository—as was the case in the United States prior to the late 1970s—or from the continuing attitude that there were no serial killers in the Soviet Union. Regardless, the murders continued.

The task force secured the assistance of a psychiatrist, the first such request for clinical help in a Soviet police investigation. The police continued to use decoys in patrolling the rail and bus stations, but to no avail, and the murders continued. It appeared that the unknown serial killer was playing a game of "cat and mouse" with the police, committing murders far from the patrolled areas. In 1988, Chikatilo murdered nine more persons, including one woman in Krasny-Sulin and two in Shakhty. Official records indicate that Chikatilo did not commit any murders in 1989, but this author suggests that it would have been impossible for him to stop murdering, because rape, mutilation, and murder met his intrinsic psychological needs. He would have been incapable of shutting off his psychological needs. It is more likely that he committed murders further away from his normal "hunting grounds" and successfully discarded his victims' bodies—or that the Soviet Task force continued to deny that the murders were happening.

In 1990 a resurgence of the murders occurred. Chikatilo would murder seven boys and two women. On November 6, 1990, he murdered and mutilated Sveta Korostik. As he was exiting the forest crime scene he was observed by a police officer who was patrolling the Leskhoz train station. Despite the suspicious nature of Chikatilo's clothing, the officer checked his papers and did not detain him. The officer filed his paperwork, noting the incident with Chikatilo and recording his name. The police subsequently found two bodies near the Leskhoz train station. However, there was insufficient evidence to arrest Chikatilo. The police did, however, place him under 24-hour undercover surveillance. On November 20, 1990, police arrested Chikatilo for soliciting children with beer. Unable to hold him for longer than 10 days, they released him, but kept him under surveillance. It appeared that a struggle had taken place at the crime scene of one of the last victims, and as Chikatilo had a fresh bite wound on his hand, he was taken back into custody.

While in custody, the police enlisted the assistance of a psychiatrist in the interrogation of Chikatilo. Following a long interrogation, Chikatilo confessed to 56 murders. As the confession alone was insufficient, Chikatilo described the murders and the locations of bodies that had not been discovered to date.

Chikatilo's trial began on April 14, 1992. The prosecutors charged Chikatilo with 34 counts of murder although he had confessed to 56. His behavior in court was bizarre but not sufficiently deranged for the judge to determine him insane. Chikatilo was found guilty in July, sentenced in November, and executed on February 14, 1994.

EVALUATION

The psychological diagnosis of Andrei Chikatilo is relatively straightforward. Despite his bizarre outbursts in court, it is obvious that he was not mentally ill. Chikatilo faked the symptoms of mental illness to avoid prosecution and the death penalty. While his behaviors of murder, rape, and mutilation and the number of heinous crimes committed might suggest insanity, his careful manipulation of the geography of his murders in relationship to the task force's deployment of officers demonstrates his ability for rational, critical planning. Andrei Chikatilo was a psychopath. His conscience deficiency enabled him to abduct, rape, mutilate, and murder at will with no sense of guilt or remorse for his behavior. He demonstrated a complete lack of empathy for his victims, and his overwhelming need for stimulation was manifested in the aggregate number of people he killed. His mutilation of victims was an activity that emerged later in his career, and suggests his ever-increasing need for heightened stimulation.

It is questionable whether Chikatilo was afflicted with sexual sadism because much of his sexual conduct and mutilation was postmortem. He was not afflicted with pedophilia, hebephilia, or an insatiable need for a particular age and gender fantasy group. Chikatilo was an equal opportunity murderer. He murdered men, women, boys, and girls. Chikatilo was recurrently, intensely sexually aroused over the murder of his victims. He was unable to achieve sexual arousal until the victim was dead, and consequently he is diagnosed with necrophilia—unfortunately, the worst type of necrophiliac. Other persons afflicted with necrophilia are sexually aroused by sex with corpses; Chikatilo was sexually aroused by sexual activity with persons he murdered.

An accurate assessment of the etiology of Chikatilo's pathology will never be possible because of the lack of cooperation and collaboration with the authorities of Russia. It is reasonable to assume that Chikatilo's pathology was a manifestation of posttraumatic stress syndrome from his experiences of World War II.

Bibliography and Suggested Reading

American Psychiatric Association. (2000). *Diagnostic and Statistical Manual of Mental Disorders* (Rev. 4th ed.). Arlington, VA: Author.

Clarkson, W. (2005). *Evil Beyond Belief.* London: Blake.

Conradi, P. (1992). *The Red Ripper: Inside the Mind of Russia's Most Brutal Serial Killer.* New York: Dell.

Cullen, R. (1993) *Killer Department.* UK: Gollancz.

Dobbert, D. L. (2004). *Halting the Sexual Predators among Us.* Westport, CT: Praeger.

Dobbert, D. L. (2007). *Understanding Personality Disorders.* Westport, CT: Praeger.

Krivich, M., & Ol'Gin, O. (1993). *Comrade Chikatilo: The Psychopathology of Russia's Notorious Serial Killer.* Fort Lee: Barricade.

Lourie, R. (1993). *Hunting the Devil: The Pursuit, Capture and Confession of the Most Savage Serial Killer in History.* New York: HarperCollins.

10

Carroll Edward Cole
(1938–1985)

Carroll Edward Cole was born on May 9, 1938, and was the first person executed by lethal injection in Nevada, on December 6, 1985. Cole was convicted of 13 lust homicides, but by his own admission, the full number was more like 34 or 35. The Carroll Cole case is very significant as a demonstration of the failure of the criminal justice system. While there were numerous instances of malfeasance in the case, the true culprit was a system that lacked contemporary technology. Cole committed dozens, if not hundreds, of crimes, in addition to the murders, throughout the United States. He was convicted in numerous local, state, and federal jurisdictions, but was commonly a first offender because of the lack of a central depository of criminal behavior. As this case study demonstrates, Cole began manifesting violent behavior at an early age, and prior to that time was a victim of child abuse.

The Federal Bureau of Investigation initiated the Violent Criminal Apprehension Program (VICAP) in 1985. Prior to VICAP there was no central depository on violent crime. There was no mechanism for sharing information on violent crimes, solved and unsolved. Consequently, if an offender was sufficiently mobile, he would be considered a first offender in every jurisdiction in which he violated the law. This case study will demonstrate not only the pathology that motivated Carroll Cole to commit his heinous crimes, but also how current technology would have prevented him from continuing a career of violent crime that spanned close to four decades.

Carroll Edward Cole was the third child of Laverne and Vesta Cole. The Great Depression forced Laverne Cole to move his family west in search for work. While the West Coast was the goal, Laverne found work in Richmond at the Kaiser Shipyard. Laverne joined the armed forces with the United States' entry into World War II. Vesta enjoyed the "company" of other men during her husband's absence, and would require Carroll to visit their homes while she participated in extramarital affairs. Carroll was sworn to secrecy under the threat of severe beatings. Vesta was physically and emotionally abusive of Carroll. She would dress him up in one of his sister's frilly dresses, refer to him as her little girl, tease him about his feminine name, and make him serve refreshments to guests she invited to the family home. Vesta, in violation of California law, also refused to send Carroll to school. At an early age, a young female acquaintance aggressively knocked Carroll to the ground and sat on his face. When Vesta observed the activity she pulled the girl off of Carroll and then proceeded to strike him in the face as if he was the aggressor rather than the victim. In a rage, Carroll crawled beneath the porch where he found and strangled a puppy.

As an adolescent, Carroll was being teased about his "girl's name" by a neighborhood boy. He struck out in anger, but the fight was broken up by others. Later he would drown the same boy while they were swimming, in retaliation for the teasing. Carroll Cole's official criminal record began in 1955, when, at the age of 17, he began to break into a local liquor store and steal beer. He was apprehended and sentenced to two weeks in the juvenile detention center. Following his release, his arrests for curfew violations and underage drinking increased. Typical of that era, the sentencing judge suspended Cole's commitment to the California Youth Authority on the condition that Cole agreed to move out of state. Cole moved in with his brother and his brother's wife in Elko, Nevada. At the age of 18, Cole enlisted and reported for duty on the USS *Ingersoll* docked in San Diego.

The military did not provide the necessary parameters to control Cole's behavior, and he stole two military-issue handguns which he later sold to taxicab drivers in order to have money for alcohol. Cole was apprehended for the theft and stood to court martial. He was sentenced to 90 days in the brig and dishonorable discharge upon release. Cole returned to Richmond only to be arrested in December 1959 for driving without a license, driving under the influence of alcohol, and theft. He was sentenced to 30 days at the County Work Farm. He was arrested again in May 1960 for providing alcohol to minors. In June 1960, while cruising, he found a parked car with a couple engaged in "necking." He withdrew a claw hammer from under his car seat and approached the vehicle. He smashed in the back window of the car but the hammer was wrestled away from him before he could injure anyone. Cole fled the scene, but was arrested the next day for assault with a deadly weapon. Once again, Cole was sentenced to 30 days at the County Work Farm.

In January 1961, Cole flagged down law enforcement officers and informed them of his obsessive desire to find a woman to rape and strangle to death. Cole was subsequently admitted to the Napa State Hospital for psychiatric evaluation. Interestingly, one clinician diagnosed Cole with schizophrenia, undifferentiated type, while a second clinician believed that Cole was manifesting behaviors symptomatic of sociopathic personality disorder (psychopathy or antisocial personality disorder in contemporary terminology). Both clinicians did concur that Cole displayed a need to demonstrate his "manliness" as if to prove his gender, suggesting gender identity disorder. In March, Cole was released from the hospital, diagnosed as having a personality disorder and as a probable sexual psychopath potentially dangerous to others. However, under the mandates and jurisdiction of the state mental hospital, he was not mentally ill and therefore could not stay in residence. He was released with a recommendation to seek out patient therapy. Though the obvious conclusion was that he was sadistic and dangerous, the mental health system terminated its involvement with him because he was not diagnosed with a mental illness. Society would continue to be victimized by Carroll Cole.

On July 13 of the same year, Cole was sentenced to 90 days at the County Work Farm for auto theft. During his sentence at the County Work Farm, he acknowledged to others his obsessive desire to abduct, rape, and murder women, and to then have intercourse with the dead body. A motion to move Cole to a mental health facility was filed in court and he was admitted to Atascadero State Hospital. Clinicians continued to disagree on a diagnosis, but concurred on his preoccupation with rape and murder. Cole was transferred to the Stockton State Hospital on September 12, 1962. The attending psychiatrist indicated that Cole was more than likely psychopathic and not mentally ill, and thus was unsuitable for treatment. Cole was released back into the community. Cole's community behavior was characterized by drunkenness and disturbing the peace. He also attempted suicide by overdosing on prescription medication. The attending psychiatrist released Cole with a referral for follow-up with the state mental health system, which was ignored.

In November 1963, Cole married "Billy" Whitmore, and there then appeared to be a hiatus from his criminal activities. Cole was not arrested again until August 1965 in Texas, where he was found guilty of arson, having attempted to burn down a house where he believed Billy was engaged in extramarital affairs. The State of Texas sentenced Cole to two years' imprisonment following a psychiatric evaluation. Received at the Wynee Unit for psychiatric evaluation, Cole was diagnosed as schizophrenic, but was later determined to be free of mental illness and remanded to Eastman Prison

Farm. Cole was released less than a year later only to be charged with soliciting for prostitution in Oklahoma City. As a first offender he was ordered to a pay a $20 fine and was released.

Shortly thereafter, Cole was charged with the attempted murder of an 11-year-old girl in Lake Ozark. He entered a plea of not guilty by reason of insanity, and was ordered into Fulton State Hospital for a 90-day evaluation. Psychiatrists at Fulton found Cole sane and competent to stand trial. He was sentenced to five years' imprisonment. He was released from the Missouri State Penal System on May 1, 1970. Upon release he was given a bus ticket to Charlotte, North Carolina, where he attended and graduated from a vocational program in heavy machinery operation. Cole disappeared following his graduation from the program until he entered a police station in Reno, Nevada, informing the desk officer that he desired to rape and strangle every woman he could find. Cole was remanded to a state psychiatric facility in Sparks, Nevada. Attending clinicians concluded that Cole had a psychopathic personality disorder, and would confess to his obsession when he was out of money and wanted food and shelter other than a jail cell. They indicated that he was manipulating the system. He was released from the hospital and he traveled to San Diego looking for work.

Unable to find work in heavy machinery, Cole took employment as a nurse's aide, at which time he became acquainted with Essie Buck. Following an evening of drinking, Cole convinced Buck to go somewhere private with him. While kissing in the car, Cole strangled her and ripped off her clothing. He indicated later that he did not want to rape her, only to humiliate her, but that he decided to strangle her because of the fecal material released from the body during the strangulation. He dumped her body in the trunk, her clothing in the ditch, and her purse in a dumpster. Cole disposed of the body in the country the next day, May 9, 1971. Buck's body was found and the coroner indicated that the victim had been legally drunk, showed no signs of sexual assault, and had been strangled, stripped, and dumped. Buck's mother filed a missing persons report, and it was determined that the last time Buck was seen was on May 7, leaving a tavern with a male nurse, C. Edward Cole from Sharpe Memorial Hospital.

Cole murdered another woman and drove to near the Mexican border to bury the body. He returned to the same tavern and murdered another woman a week later. Again, he drove to near the border to bury this woman next to the one he had murdered the previous week. On June 1, 1971, Cole was arrested on his third violation for driving under the influence of alcohol in a month, and received a 30-day jail sentence. Immediately upon his release he wrote fraudulent checks and was arrested. While sitting in jail, he was interviewed by the detective investigating Essie Buck's murder. The investigating detective did not believe Cole's alibi, but lacked sufficient evidence to produce an arrest warrant for the murder. Cole was sentenced to one year for check uttering and publishing. He was transferred to the honor farm to complete his sentence on July 23, 1971. Following release from the honor farm, Cole met two Latino women in a restaurant and offered them a ride. He murdered one by striking her on the head with the claw end of a claw hammer, and strangled the other. He buried them at the site of the murders.

During the summer of 1972, Cole established a relationship with Diana Pashal, an alcoholic bartender. Despite living together, Cole and Pashal were not monogamous. They married July 1973. The marriage was doomed to failure as they both continued their extramarital affairs. In an effort to save the marriage they decided to relocate to Las Vegas. Between the time of his release from the honor farm and January 15, 1973, Cole commited the murders of these two Latino women, served 30 more days on a drunken driving charge, and served six months on another uttering and publishing conviction. On January 15, 1973, Cole was pulled over by a patrol officer who found an outstanding warrant for his arrest on a charge of escaping lawful custody. Cole was sentenced to another six months at the county honor farm. However, he wrote to the judge and asked to be released on his birthday, May 9. The judge, impressed with Cole's behavior at the farm, agreed.

Unless there was an unidentified, unsolved murder, Cole did not commit his next homicide until August 1975. Cole met Myrlene Hamer in a tavern in Mills, Wyoming; he raped and strangled her, and dumped her body. Hamer's body was discovered on August 9. Robbery was ruled out because of the signs of sexual assault and strangulation, and because Hamer was still wearing a ring valued at $1,500. The tavern bartender was able to assist sketch artists in reconstructing the last hours of Hamer's life. However, the disposition was apparent homicide, with no suspects.

Cole returned to San Diego, where he stole a government check and was charged with mail theft. He escaped from custody and, following apprehension, was sentenced in February 1977 to a year in jail. He was paroled in April and moved to Las Vegas in violation of his parole. While in Vegas, Cole met and strangled prostitute Kathlyn Blum. Her body was discovered on May 14, 1977. Cole remained in Las Vegas as the police had no clues on the Blum murder.

Cole relocated to Oklahoma City, and the night before Thanksgiving he picked up a woman at a bar. They spent the night together and when Cole awoke he found her dead. Cole had strangled the woman and severed her feet and one arm. He also excised a piece of her buttocks, which he fried in a skillet. He dismembered the body and disposed of it. Cole fled from Oklahoma City to Denver City, Texas where he was arrested on a drunk and disorderly charge. Upon booking the authorities found an outstanding federal warrant for Cole's arrest. He was returned to San Diego in restraints.

Cole was released on probation on June 16, 1978. Despite his conditional release, he continued with his drinking until he was arrested for public drunkenness on October 25 and November 8. Following a probation violation hearing in March 1979, Cole was not incarcerated, but remanded back to probation status. Probation was not a deterrent for Cole and he continued to drink and look for female companionship. He met a local prostitute, Bonnie Sue O'Neil. Following their sexual encounter, she indicated that she needed to contact her husband, thus driving Cole into a rage. He strangled O'Neil and dumped her body. The medical examiner ruled the cause of death as natural due to advanced stages of alcoholism. Obviously, the medical examiner did not examine the body or consider that it been unceremoniously dumped naked.

The arguments with Diane became more frequent and more intense and finally, on September 17, 1979, after a night of lovemaking, Cole strangled his wife, wrapped her body, and placed it in a closet. Cole was found digging a grave in his crawl space and the police took him to a detox center. Diana's mother found her daughter's corpse and, as had happened with Bonnie Sue O'Neil, the medical examiner determined that Diane had died from alcohol poisoning. Believing that the authorities were searching for him on a murder warrant, Cole left the rehab center and took a bus headed for Las Vegas. He found employment driving trucks and began dating another employee, Sharla Floyd, who he would eventually marry. However, this relationship did not keep him from finding other women. On November 3, 1979, Cole met and murdered Marie Cushman.

Cole married Sharla Floyd on December 16, 1979, and the two of them traveled from Las Vegas to Denver City, Texas. Officers identified Cole's fugitive warrants following a traffic stop. Cole was arrested turned over to the federal authorities on January 17, 1980. He was sentenced to one year. During his incarceration he received another psychiatric evaluation. Once again he was diagnosed with psychopathy and determined to be dangerous to others. He was released to a Dallas Texas parole halfway house on October 4, 1980. Cole murdered three women between his release and November 30, 1980. On November 2, he strangled Dorothy King and raped her corpse. Once again, a medical examiner ruled that the cause of death was alcohol abuse.

On November 12, 1980, a naked and strangled body was found in inner-city Dallas. The woman's clothing was found hidden in the bushes. Her driver's license identified her as 32-year-old Wanda Roberts. A bartender recalled that Roberts, a regular customer and heavy drinker, had left with a man named Eddie on the evening of her murder. No additional clues were found. On November 30, 1980, the sons of 43-year-old Sally Thompson visited their mother. A stranger opened the door of their mother's home. They observed their mother's body lying on the floor with her slacks and underwear pulled down around her ankles. The sons fled their mother's house and called the police, who responded immediately before Cole could escape. Cole indicated that he and Thompson were beginning to engage in sex when she suddenly collapsed. The medical examiner ruled the cause of death unknown and Cole was released. The detective investigating the case noticed that Cole's address was a parole halfway house, and also wondered why Cole used a short version of his middle name, "Eddie." The detective had Cole brought in on December 1, 1980, for subsequent questioning, and Cole began to confess.

Cole's confession lasted throughout the day and night of December 1. Cole confessed to all of the murders he could remember. Cole was booked in the Dallas jail, where he would remain until his trial for the three Dallas murders. Psychiatrists found Cole sane and competent to stand trial. During the trial, he confessed to other murders that he had not recalled earlier, including the cannibalism of the woman in Oklahoma City on Thanksgiving eve. Jurors found Cole guilty of the three Dallas murders, and he was sentenced to life imprisonment. Nevada authorities charged Cole with capital murder and stated their intent to request extradition. Incredibly, Cole waived extradition, and was transported to the Clark County (Las Vegas) jail on April 11, 1984.

Psychiatrists concurred that Cole had waived extradition so he could stand trial for capital murder and receive the death penalty. Cole had decided he wanted to die rather than spend the rest of his life in prison. He pled guilty to the two Las Vegas murders, and during the sentencing phase he informed the sentencing judges that he was eligible for parole in Texas in 5 years. Cole was sentenced to death. He was transferred to death row in Carson City on November 6, 1984. Despite Cole's interest in dying, outside parties that disagreed with the death penalty filed appeals on his behalf. Cole was the first inmate in Nevada to die by lethal injection on December 6, 1985.

EVALUATION

The case of Carroll Edward Cole is a story that demonstrates the hideous nature of psychopathy, particularly when cormorbid with sexual sadism and necrophilia. It is also a story that shames the systems of jurisprudence and mental health. Additionally, it demonstrates that alcoholic female prostitutes do not receive justice. Cole raped and murdered 16 women over his career. The additional number of rapes will never be known. He manipulated a system with statements of his mental illness and compulsive desire to abduct, rape, and murder every woman he could locate. Only one clinician acknowledged that Cole was a danger to society, and every time Cole needed to avoid the law or wanted to spend his time in a mental health facility rather than jail, he would play the "mentally ill" card. The system of jurisprudence, already overwhelmed with cases, was enthusiastically responsive to the mental health system taking care of the case. The mental health system continued to indicate that Cole was not suitable for mental health intervention, and repeatedly released him back to the community.

Finally, the criminal justice system also failed because of its inability and unwillingness to share information across jurisdictional lines. The system played the "out of sight, out of mind" game, and Cole was able to commit 16 murders and countless rapes.

Carroll Edward Cole was physically and emotionally abused, and this abuse was instrumental in the development of his intense egocentricity, which in turn developed into psychopathy. Cole regarded his own interests and desires as paramount to the interests and desires of others, and demonstrated no empathy for others or remorse for his behavior. He was conscience-deficient. This conscience deficiency allowed him to do anything he wanted free of guilt and anxiety. He was a pure psychopath.

While Cole's psychopathy allowed him to engage in his heinous behaviors, it was obsession with sex and sexual sadism that motivated him to the specific behaviors he pursued. Cole was recurrently, intensely sexually aroused through the delivery of humiliation and pain to his victims. He was also aroused in delivering death through strangulation. He didn't use a weapon, but rather used his hands and garrotes, and he looked into the eyes of his victims as they died. He desired seeing the terror in their eyes.

Finally, it was a society that viewed alcoholic women as having inferior worth that permitted Cole to continue. Medical examiners chose not to provide the usual level of examination, and did not produce the cause-of-death determinations that would have demonstrated wrongful treatment of Cole's victims.

Bibliography and Suggested Readings

American Psychiatric Association. (2000). *Diagnostic and Statistical Manual of Mental Disorders* (Rev. 4th ed.). Arlington, VA: Author.

Bowman, C. (1985, December 7). *Bee Sierra Bureau*. Sacramento, CA: Author.

Cole v. State of Nevada. NRS 200.003(2).

Dobbert, D. L. (2004). *Halting the Sexual Predators among Us*. Westport, CT: Praeger.

Dobbert, D. L. (2007). *Understanding Personality Disorders*. Westport, CT: Praeger.

Murderer Won't Appeal. (1985, November 28). *The Chronicle Telegram.* Lorraine, OH.
Newton, M. (1994). *Silent Rage: The 30 Year Odyssey of a Serial Killer.* New York: Dell.
Schechter, H. (2003). *The Serial Killer Files: The Who, What, Where, How, and Why of the World's Most Terrifying Killers.* New York: Ballantine.
Wright, J., & Hensley, C. (2003). From Animal Cruelty to Serial Murder: Applying the Graduation Hypothesis. *International Journal of Offender Therapy and Comparative Criminology, 7*(1).

11

Robert Hansen (1939–)

Robert Hansen is the nonfiction equivalent of General Zaroff in Richard Connell's 1989 best-selling story, *The Most Dangerous Game*. Hansen was convicted of the murder of four women in 1984 and sentenced to 461 years in prison. Hansen also led investigating authorities to the graves of an additional 12 women in the Alaskan wilderness. Like the fictitious General Zaroff, Hansen would release his abducted women in the wilderness and then hunt them down like wild game.

Robert Hansen was born on February 15, 1939, to Christian and Edna Hansen, Dutch immigrants residing in Esterville, Iowa. The family moved to Pocahontas, Iowa, when Hansen was ten years old, and his father opened a bakery there. As the oldest son, Hansen was required to work long hours in the family-owned bakery even while attending school. Hansen's father was a stern and demanding man who allowed little opportunity for Hansen to associate with his school peers, while Hansen's mother attempted to shield him from his father's abuse. Further, Hansen was afflicted with severe stuttering and facial acne. These two characteristics caused Hansen to be the subject of his peers' teasing and degrading remarks. Hansen developed a dichotomized view of women. Goodness was an admirable trait as exhibited by his mother, but the ridicule and humiliation he received at the hands of female peers inspired a hatred growing inside him.

In 1957, Hansen graduated from high school and enlisted in the armed forces reserves. During his enlistment basic training period, Hansen contracted sex with prostitutes. Upon completion of his basic training, he returned to Pocahontas and married a local girl in 1960. His resentment of the people of the community, and particularly the superintendent of the Pocahontas schools, resulted in a retaliatory strike in which Hansen set the school bus garage on fire. Hansen was arrested, convicted of arson, and sentenced to three years in prison. His wife filed for divorce shortly after he was imprisoned. Hansen served 20 months of the three-year sentence.

Following his release from prison, Hansen jumped from job to job. He also met and married another young woman in 1963. The next few years were marked by instability in work and by arrests for thefts from his employers, from stores, and from others' homes. Hansen's arrest and work records posed a problem for him, and he and his wife moved to Alaska in 1967. Hansen spent his free time hunting in the nearby Alaskan wilderness. His prowess with archery was recognized by the hunters of the area, and by the International Pope and Young World Record Book for Archery, as four of his trophies were entered.

Hansen's interest in prostitutes continued in Anchorage. In November 1971, he followed Susan Heppeard home to her apartment, where he accosted her at gun point, telling her he would kill her if she did not come with him. Susan's scream was heard by her roommates who in turn called 911. Police arrested Hansen in possession of the weapon several blocks away. Hansen informed the officers that he was suffering from a blackout and did not know what had happened. He was evaluated by a court-appointed psychiatrist and released from custody to stand trial in early 1972.

Before Hansen appeared in court, he abducted Barbara Fields at gunpoint, took her to a motel, and raped her. She pleaded with him and he released her. At the trial, scheduled in January, 1972, Hansen was charged with the attempted abduction of Susan Heppeard and the kidnapping and rape of Barbara Fields. As a victim's character reference was allowed into evidence in 1972, defense counsel entered Fields' reputation as a prostitute into evidence and Hansen's charges of kidnapping and rape of Barbara Fields were dropped. Hansen agreed to a plea bargain on the Susan Heppeard charges and was sentenced to five years in prison, but was eligible for parole following a psychiatric evaluation, with an order to receive intense counseling for three years. Despite his lack of relevant symptoms, Hansen was diagnosed as schizophrenic, released to a parole halfway house after a mere three months, and then released from the halfway house before the end of 1972.

Allegations regarding rapes of young women continued; however, Hansen was not charged. In 1977, he was charged with the theft of a chainsaw and sentenced to five years in prison. While incarcerated Hansen received a psychiatric evaluation, and was initially diagnosed as antisocial and afflicted with paranoid schizophrenia, with this diagnosis later revised to bipolar affective disorder with a danger to society. Regardless of the diagnosis, Hansen was released from prison after one year. Following his release, allegations of rape continued, but no charges were brought forth. In the early 1980s, Hansen committed fraud by reporting the theft of his mounted hunting trophies. He received a $13,000 check from the insurance company. Hansen used this check to open a bakery. The bakery was successful, and following a couple of years of profit, Hansen purchased a bush plane for his wilderness hunting adventures.

Hansen's secretive life of abduction, rape, and murder began to unravel in 1982, when hunters discovered human skeletal remains in the Knik River Valley wilderness. Crime scene investigators exhumed the remains from the shallow grave and also found a spent .223 cartridge. Following examination of the badly decomposed body in Anchorage, it was determined that the victim was Sherry Morrow, a 24-year-old exotic dancer from the Wild Cherry Bar who had been missing since November 17, 1981. Ms. Morrow had died from three .223 gunshot wounds. Witnesses reported that when she was last seen she indicated that she was meeting a man who was offering her money to pose for pictures.

In the few months prior to the discovery of Sherry Morrow's body, there had been a number of missing persons reports filed on exotic dancers and prostitutes. Considering the lack of evidence to suggest foul play and the transient living patterns of exotic dancers and prostitutes, the Anchorage police had few leads. The discovery of Morrow's body and determination of wrongful death led the authorities to contemplate that the women's disappearances were the act of a serial killer. The Anchorage City Police, in collaboration with the Alaskan State Police, considered two female bodies found in 1980 by construction workers. Both women had been found in shallow graves. The first was heavily decomposed with most of the skeletal remains removed by animals, so identification was not possible. The second woman was identified as Joanne Messina, a topless dancer. There was insufficient evidence to develop solid investigative leads from these bodies.

The Alaskan authorities became convinced that the deaths and the missing women were connected to the work of a single killer, and requested assistance from the Federal Bureau of Investigation (FBI). The recently formed Behavioral Science Unit of the FBI was charged with the mandate of examining, and providing consulting services to, local and state law enforcement agencies working high-profile and violent cases. The FBI's Violent Criminal Apprehension Program (VICAP), initiated in 1985, received violent crime data from throughout the United States, and the Behavioral Science Unit was the central depository. By comparing the baseline data created through VICAP with the characteristics of the specific crime in question, the FBI can provide a statistical profile of the potential perpetrator of the crime. The profile is generally demographic in nature.

In June 1983, a trucker found a young woman wearing handcuffs standing in the middle of the highway attempting to flag him down. The trucker stopped to assist the young woman and she reported that she was being chased by a man. The young woman reported to the police that she was a prostitute and had agreed to provide oral sex on a man for a fee. He pulled a gun and handcuffed her. He then drove her to a house in an upper-class neighborhood where he raped and violently sexually assaulted her. He told her that he was going to take her to his cabin in a more remote location where he would release her unharmed if she cooperated. As he was loading his plane, she escaped and ran down the highway with him in pursuit. He abandoned his pursuit when she flagged down the trucker. She took the police back to the airport and identified the plane that her attacker had been loading. The plane was registered to Robert Hansen. Authorities immediately drove to Hansen's home where they confronted him with the allegation. Hansen protested the allegation and told him that he had been with friends the entire evening. Hansen's friends lied to police and confirmed that he was in their presence that evening. No charges were brought against Hansen.

On September 2, 1983, the decomposing body of Paula Golding, age 17, was found in a shallow grave in the Knik River Valley wilderness. Golding, a topless dancer and prostitute, had been reported missing in April 1983, and she had been murdered with a .223 caliber weapon. The Alaskan authorities contacted John Douglas, director of the FBI's Behavioral Science Unit, and requested additional assistance. They had concluded that Robert Hansen was a viable subject and wanted Douglas's opinion. In route to investigating the Green River Murders, Douglas stopped and consulted with the Alaskan law enforcement officers. Douglas confirmed that despite his alibi for the kidnapping and rape of the young prostitute, Hansen was a viable suspect. He suggested that the officers put pressure on Hansen's friends; if they recanted their alibi they could turn state's evidence and not be charged as accomplices after the fact. The friends not only recanted their alibi for Hansen but also advised the authorities that Hansen had committed insurance fraud on the alleged theft of his mounted trophies, which were still in the basement of his house. Following the advice of John Douglas, the police requested and obtained search warrants.

On October 27, 1983, the police asked Hansen to come in for questioning. Hansen complied and as he was being interrogated at the police station, officers executed the search warrants. The search of Hansen's house produced numerous items that directly tied Hansen to the murders, including a .223 caliber rifle that would be established through ballistics to be the murder weapon. Hansen's cache also included maps of Alaskan wilderness areas with designating marks. These marks would later prove to be the grave sites of 15 murdered women.

Hansen pled not guilty. However, on November 3, 1983, he was bound over for trial on four criminal counts, including kidnapping, criminal sexual assault, and insurance fraud. Hansen, unable to make the $500,000 bail, was held pending trial. On November 20, 1983, the FBI reported the ballistic tests on the .223 rifle, confirming that it was the murder weapon. Recognizing that the incriminating evidence was overwhelming, Hansen accepted a deal to plead guilty to the four murders in exchange for serving his sentence in a federal penal institution rather than the maximum security Alaskan penitentiary.

Hansen confessed to the murders and took authorities to the graves of 15 women. Hansen informed the authorities that he would abduct the women—not "good" women, but rather exotic dancers and prostitutes—and take them to his remote cabin, where he would torture and rape them. He would then release them naked and hunt them down as he would trophy game.

Robert Hansen was sentenced to 461 years in prison.

EVALUATION

Robert Hansen's case is riddled with inaccurate diagnoses of mental illness. These inaccurate diagnoses contributed to the extended time for which Hansen was allowed to live freely in society. Much of his early behavior erroneously excused by attribution to inaccurately diagnosed mental illnesses. In addition, society's pervasive negative attitude about prostitution and exotic dancing facilitated the duration of Hansen's repugnant and murderous behavior.

One must contemplate whether the circumstances would have been different if the young women had been abducted from college campuses, rather than from the parking lots of exotic dancing clubs or from streets lined with prostitutes. Police ignored the complaints of women who were raped by Hansen because they had questionable credibility given their socially unacceptable professions.

Even the word of a recidivist felon was accepted over the word of these young women. These women were sentenced to be victims, because of their status as "women of the night and the streets." The court's decision to dismiss Barbara Fields's complaint of abduction and rape because of her reputation is indicative of this pervasive attitude.

This author suggests that Robert Hansen was not afflicted with schizophrenia or borderline affective disorder. Rather, Hansen was afflicted with psychopathy. Hansen, with premeditation, stalked, abducted, raped, and murdered his victims. He exhibited most of the criteria requisite for a diagnosis of psychopathy. His thefts and arson are indicative of the behaviors of a psychopathic personality and conduct-disordered person. He demonstrated his egocentricity in taking things that met his desires without regard for the persons from whom he was stealing, as well as in his destruction of the property of others as a means of retaliation. He manipulated others to meet his desires and excuse his own behavior. He committed insurance fraud in order to obtain money that he needed to open his bakery.

Hansen demonstrated no empathy for others or remorse for his behaviors that caused others pain or injury. His needs were paramount, and the needs of others insignificant. His premeditated torturous behaviors demonstrate that he was conscience-deficient.

Hansen was also afflicted with sexual sadism. He was recurrently, intensely sexually aroused at the thoughts, behaviors, and memories of delivering pain and humiliation to others. He delighted in instilling fear into his victims, and used that fear to coerce them to go along with the abduction and rape in the hope that he would let them live. He delighted in humiliating them by forcing them to undress. He delighted in seeing their terror when telling them that he would give them a head start before he came to hunt them down. Finally, he delighted in killing them.

It is obvious that Robert Hansen was afflicted with psychopathy and sexual sadism, and that these afflictions were the motivating forces driving him to his repugnant, torturous lust homicides. Additionally, a system that denigrates women was responsible for the continuation of Hansen's murders.

Bibliography and Suggested Readings

American Psychiatric Association. (2000). *Diagnostic and Statistical Manual of Mental Disorders* (Rev. 4th ed.). Arlington, VA: Author.

Connell, R. (1989). *The Most Dangerous Game.* Amherst, ME: Creative Education.

Dobbert, D. L. (2004). *Halting the Sexual Predators among Us.* Westport, CT: Praeger.

Dobbert, D. L. (2007). *Understanding Personality Disorders.* Westport, CT: Praeger.

Douglas, J., & Olshaker, M. K. (1996). *Mindhunter: Inside the FBI's Elite Serial Crime Unit.* New York: Pocket.

DuClos, B. (1993). *Fair Game.* New York: St. Martin's.

Gilmour, W., & Hale, L. (1991). *Butcher Baker.* New York: Penguin.

Newton, M. (1991). *Hunting Humans.* Port Townsend, WA: Breakout.

12

Jerome Brudos (1939–2006)

The case history of Jerome Brudos is an interesting, yet repugnant, study of sexual deviance, personality disorder, and lust homicide. While authors of serial killer encyclopedias suggest a relationship between Brudos's acts and the movie *Psycho,* the reality of his behavioral manifestation is more clearly understood with clinical interpretation. Brudos's motivation for abduction, rape, and body mutilation is related to his psychopathy, his gender identity disorder, and his paraphilias of necrophilia and transvestic fetishism. The etiology of his pathology can be correlated to his psychosexual development.

Jerome H. Brudos was born on January 31, 1939, to Henry and Eileen Brudos. Eileen had birthed two older boys and had hoped for a daughter. Consequently, she was disappointed by her youngest child's gender. She exhibited her disappointment through her belittling, emotional neglect, and abuse of Jerry. It is logical to assume that Jerry probably developed a gender identity disorder at a young age, in hopes of meeting his mother's desires for a daughter and winning her love and acceptance. Evidence supporting this hypothesis includes his early interest in women's clothing. Jerry paraded around in front of his family wearing a pair of women's high-heel shoes that he had found. The shoe-wearing incident resulted in an angry response from his mother, but in the cases of many emotionally neglected and abused children, any form of attention is desired. Furthermore, this incident took place when Jerry Brudos was at a preschool age, and consequently, as a prepubertal behavior, would not have had a sexual motivation.

Brudos's fascination with women's clothing continued throughout his life. Others have suggested that he was afflicted with the paraphilia of fetishism, with the fetish objects of women's shoes and underwear. Incidents later in his life suggest that Brudos was not recurrently, intensely sexually aroused by these specific objects, but rather by wearing them himself; this is indicative of a diagnosis of transvestic fetishism. Jerry Brudos was recurrently, intensely sexually aroused over the thought of being a woman when he wore women's clothing. This, coupled with the development of psychopathy, was the motivation behind his lust homicides.

Brudos also stole his kindergarten teacher's shoes. On the surface this suggests the early development of a "shoe fetish," yet critical thought indicates that early elementary children do not experience sexual arousal as is required for a diagnosis of any of the paraphilias. Furthermore, Brudos had relatively easy access to women's shoes; obtaining other articles of women's clothing, particularly underwear, would have been far more difficult. Shoes, in contrast with underwear, are discarded with little thought of privacy. Consequently, Brudos, at an early age, could collect women's shoes and wear them with the thought of looking like a girl to please his mother.

As Brudos entered adolescence and puberty, he began to find that he was sexually aroused by women's clothing—not the clothing specifically, but rather the thought of wearing women's clothing and personally admiring himself as a woman. This forced Brudos into new arenas of curiosity as he was interested in viewing women's bodies. Brudos began to exhibit symptoms of voyeurism, attempting to watch women in his neighborhood in the acts of dressing and disrobing, bathing, and engaging in sexual activity. Brudos also secretively entered his neighbors' houses and stole women's shoes and underwear. Using this clothing, along with an extensive collection of photos of naked women, he fantasized, became sexually aroused, and sexually gratified himself. The use of nude photos of women and adult magazines is a normal activity in male adolescent development and autoerotic gratification. Arousal from thought of wearing women's clothing is not normal adolescent psychosexual development, and thus continues to support the hypothesis that Brudos was afflicted with gender identity disorder and transvestic fetishism.

In 1955, when Brudos was 16 years old, he invited a neighborhood girl to his house where she encountered a masked man with a knife who demanded that she remove her clothing so he could photograph her. After the masked man left, the girl met Brudos, who indicated that he been locked in the barn by someone. In 1956, Brudos forced a young woman into his car, drove to an abandoned building, and, when she refused to remove her clothing, beat her. His assault was interrupted by neighbors and the young woman filed a police complaint. During the ensuing investigation, police found a number of photos of terrified young women wearing their underwear. Brudos was remanded to the Oregon State Hospital where he resided for nine months.

Following his discharge, Brudos finished high school and then attended trade school, studying to become an electronics technician. He joined the armed forces but was discharged for medical reasons—specifically, mental health concerns. Brudos then began a career as an electronic technician. In 1961, 22-year-old Brudos met and married Darcie, a 17-year-old. Their marriage was marred by Brudos's strange behavior. He would ask his wife to clean the house dressed only in high heels or clothed in lingerie, and he would photograph her. Brudos also posed for pictures himself wearing women's undergarments. Despite his bizarre behavior and requests of her, Darcie stayed with him and bore two children with him.

Brudos entered the next phase of his sexually motivated conduct when he abducted a young woman who was selling encyclopedias as a source of revenue to pay for her college education. On January 26, 1968, Linda Slawson, age 19, approached Brudos at his home intent upon selling him a set of reference books. Brudos coerced her to come back to his workshop in the backyard to discuss the sale. She readily agreed, and in the workshop Brudos struck her with a board, rendering her unconscious. He subsequently strangled the young woman and continued to play with the corpse in his workshop. He sent his wife, two children, and mother out for dinner so that he could have some uninterrupted time with the body. Brudos undressed Slawson carefully, examining her underwear. He then redressed her with clothing from his collection and photographed her. Brudos removed her foot with a hacksaw and put it in the freezer. He would later put shoes from his collection on the foot and photograph it. After mutilating Slawson's body, he weighted down the corpse by tying it to a heavy automobile part and dumped it into the Willamette River. After the severed foot began to decompose he discarded it in similar fashion.

Brudos committed his second murder on November 28, 1968. Jan Whitney, age 23, had problems with her automobile as she was driving home for Thanksgiving. She flagged down a passing motorist, who to Whitney's misfortune was Jerry Brudos. Brudos picked up Whitney and told her he would fix her car, but would need to retrieve some tools from his house. He took her to his home, told her to stay in the car, and told his wife he was going out to fix this person's car. He strangled Whitney in her car and then had sex with her lifeless body. Brudos then took the body to his workshop, took photos of her in her clothes as well as clothing from his collection, and had repeated sex with the corpse. Utilizing a hoist and hook, he raised the corpse to the ceiling of his workshop. He covered the body with plastic and left it to hang there for several days, visiting it regularly for sex and photography. Before he discarded Whitney's body he removed her breast with the intent of making a plastic mold of it to produce paperweights. Using a method similar to the one he used in disposal of Slawson's body, Brudos weighted down Whitney's body with a heavy auto part and dumped it into the Willamette River.

On March 27, 1969, Karen Sprinker, age 19, was abducted at gunpoint by Brudos in a parking garage. After her mother reported her missing, Sprinker's car was located in the parking garage near the restaurant where she was to meet her mother for lunch. Investigators identified witnesses who had not observed the abduction, but had seen a tall, strange-looking woman who appeared to be a man dressed in women's clothing. Brudos took Sprinker back to his workshop where he raped and photographed her in clothing from his collection. Brudos murdered Sprinker by hanging her from her neck on the hoist and hook. He mutilated the body by removing both breasts. Brudos dressed the corpse in a long waist bra and stuffed the bra with paper towels to fill the breast cups and absorb blood. Brudos dumped the body in the Long Tom River in Corvallis, Oregon.

Brudos committed his final abduction and murder four weeks after the Sprinker murder. Brudos abducted Linda Salee, age 22, after using a police badge to arrest her for shoplifting at a shopping mall. Brudos took Salee back to his workshop where he bound and raped her as he was strangling her. After her death he attempted to resurrect movement in the lifeless body by attaching electrical cables to the body and sending electrical current through the corpse as he was raping it. Brudos dumped the body, attached to a automobile transmission, in the Long Tom River, south of Corvallis.

In mid-May 1969, a man fishing the Long Tom River found decomposing flesh floating in the river and notified authorities. The body was found tied to an automobile transmission to weight it down in the current. Dental records would identify the victim as Linda Salee. Further search of the river uncovered the body of Karen Sprinker, tied with similar rope and exotic knotting to an automobile engine.

Law enforcement officers initiated an investigation at Oregon State University in Corvallis, as Karen Sprinker was enrolled at that university. Their investigation turned up female students who had reported receiving unsolicited calls from a man attempting to lure them out to meet him. Others reported seeing a pudgy, red-haired man, obviously not of college age and not known to be a university employee, hanging around campus. One witness informed the officers that she had met a pudgy man with red hair, who claimed he was a Vietnam veteran and was looking for companionship. Further, he had said to her, "Aren't you afraid I might strangle you?" This information was sufficient for the police to ask the witness to make plans to see Brudos if he contacted her, and then to contact the police. Brudos did call and make a date with the young woman. Police met Brudos for the date and released him with no evidence to hold him. However, they did arrest Brudos five days later. Their subsequent investigation of Brudos led to his arrest on May 30, 1969. On June 2, he was charged with the abduction and murder of Karen Sprinker. A subsequent search warrant and search of his workshop provided sufficient evidence to charge him with the murders of Whitney and Salee.

Brudos's confession and the physical evidence from the workshop were sufficiently damaging to force his attorneys to advise Brudos to plead not guilty by reason of insanity. Psychiatrists appointed to evaluate Brudos found him free from mental defect, but afflicted with antisocial personality disorder (psychopathy) and sexual paraphilias. Brudos was found guilty of the charges and sentenced to three consecutive life sentences.

EVALUATION

The psychiatrists that evaluated Jerry Brudos at the time of trial determined that he was free from mental defect, but was afflicted with antisocial personality disorder and sexual paraphilias. As discussed earlier, the term psychopathy is used in this study as a synonym for psychopathic personality disorder, sociopathic personality, and antisocial personality disorder. Jerry Brudos exhibited sufficient diagnostic criteria for a diagnosis of psychopathy. He presented unlawful behavior, pathological lying, disregard for others, and absolutely no empathy for his victims, nor remorse for his actions. He exercised methods of stalking to procure his victims.

Brudos's acts were premeditated and carried out in the absence of any thought or concern for his victims or their families. His behaviors indicate that his intrinsic psychological needs for pleasure were paramount to the needs of his victims. Even after death Brudos continued to humiliate his victims with his photography of them in sexually seductive positions and his mutilation of their bodies. Further, he did not exhibit anxiety when he abducted and restrained them in his workshop and then went into the house to have dinner with his family. His lack of empathy for his victims and his lack of remorse clearly demonstrate deficiency in conscience, a prerequisite criterion for the diagnosis of psychopathy.

As discussed in the case study, Brudos was afflicted with paraphilias that were motivating variables that precipitated his behavior. The specific paraphilias are not as clearly delineated. Other clinicians, criminologists, and authors suggest that he was afflicted with fetishism and the specific fetish of feet, because he obsessed over women's shoes and the surgical removal and preservation of Linda Slawson's left foot. Clinically speaking, a person afflicted with fetishism is recurrently, intensely sexually aroused by an inanimate object—in Brudos's case, shoes and women's undergarments. Consequently, Brudos cannot have had a "foot" fetish, and might rather have had a shoe and underwear fetish. If Brudos was recurrently, intensely sexually aroused over feet, he would have been afflicted with the paraphilia partialism. This author suggests that Brudos was afflicted not with either fetishism or partialism, but rather with transvestic fetishism.

A person afflicted with transvestic fetishism is recurrently, intensely sexually aroused over the behavior of cross-dressing. Brudos demonstrated this paraphilia. He paraded around his home, in front of his wife, while wearing women's underwear. He was wearing woman's panties when he was arrested for the murders. From a very young age, Brudos was fascinated with women's clothing. He started wearing a pair of women's spike heels at prepubescence. This is significant because a person cannot have sexual arousal as a prepubescent, and therefore cannot be diagnosed with a paraphilia. However, a prepubescent boy who exhibits a fascination with women's shoes and clothing is more apt to be afflicted with gender identity disorder.

Brudos's mother demonstrated her discontent over his gender when he was born. She already had two sons and had hoped that her next child would be a girl. She obviously communicated in different fashions her desire that Brudos be a girl, and consequently, to win her favor and reduce the belittling, he wished he was a girl. The overt manifestation of this gender identity disorder was Brudos's wearing the clothing of the opposite gender. Brudos carried these manifestations through adolescence into adulthood.

As Brudos came to adolescence, he became sexually aroused over the thoughts, urges, and behaviors associated with being a woman. This affliction was the motivating factor behind his illegal entry into women's homes to steal their clothing, and his extensive collection of women's shoes and lingerie. Further, witnesses indicated that prior to and at the time of the abduction of Karen Sprinker, they saw a tall, strange-looking woman lurking in the area of the abduction. One witness indicated that when this woman came close to her, it was obviously a man in drag. The obvious conclusion is that Brudos's gender identity disorder developed into transvestic fetishism after sexual maturity.

The age of Brudos's victims demonstrates his fantasy love group as well as his transvestic interest in being a woman of this age. Following the victims' deaths he would dress them in different lingerie and photograph them. Many of his photographs were shot so as to "cut off" the heads of his victims. Obviously, Brudos could substitute his own head, either "really" or via a delusion, as he was recurrently, intensely sexually aroused by the idea of himself as a "woman."

Brudos's sex with the corpses fits the diagnostic criteria for necrophilia. However, this author suggests that this behavior is more likely to be an extension of Brudos's transvestic fetishism. Brudos was sexually aroused by the thought of wearing the clothes of women, and by dressing his victims in his preferred collection of clothing. When he reached sexual arousal, he was sexually gratified by raping the corpse rather than masturbating.

It is ludicrous to believe that Brudos's mutilation of the corpses and preserving of body parts was a means of keeping a "trophy," as suggested by others. Brudos kept body parts to sexually arouse himself in the absence of a "fresh" victim. He preserved body parts in the freezer so he could bring them out, fondle them, dress them, become sexually aroused, and then achieve sexual gratification through masturbation. Interestingly, his surgical removal of the breast of Jan Whitney and both breasts of Karen Sprinker was performed not to keep trophies from his conquests, but rather so that the removed breasts could serve as models for constructing his own.

Jerome Brudos is an extreme example of the potential implications of a child growing up in an environment where they experience perpetual emotional abuse and neglect because of their gender. Most others who experience gender abuse and neglect do not develop the depravity of Brudos, but many will develop disturbances that influence their lives.

Bibliography and Suggested Readings

American Psychiatric Association. (2000). *Diagnostic and Statistical Manual of Mental Disorders* (Rev. 4th ed.). Arlington, VA: Author.

Dobbert, D. L. (2004). *Halting the Sexual Predators among Us.* Westport, CT: Praeger.

Dobbert, D. L. (2007). *Understanding Personality Disorders.* Westport, CT: Praeger.

Fraser, D. (1996). *Murder Cases of the Twentieth Century.* Jefferson, NC: McFarland

Hickey, E. (1998). *Serial Murders and Their Victims.* Belmont, CDA: Wadsworth.

Jerome Brudos: A Brutal Killer. (1994, April 21). *The Oregonian.* Portland, OR.

Rule, A. (1983). *The Lust Killer.* New York: New American Library.

Schechter, H. (2003). *The Serial Killer Files.* New York: Ballantine.

Vronsky, P. (2004). *Serial Killers.* New York: Berkley.

13

John Wayne Gacy (1942–1994)

John Wayne Gacy is one of the contemporary serial killers whose name is well known to mainstream America. Much of that notoriety is based upon his execution on May 10, 1994. Due to Gacy's pending execution, the media refreshed society's memory of the man who murdered 33 adolescent males and buried 27 of them in the crawl space of his house in suburban Chicago.

John Wayne Gacy was born on March 17, 1942, and was raised in North Side Chicago. He was the middle child of John and Marion Gacy. John had a sister 28 months older and a sister 28 months younger. He was devoted to his older sister. John Gacy Sr. was a violent drunk who dealt out severe razor strop beatings to John Jr. and humiliated him for not meeting his expectations. Marion had no control over her husband and was unable to prevent the humiliation and beatings. John Jr. developed an interest and elementary skills in building; however, his father would destroy all of his carefully constructed "forts," with the exception of a hidden one that John built under the front porch. This fort became John's place of solitude and safety from his cruel father. John was unlike other boys his age and developed interests in flowers and landscaping, probably due to the influence of his older sister. He did not enjoy or engage in sports, much to his father's anger and wrath. His father's contempt developed John's poor self worth and feelings of being "not good enough." He was a loner, and was disliked by boys his age. His father told him that he was sickly, weak, uncoordinated, and flabby, suggesting that he was probably a "queer."

During his formative years, John was alleged to have been sexually molested by a 15-year-old girl, and was also caught playing naked with a neighbor boy and the neighbor's younger sister. When John was six or seven years of age, his father discovered the fort under the front porch. He also found a bag containing John's mother's underwear, of which John enjoyed feeling the texture. Following the common razor strop beating, John was required to wear his mother's underwear for continued humiliation. Marion was unable to control her husband's brutality toward her son, because she was a victim of domestic violence. John Sr. would dish out various forms of violence to Marion, and despite her taking the children and leaving John Sr., she would later return and pretend that all was well in the family home.

The Gacy family moved into a larger home when John was 10 years old. His father spent hours in the basement, and the rest of the family was prohibited from going there. John Sr. would come up from the basement drunk and the family would hide in fear of his brutality. Marion, continuing in her efforts to portray a normal family life, would tell her children that their father suffered from a brain tumor, and that while the alcohol served to reduce the pain, it also produced his violent behavior. Marion also utilized physical illness as an explanation for John Jr.'s frail condition. She informed John Jr. that he suffered from a serious heart condition from birth and that this condition caused his physical problems. John became extremely concerned about his physical health, and imposed further restrictions on his own activities. His mother's attempts at helping John understand why he was different from others produced hypochondria in her son.

John began to experience seizures, and despite a number of hospitalizations, no diagnosis explaining the seizures was identified. This incurred the wrath of his father, who believed John had faked the seizures to gain attention. At 15 years of age, John had a tonsillectomy, and while hospitalized began to complain of stomach aches. His father dismissed his complaints as attention-seeking and took him home. John was later admitted to the hospital with a burst appendix, which nearly cost him his life. John's seizures continued, and finally a physician recommended a psychiatric evaluation. However, John's parents did not follow through with the evaluation.

High school was relatively unremarkable, except that John joined the Civil Defense and enjoyed driving around the neighborhoods with his portable blue emergency light flashing on his dashboard. John became involved with Chicago local politics because of his association with his parish. He organized a youth group and volunteer activities. During this period of time, John contemplated becoming a priest. This interest solidified his father's opinion that John was becoming a "queer." Years later, John's mother would indicate that his father was homophobic and would have killed John if he learned of his son's homosexuality.

No longer capable of enduring his father's physical and emotional abuse, John, at age 20, ran away from home and found employment at a mortuary in Las Vegas, Nevada. He remained in Las Vegas for three months. Following his convictions, John Wayne Gacy would admit that he fulfilled his curiosity and fantasies with some of the corpses, including crawling into the casket of a young boy to experience the feeling of death.

Following his return home, Gacy persuaded a local business college to admit him, even though he did not possess a high school diploma. After graduation from this business school, he accepted employment as a shoe salesman, and was shortly thereafter transferred to Springfield, Illinois. While in Springfield, Gacy joined the Jaycees and was elected "Jaycee of the Year," an award designated for the individual most involved in volunteer community activities. He also married Marlynn Myers in September 1964. Marlynn would later indicate that Gacy was a likable person and an extremely good salesman.

In 1964, Gacy and Marlynn moved to Waterloo, Iowa, and accepted a job working for Marlynn's father, managing his three Kentucky Fried Chicken franchises. Gacy continued his involvement with the Jaycees by affiliating with the Waterloo chapter. Waterloo Jaycees would describe Gacy as one of the hardest-working Jaycees in the chapter, but while a valued member of the chapter, he was a little overbearing and offensive. Replicating his activities in high school, Gacy became an auxiliary member of the local police department and enjoyed carrying a gun and running his emergency flashers.

A son was born to the Gacys in 1966, and a daughter a year later. They appeared as the average American married couple. However, the Waterloo prosecuting attorney's office began to receive complaints that Gacy was holding parties for the underage males that were his employees at the restaurants. The complaints indicated that Gacy was providing alcohol to the boys and then encouraging them to participate in sexual activities. One complaint held that Gacy would play billiards with a boy, and if the boy lost he would have to perform a sexual act. If the boy refused, Gacy would tie him up and force him to participate. In May 1968, Gacy was arrested for sodomy of the son of a fellow Jaycee. Gacy was convicted of the charge and sentenced to 10 years in prison. Other Jaycees and family members were shocked at the allegation and subsequent conviction. Gacy maintained his innocence and stated he had been framed. Marlynn divorced Gacy in 1969 when he was incarcerated.

As is common practice in all penal systems, Gacy underwent a physical and psychiatric evaluation to determine his mental and physical health, as well as his threat to security and the likelihood that he would engage in violence or truancy. The reception center physicians could not find a heart condition, which confirmed Gacy's father's previous contention that his son was faking his physical ailments. The psychiatrists diagnosed Gacy as having antisocial personality disorder with manipulative social intelligence. Gacy was remanded to the Iowa State Reformatory. True to his diagnosis, Gacy began his manipulation of the other inmates. Much to the delight of the warden, Gacy organized a prison Jaycee chapter and his good behavior was rewarded with a work assignment as a prison cook. This position allowed him to provide favors to specific inmates and he utilized his position to arrange for a number of bodyguards. One inmate indicated that Gacy hated homosexuals and he feared being raped. His bodyguards protected him throughout his stay at the State Reformatory. Gacy was released on parole after serving a mere 18 months of his sentence.

Gacy moved back to Chicago, and in February 1971, eight months after his release from prison, he was arrested for soliciting sex from a teenage boy he picked up at the Chicago downtown Greyhound bus station. As the boy did not show up for the trial, the charges were dismissed and Gacy's parole remained in effect.

In 1972, Gacy found employment as a chef, and as his father had died when he was in prison, he and his mother moved into a house together in Norwood Park Township, a neighborhood of Chicago. The home was built on a crawl space, but because the crawl space would frequently flood, it could not be used for storage. On July 1, 1972, Gacy married Carol Lofgren, a divorcee with two young girls. Gacy informed Carol that he was bisexual, but she questioned this because he demonstrated such hatred of homosexuals. However, just prior to the wedding, Gacy was arrested for aggravated battery and assault on a boy whom he forced into his car by identifying himself as a police officer. Gacy forced the boy to perform oral sex, but the boy was able to escape. These charges did not proceed to trial.

In 1975, Gacy opened a building contracting company and became active in local politics, eventually rising to the position of precinct captain. In that capacity he was responsible for the annual Polish Constitution Day parade, and during the 1978 parade he was photographed with Rosalynn Carter, President Jimmy Carter's wife. Gacy was well liked in his community and would frequently hold block parties at which he would dress as "Pogo the Clown" and entertain the children. Later Gacy would be nicknamed "the Clown Killer." Following the opening of his construction company, Gacy's marriage began to deteriorate. Gacy began coming home late and offering no excuses for his absence, and his wife found gay pornography in the home as well as wallets with identification of young men and boys. Carol divorced Gacy in March 1976.

Between 1972 and 1978, Gacy would murder 33 boys. Gacy would locate his victims through employment advertisements for his company, as well as by "trolling" the tenderloin district of downtown Chicago looking for young gay prostitutes. He would also frequent the downtown Chicago Greyhound bus station looking for young runaway boys to befriend. Gacy would entice the boys into his car and, if necessary, use chloroform to force them unconscious. He would then take the boys back to his home, where he would entertain them with alcohol and drugs and then force them into nonconsensual sex. Most of the boys were killed through the use of Gacy's "rope trick." Utilizing a rope as a garrote, he would cut off their air supply while engaged in sex with them. Some of the boys would experience enhanced orgasm as the rope garrote was released at the time of orgasm, producing the simultaneous flow of oxygen to the body. During his trial, Gacy would indicate that he had not murdered these boys as they merely died from autoerotic oxygen restriction. In fact, the boys died because Gacy would not release the garrote and they were strangled.

Gacy buried 27 bodies in the crawl space of his house, covering each with lye to reduce the odor of the decomposing bodies. After his basement filled with the bodies, he began to dump the subsequent victims in the Des Plaines River. The murder that resulted in the investigation of John Wayne Gacy was the disappearance of Robert Piest, 15 years old, who worked for Gacy at a pharmacy construction job after work. Piest's parents contacted the Des Plaines police, who found Gacy's previous record for sodomy. An initial search warrant of Gacy's home turned up physical evidence suggesting his involvement in the disappearances of Piest and others, as well as an offensive odor. A second search warrant found the bodies buried in the crawl space.

The victims were all boys and ranged in age from 14 to 21, suggesting a diagnosis of hebephilia:

- Timothy McCoy, age 18, missing January 3, 1972
- John Butkovitch, age 17, missing July 21, 1975
- Darrell Sampson, age 18, missing April 6, 1976
- Randall Reffett, age 15, missing May 14, 1976
- Sam Stapleton, age 14, missing May 14, 1976
- Michael Bonnin, age 17, missing June 3, 1976
- William Carroll, age 16, missing June 13, 1976
- Rick Johnston, age 17, missing August 6, 1976
- Kenneth Parker, age 16, missing October 25, 1976
- Michael Marino, age 14, missing October 25, 1976
- Gregory Godzik, age 17, missing December 12, 1976
- John Szye, age 19, January 20, 1977
- Jon Prestidge, age 20, missing March 15, 1977
- Matthew Bowman, age 19, missing July 5, 1977
- Robert Gilroy, age 18, missing September 15, 1977

- John Mowery, age 19, missing September 25, 1977
- Russell Nelson, age 21, missing October 17, 1977
- Robert Winch, age 16, missing November 1, 1977
- Tommy Boling, age 20, missing November 18, 1977
- David Talsma, age 19, missing December 9, 1977
- William Kindred, age 19, missing February 16, 1978
- Timothy O'Rourke, age 20, missing June 1978
- Frank Landingin, age 19, missing November 4, 1978
- James Mazzara, age 21, missing November 24, 1978
- Robert Piest, age 21, missing December 11, 1978

John Wayne Gacy's plea of temporary insanity was rejected outright, and he was convicted of capital murder. Gacy was executed on May 10, 1994.

EVALUATION

John Wayne Gacy clearly manifested many of the symptoms characteristic of psychopathic personality disorder. First and foremost, Gacy exhibited a lack of conscience in his ability to commit a great many homicides. He demonstrated no empathy for his victims or remorse for his behavior. He abducted the youths, drugged them, and tortured, raped, and murdered them with impunity. In further demonstration of his absolute disregard for his victims, he discarded them in a calculated manner in order to avoid detection. Gacy also demonstrates the gregarious, intelligent, manipulative characteristics of the psychopath. He charmed young men into his vehicle, offered them money for sex, befriended them as runaways, and offered employment in construction—a relatively lucrative type of employment uncommon for youths of this age and skill level. Gacy's intelligence was frequently demonstrated early in his murderous career, as he sought out young male prostitutes and runaways. These youths are less apt to be missed or identified.

The list of the names, ages, and dates of disappearance of the youths identified as missing is very informative. First, and most important, the age and gender of the victims demonstrates Gacy's fantasy love group and preferred sexual group. He is easily diagnosed with the paraphilia of hebephilia. Whereas a pedophile is recurrently, intensely sexually aroused by prepubescent children, a hebephile is recurrently, intensely sexually aroused by children who have arrived at puberty. While most hebephiles are aroused by youths that are close to pubescence due to the illusion of purity and virginity, Gacy demonstrated later that he had a preference for homosexual males in their late teens and even as old as 21 years. This may have been due merely to a preference for this slightly older age group, which is likely to have more interest and experience in sex, while still being young and small enough for Gacy to control.

It has been suggested by investigators that there may be more victims. This author concurs with that suggestion. There are many gaps in the 1972–1978 timeframe for the murders. An individual afflicted with psychopathy cormorbid with hebephilia would generally experience an ever-increasing need for higher levels of stimulation. One can notice from the dates of the missing youths that there were occasions when two youths would go missing on the same day, and a number of occasions where there were but a few days to a week between abductions. This pattern is consistent with Gacy's pathology; however, gaps of two to five months are an anomaly. He would not have been able to restrain his activity for those periods of time. Furthermore, Gacy's construction remodeling company would take him to locations outside of his normal work area. Consequently, it is this author's opinion that there are probably many more youths who died at Gacy's hands. When outside Chicago, he would have maintained a pattern of locating his victims similar to the one he used in Chicago. Therefore, on a contracting remodeling job in a different town and/or state, he would have looked for runaway youths, befriended them, and offered them employment. His profession also provided him the opportunity to discard bodies in newly poured foundations. In the absence of bodies, the runaway youths remain on the records as having whereabouts unknown.

Although Gacy demonstrated his lack of remorse and empathy for his victims, there is some question whether he would have been as a sexual sadist. The rope Gacy used as a garrote was a "sex toy," later employed as a mechanism to murder his lover. This author suggests that Gacy was probably not sexually aroused by the delivering of pain, but rather by the sexual activity with the fantasy love group.

The etiology of Gacy's pathology appears to be relatively straightforward. His father seriously emotionally abused and neglected him, called him a sissy, and suggested he was probably homosexual. His mother defended him as best she could, and he developed a dependency upon her as well as a devotion to his older sister. While the emotional abuse and his sister's and mother's pampering probably did not generate a gender identity disorder, it probably did make Gacy question his gender preference. His enjoyment of hobbies and interests not recognized as masculine, combined with his father's accusations of homosexuality, certainly were influential in determining Gacy's age and gender preferences. Gacy's overt statements of disgust for homosexual males prevented him from establishing consensual gay relationships, which would have confirmed his father's accusations. By contrast, sexual involvement with young boys who were later murdered and discarded could not demonstrate Gacy's homosexuality. This response to his father's accusations also explains Gacy's failure to frequent adult gay taverns, and his very active participation in the Jaycees, a commonly recognized heterosexual community organization.

Bibliography and Suggested Readings

American Psychiatric Association. (2000). *Diagnostic and Statistical Manual of Mental Disorders* (Rev. 4th ed.). Arlington, VA: Author.

Dobbert, D. L. (2004). *Halting the Sexual Predators among Us.* Westport, CT: Praeger.

Dobbert, D. L. (2007). *Understanding Personality Disorders.* Westport, CT: Praeger.

Doyle, R., & Cave, J. (1992). *Crawlspace.* Alexandria, VA: Time Life Books.

Sullivan, S., & Maiken, P. (1983). *Killer Clown: The John Wayne Gacy Murders.* New York: Grossett & Dunlap.

Wilson, C., & Seaman, D. (1988). *The Encyclopedia of Modern Murder.* New York: Arlington House.

Wilson, J., & Herrnstein, R. (1985). *Crime and Human Nature.* New York: Simon & Schuster.

14

Dennis Nilsen (1945–)

Dennis Nilsen is often characterized as the United Kingdom's Jeffrey Dahmer. Nilsen's string of murders from 1978 through 1983 were marked by bizarre behaviors that recall the repugnant behavior exhibited by Jeffrey Dahmer in his Milwaukee, Wisconsin, apartment.

Dennis Nilsen was born on November 23, 1945, in Fraserburgh, Scotland, to Olav and Betty Nilsen. Dennis, his brother, Olav, Jr., and his sister, Sylvia, were the products of brief visits between their mother and father. Olav was a serious alcoholic, and his extended time away from the marital home, and drunkenness when home, led to the couple's divorce in 1949.

Betty and the children continued to live in Fraserburgh, a small fishing village in the northeast of Scotland. Betty was tormented over the circumstances of her life, marriage, and divorce. Betty's father, Andrew, was a fisherman, and, following Olav's departure, became the only male adult figure in Dennis's life. Dennis developed a close and dependent relationship on his grandfather and would miss him terribly when he was at sea on a fishing trip. Dennis and his grandfather spent many enjoyable hours together, and when Andrew would leave for fishing trips, Dennis would slip into a deep depression and withdraw from contact with his mother, grandmother, and siblings. Dennis's mood would turn to one of joy and excitement when his grandfather returned with stories of the sea.

While at sea on a fishing trip, on October 31, 1951, Andrew suffered a heart attack and died. When his body was returned to Fraserburgh, it was laid in repose in the bedroom of the home. Initially Dennis was not told about Andrew's death. Dennis's mother believed that the death of his grandfather would have a traumatic affect on him, and therefore, when the children were taken in to observe their grandfather before the funeral, they were told that their grandfather was sleeping. Later Dennis was told that his grandfather was no longer with them and that he was living in a much nicer place. In the hope of not traumatizing Dennis, Betty inadvertently produced the delusion that his grandfather had found a better place to live away from Dennis. Dennis was devastated by this thought and slipped deeper into depression and isolation from his family. As Dennis aged the delusion changed and Dennis believed that death was a better place to live.

Betty remarried in 1952 and had four additional children with Dennis's stepfather. Dennis retreated into isolation from all of the family members. His childhood and adolescence were characterized by isolation, introversion, and depression. He did not have any sexual experiences, but did notice that he was attracted to boys rather than girls. On one occasion Dennis observed the naked body of his brother while he was sleeping and fondled his brother's genitalia. Dennis felt shame and confusion over his attraction to boys. His mother's and stepfather's lectures on "sins of the flesh" haunted him. During adolescence, Dennis found himself attracted to a painting of a boy in a book. Dennis would fantasize about a sexual relationship with this boy. He also began to visually explore his own naked body in the mirror, finding himself sexually aroused as he stroked his own body. He would become sexually aroused by the picture of the boy and by his own naked body in the mirror. Dennis would masturbate imagining he was in a relationship with the boy in the painting, who now, curiously, looked like his own image in the mirror.

Having little interest in his family and Fraserburgh, Dennis Nilsen quit school and enlisted in the army in 1961 at the tender age of 15. Enlisting in the armed forces turned out to be a good decision for Nilsen, as he was promoted to a noncommissioned rank in the army catering corps. Nilsen was trained as a butcher, a skill that would serve him well throughout his enlistment and well into his life. As a noncommissioned officer, he lived in a private room and could continue his autoerotic behaviors. Nilsen would position a mirror so he could view himself and pretend he was lying with that person in the mirror. He would masturbate to achieve sexual satisfaction. Nilsen drank heavily to stave the feeling of loneliness and to assist his delusion in achieving sexual arousal.

Venturing out into the world was difficult for Dennis, but he was able to find a companion who biographers have referred to as "Terry Finch." Dennis fell in love with Terry, but as Terry was not homosexual, they did not have a sexual relationship. However, they did make home movies depicting themselves in death. When Finch suspected that Nilsen wanted to take the relationship to the next level, he left and broke Nilsen's heart. Nilsen burned the home movies and returned to heavy drinking to deal with the perceived abandonment by Finch. Nilsen slipped into the deep recesses of depression over Finch's abandonment.

Nilsen left the army after 11 years of service and returned to Fraserburgh. He could not stand the boredom there, so he moved and trained to be a constable. Following a year of employment, he resigned his position, and began to search for a new job. Nilsen moved to London and took a position with the Department of Employment, where he would remain working until his arrest.

Nilsen's life was a series of one night stands with homosexual males that he would find at the local taverns where gay men would congregate. Nilsen longed for a long-term relationship with commitment. His relationship with his own image continued to grow more bizarre, and began to take on elements of his past fascination with death. Nilsen would rub his body with talc, giving the impression of death. He was sexually aroused at the thought of having sexual activity with a corpse.

In November 1975, Nilsen met David Gallichan and they moved into a London flat. Setting up house together, they bought a dog and cat, and Nilsen believed that his dream of a lasting loving relationship had been fulfilled. However, Nilsen continued his bizarre necrophiliac-like relationship with his own body. His interest in the macabre and in death strained Nilsen's and Gallichan's relationship, and after two years together, Gallichan left at Nilsen's request. Although the strained relationship caused great heartache, Gallichan's absence was more traumatic for Nilsen. He fell back into the pattern of heavy drinking and autoeroticism.

Nilsen's mirror fantasies and homosexual encounters began to blend after Gallichan departed, and Nilsen would have difficulty separating fantasy from reality. This blending of the macabre mirror autoeroticism and homosexual encounters resulted in the murders of 15 men and boys.

Nilsen's killing spree began in late 1978, when he brought home a young man from a gay bar. They drank heavily and then went to sleep. Nilsen expected that the young man would leave after he awoke. Not wanting his lover to leave, he strangled him till he was unconscious and then drowned him by sticking his head into a bucket. He bathed the boy and put him back in bed. Unable to discard the body, he dressed it in clean clothing, lay down alongside it, and had sex with the corpse. Each time that Nilsen would contemplate dismembering the body he would become sexually aroused, and he realized that he could not discard the boy. Consequently, he would bathe and dress the body again. Nilsen pried loose the floorboards of his garden flat and stored the body beneath the floor. He kept the body of this young man for seven months, retrieving it to hold and masturbate over. At the end of the seven months Nilsen removed the body and burned it in a bonfire in his backyard.

Between late 1978 and 1983, Nilsen would commit 15 murders, all with a similar modus operandi as the first. Nilsen would strangle the men, bathe them, photograph them in seductive poses, and engage in sexual activity with the corpses. He would store their bodies under the floorboards of his flat. At times during his killing spree, Nilsen would have a half a dozen bodies stored in the cupboard or under the floor boards. He would bring them out, arrange them, and then engage in sex with their corpses. No one left of their own accord. Nilsen would not be abandoned again.

Nilsen would spray his apartment twice a day to keep the flies away and mask the stench of the decomposing flesh. It finally became necessary for Nilsen to discard some of the bodies. Nilsen would dismember the bodies in his stone-floor kitchen, bury some of the body parts, discard entrails over his garden fence for animals to eat, and burn remaining parts in a bonfire. Following his arrest, law enforcement officers located over a thousand bone fragments in his garden. Nilsen would use three bonfires to destroy the remains of his victims.

Nilsen moved from his garden flat to an attic flat in a building with six apartments, thus losing access to his floorboards and garden. This did not deter Nilsen from his grisly activity. Three more men would die in the new attic flat. Discarding the dismembered bodies was more difficult, as Nilsen would cut them into smaller pieces and flush them down the toilet. This became too time-consuming, so he began to boil the flesh from the bones and stuff the bones into bags to go with the trash.

Nilsen's final victim was Stephen Sinclair, who was discarded in the same dismemberment process as the other two men that had visited Nilsen's attic flat. Nilsen boiled body parts, put the bones in the trash, and flushed some flesh and entrails down the toilet. The toilets in the apartment building backed up and a plumber was summoned. The plumber found sludge containing rotting flesh. The plumber left and reported the incident to his supervisor, and during his absence, Nilsen cleaned out the backed up rotting flesh from the sewer. However, one piece of decomposing flesh was found by the returning plumber, who subsequently called the police.

The police searched Nilsen's attic flat and found bags containing human remains. Once in custody, Nilsen confessed to the murders and mutilations, and directed police to the bodies of the 12 men at the garden flat.

Nilsen was indicted on six counts of murder and two counts of attempted murder. At the urging of his defense team, Nilsen pled not guilty to all of the charges with the presumption of mental defect. Following extensive psychiatric evaluations, the presiding Judge determined that Nilsen was free from mental defect and competent to stand trial.

On November 4, 1983, Dennis Nilsen was found guilty of six counts of murder and two counts of attempted murder, and sentenced to life in prison with no opportunity for parole for 25 years. This was a short sentence considering the number of murders he committed.

EVALUATION

Evaluation of Dennis Nilsen is not as straightforward as we find with most of the other serial killers. Nilsen exhibits diagnostic criteria for a number of different diagnoses.

Schizophrenia

Despite the fact that the psychiatrist assigned by the Court to examine Nilsen found him free of mental defect, Nilsen manifested symptoms of schizophrenia. He exhibited distortions in thought content pertaining to death. Following the death of his grandfather and his mother's failure to assist in him in understanding the nature of death, Nilsen developed an inaccurate perception of death and of the presence of the dead. Throughout his adult life, he displayed a relationship with death that was abnormal and delusional. He appears to have maintained an extraordinary delusion that the men he had murdered continued to "live" with him in more than memory.

Retaining a memory of a deceased loved one is normal, and most persons keep photographs and mementos, including cremation ashes, that help refresh the memory of their deceased loved ones. However, the practice of retaining the unpreserved corpse and "spending time" with it is abnormal and bizarre. Nilsen kept his first murdered lover for over seven months under the floorboards of his flat. He would regularly retrieve the corpse, bathe it, change it into clean clothes, place it on the couch next to him while he watched TV, and have sex with it. He would then bathe the corpse again and place it back under the floorboards. This behavior is not the behavior of a person who has a rational view of life and death.

Prior to the first murder, Nilsen found his mirrored image sexually arousing, and he could view his image as a person other than himself. Sexually aroused, he would masturbate while viewing the mirrored image and would sense that he was "making love" to a different person. As this was a repeated behavior, one must conclude that it truly was delusional. Nilsen blended his delusion regarding death with his delusion of the lover in the mirror, and began to put talc on his body to give it the appearance of death. He was capable of separating the image in the mirror from the reality that it was himself, and of having a sexual experience with the deceased person in the mirror.

Borderline Personality Disorder

Nilsen also manifested behaviors that are characteristic of borderline personality disorder. Despite his young age, he experienced depression, a sense of emptiness, and hermit-like isolation following the death of his grandfather. Nilsen also had a great deal of difficulty in developing meaningful relationships with others. He exhibited promiscuous behavior in soliciting sexual encounters from gay men on a regular basis. He appeared to be searching for a perfect lover who would stay with him forever. When Nilsen found and developed a relationship with David Gallichan, he set up a household in the garden flat. Fearful of abandonment, he monopolized Gallichan, and exhibited bouts of suspiciousness of Gallichan's commitment to the relationship. Nilsen eventually told Gallichan to leave; however, his subsequent behaviors indicate that he probably did not want Gallichan to leave, but rather to demonstrate total unconditional acceptance.

Nilsen immediately attempted to fill the void in his life. He reverted back to heavy drinking and to his relationship with the "man in the mirror." He also solicited numerous one-night encounters in hopes of finding a replacement lover. When he does find a suitable replacement, he murders him and retains the body to be his companion that will never abandon him. Nilsen's mirror image delusion also reflects the diagnostic criterion of marked disturbance in self image. This behavior also suggests the possibility of dissociative symptoms.

Schizoid Personality Disorder

From an early age on, Nilsen presented symptoms characteristic of schizoid personality disorder. With the exception of attempting to identify and establish a stable continuing sexual relationship, he was not interested in close relationships with family and others. He preferred his solitude to the point of isolation, and had few if any activities that he found pleasurable—with the exception of watching television and drinking, the latter probably occurring mainly as a result of his depression or as an activity requisite to finding sexual partners in taverns.

Psychopathy

Nilsen also exhibited diagnostic criteria requisite to a diagnosis of psychopathy. He was extremely egocentric to the point of narcissism, with the associated sense of entitlement. He demonstrated a lack of empathy for his victims and little to no remorse for the murders and mutilations. His behaviors met his intrinsic psychological needs at the expense of others. His needs were paramount and took precedence even over the lives of others.

Necrophilia

Nilsen's behavior with the corpses of his victims demonstrates that he was afflicted with the paraphilia necrophilia. Although the corpses with which he engaged in sexual activity were not randomly selected, he nonetheless experienced recurrent, intense sexual arousal over fantasies of, urges for, and the completion of sexual activity with dead bodies. Nilsen kept his victims' bodies for extended periods of time, long into the stages of decomposition.

Bibliography and Suggested Readings

American Psychiatric Association. (2000). *Diagnostic and Statistical Manual of Mental Disorders* (Rev. 4th ed.). Arlington, VA: Author.

Dobbert, D. L. (2004). *Halting the Sexual Predators among Us.* Westport, CT: Praeger.

Dobbert, D. L. (2007). *Understanding Personality Disorders.* Westport, CT: Praeger.

Everitt, D. (1993). *Human Monsters.* New York: Contemporary Books.

Gekoski, A. (1998). *Murder by Numbers: British Serial Killers since 1950.* London: Deutsch.

Lisners, J. (1983). *House of Horrors: Dennis Andrew Nilsen.* London: Corgi.

Masters, B. (1993). *Killing for Company: The Story of a Man Addicted to Murder.* New York: Dell.

Maxmen, J., & Ward, N. (1995). *Essential Psychopathology and Its Treatment.* New York: Norton.

McConell, B. (1983). *The Nilsen File.* London: Futura.

Odell, R. (1989). *The New Murderers' Who's Who.* London: Headline.

Szuchman, L., & Muscarella, F. (2000). *Psychological Perspectives on Human Sexuality.* New York: Wiley.

Wilson, C. (1995). *The Killers among Us.* New York: Warner.

15

Ted Bundy (1946–1989)

Ted Bundy is probably the most well-recognized American serial killer. His killing spread throughout the United States for five years. Bundy confessed to 30 murders, but estimates of his actual murder count place it between 30 and 100. His case history and psychological pathologies are significant to this study.

Ted Bundy was born on November 24, 1946, the illegitimate son of Eleanor Louise Crowell, known as Louise. As out-of-wedlock pregnancy was considered inappropriate in the 1940s and abortion was unlawful, Louise was sent to the Elizabeth Lund Home for Unwed Mothers in Burlington, Vermont. Louise's parents, irate and embarrassed by their daughter's pregnancy, brought her and the baby home and raised Ted as their own child, referring to Louise as his older sister. At an early age, Ted and his mother moved to Tacoma, Washington, from her parent's home in Philadelphia, Pennsylvania.

While in Tacoma in 1951, Louise met and married Johnny Culpepper Bundy. Johnny adopted Ted, and Ted's name was officially changed to Theodore Robert Bundy. Louise and Johnny Bundy birthed other children. While Johnny attempted to keep Ted involved in family activities, Ted found solace in his bedroom listening to late night radio talk shows. He would later indicate that he found listening in to others' conversations a pleasurable, voyeuristic activity. Ted seemed to enjoy isolation from his siblings. Despite the appearance of insecurity, he was popular in school. While not particularly athletic, he was an above-average student, active in Boy Scouts and in the Methodist Youth Fellowship of his community congregation.

While Ted Bundy superficially appeared to be a well-adjusted teenager, he later reported to author Ann Rule that he was conflicted with social expectations and found interest in literature that discussed violent sexual activity and death. He did not make friends easily and was insecure; however, he would compensate by structuring his activities, for instance through political activism.

Following graduation from high school, Bundy was awarded a scholarship to the University of Puget Sound. He enrolled in fall semester, 1965, and studied psychology and the Orient, with a concentration in Chinese. Bundy stayed at Puget Sound for two semesters and then transferred to the University of Washington in Seattle to study Chinese. While studying at the University of Washington, he also held a part-time job and volunteered for a local suicide "watch and help" line. It was at this suicide crisis line that he met Ann Rule. They would become friends, and she would collaborate to write Bundy's biography while he was on death row in Florida.

While a student at the University of Washington, Bundy met and developed an intimate relationship with Stephanie Brooks, a fellow student. Their relationship continued until Brooks graduated in 1968, moved to her familial home, and terminated her relationship with Bundy. Traumatized by this rejection and suspicious of his parentage, Bundy traveled to his birthplace and discovered his birth record identifying him as illegitimate, his father unknown, and Louise his mother, not his sister. The combination of Brooks's rejection and finding the stark reality of his parentage appears to have had a significant impact on Bundy.

Bundy returned to Seattle, where he became active in local, state, and national politics—including the presidential campaign of Nelson Rockefeller, for which Bundy attended the Republican National Convention. He also returned to the University of Washington, but changed his major from chinese language to psychology. In 1969, Bundy met Elizabeth Kloeper, a divorced woman with a young daughter. Kloeper fell madly in love with Bundy and they would maintain their relationship until 1976; however, it was obvious the relationship was one-sided. Bundy was beginning his siege of terror.

Following his graduation from the University of Washington in 1972, Bundy moved his volunteer political activism to the professional level, working for the Washington State Republican Party. He also enrolled in the University of Utah Law School in 1973. With a solid foundation of employment and the status of a law student, Bundy reappeared in the life of his first love, Stephanie Brooks. He demonstrated the maturity that Brooks felt was previously nonexistent, and, following his intense courtship, she accepted his offer of marriage. Two weeks after her acceptance of his marriage proposal and shortly after the 1974 New Year, Bundy began refusing to take Brooks's calls and broke off the relationship, in a fashion similar to her earlier rejection of him. Bundy had achieved his revenge on the only woman who had rejected him.

While there is suspicion that Bundy may have committed murder earlier in his life, there are no convictions or confessions of murder prior to 1974, after his rejection of Stephanie Brooks. Interestingly, many of Bundy's victims were similar in appearance to Brooks, and one may contemplate the murders as acts of continuing revenge on young women. In support of this hypothesis is the brutal beating and sexual assault of 18-year-old University of Washington student Joni Lenz on January 4, 1974. Bundy brutally beat Lenz with part of her dormitory bed frame, leaving her in a coma and brain-damaged. Bundy's Washington State's killing spree was just beginning.

Between the assault on Joni Lenz on January 4, 1974, and July 14, 1974, numerous young women were abducted and then sexually assaulted and murdered:

February, 1, 1974: Lynda Ann Healy, age 21, is bludgeoned while sleeping and abducted from her University of Washington room.

March 12, 1974: Sensing that authorities at the University of Washington are carefully investigating the Joni Lenz and Lynda Ann Healy crimes, Bundy moves to another Washington State University, Evergreen State College in Olympia, Washington. Here he abducts 19-year-old student Donna Gail Manson as she is walking to a jazz concert.

April 17, 1974: Moving on to another campus, Bundy kidnaps Susan Ranscourt, age 18, from Central Washington State College. It is after this abduction that part of Bundy's modus operandi is identified. Bundy had put a cast on his arm and asked female Central Washington students to help him carry books to his yellow Volkswagen Beetle.

May 6, 1974: Staying ahead of the law enforcement investigation, Bundy moves out of state to abduct Kathy Parks, age 22, a student at Oregon State University in Corvallis.

June 1, 1964: Brenda Carol Ball, age 22, disappears from the Flame Tavern in Burien, Washington.

June 11, 1964: Bundy abducts Georgeann Hawkins, age 18, of Washington State University, from the alley behind the Kappa Alpha Theta sorority house as she returns from visiting her boyfriend. Witnesses later indicate that a man with a cast on his leg was observed carrying what appeared to be a heavy briefcase, and one Washington State University student states that earlier that evening, a man with a cast on his leg had asked her to assist him in placing a heavy briefcase into his yellow Volkswagen Beetle.

July 14, 1964: Moving off campus to the Lake Sammamish State Park in Issaquah, Washington, Bundy uses his "arm in a cast" modus operandi to abduct two different women, Janice Ott, age 23, and Denise Marie Naslund, age 19, at different times on the same date. Numerous female witnesses indicate that a man named "Ted," with his arm in a cast, asked them to assist him in removing a sailboat from his Volkswagen Beetle. Others report Janice Ott leaving with the man with a cast. The remains of these two women were not discovered until September 7, 1974 one mile from the park. Interestingly, the bones of Georgeann Hawkins were also found at the scene, indicating that Hawkins's body had been mutilated and some of the bones dumped in the same location. Issaquah was a favored dump site for Bundy, as the partial remains of four of his other victims were found nearby. The partial remains support the hypothesis of postmortem mutilation.

September 2, 1964: Prior to his execution, Ted Bundy confessed to the abduction and murder of a teenage female hitchhiker in Idaho on this date. Her identity has not been established and her body has not been located.

October 2, 1964: In the fall of 1964, Bundy is enrolled at the University of Utah Law School in Salt Lake City, Utah. Nancy Holiday, age 16, disappears from her home in Hollady, Utah. She is last seen riding in a Volkswagen Beetle.

October 18, 1964: Melissa Smith, age 17, daughter of the Midvale Chief of Police, is abducted by Bundy.

October 31, 1964: Bundy, in Levi, Utah, abducts 17-year-old Laura Aime. Her body is found on Thanksgiving Day, 1964.

November 8, 1964: Bundy, posing as a police officer, attempts to abduct Carol DaRonch from a shopping mall in Murray, Utah. Bundy places handcuffs on DaRonch, but before he can strike her with a pry bar, she jumps from his moving car.

November 8, 1964: Later on the same day that he attempted to abduct Carol DaRonch, Bundy is observed in a high school parking lot in Bountiful, Utah. Debra Kent, age 17, disappears from the parking lot, and a handcuff key, found in the parking lot, proves able to open the handcuffs on DaRonch. Debra Kent has never been found.

January 12, 1975: Bundy abducts Caryn Campbell, age 23, taking her from a ski resort in Snowmass, Colorado, where she is vacationing with her fiancée.

March 15, 1975: Julie Cunningham, age 26, is abducted by Bundy in Vail, Colorado. Bundy later confessed to this crime and indicated that he utilized crutches as part of his modus operandi.

April 6, 1975: Bundy abducts Denise Oliverson, age 25, while she is cycling in Grand Junction, Colorado.

May 6, 1975: In an interesting change of age preference and location, Bundy abducts Lynette Culver, age 13, from a school playground in Pocatello, Idaho.

June 28, 1975: Bundy abducts Susan Curtis, age 15, from a summer conference at Brigham Young University in Provo, Utah.

On August 16, 1975, Ted Bundy, driving his yellow Volkswagen Beetle, was pulled over in Salt Lake City, Utah, on a routine traffic stop. Bundy's vehicle was searched, and items suspected as armed robbery and burglary tools were found in his car. While being questioned, Utah police officers tied Bundy's description and vehicle to the attempted abduction of Carol DaRonch. Bundy was identified by DaRonch in a lineup, and on March 1, 1976, was convicted of kidnapping and sentenced to 15 years' imprisonment. A search of Bundy's residence and the items found in his vehicle provided probable cause to investigate Bundy on murder charges, and he was extradited to Colorado, where he was held pending trail.

On June 7, 1977, Bundy was moved to Aspen, Colorado, to stand trial for the murder of Caryn Campbell. While in custody at the Pitkin County courthouse, Bundy jumped from a second floor window and escaped. He climbed Aspen Mountain and hid in an unoccupied hunting cabin until he ventured back down the mountain and stole a vehicle on June 13, 1977. He was apprehended in Aspen when observed driving erratically. Bundy was placed back in custody in the Glenwood Springs, Colorado, jail.

Bundy was successful in obtaining cash and a saw blade while in custody. Over the course of several weeks, he successfully cut through a vent in the ceiling of his cell. He also began a diet routine to slim down his body sufficiently to allow him to squeeze through the opening. On December 30, 1977, 10 days before the start of the Caryn Campbell murder trail, Bundy squeezed through the vent, crawled through the duct work to a location directly above the jailer's apartment, dropped down, and walked out of the jail.

Bundy stole a car only to have it break down in the mountains; hitched a ride to Vail, Colorado; caught a bus to Denver; and then boarded a flight to Chicago, Illinois. He took an Amtrak train to Ann Arbor, Michigan, rented a room at the YMCA, strolled to a local tavern, and watched the Washington Huskies beat the University of Michigan in the 1978 Rose Bowl. Bundy then stole a car, drove to Atlanta, Georgia, and took a bus to Tallahassee, Florida. Under the alias of Chris Hagan, Bundy rented a room and looked for work. Despite his freedom and disguise, Bundy could not withhold his pathological need to abduct, sexually assault, and murder women. On January 15, 1978, he broke into the Chi Omega sorority house at Florida State University. Bundy murdered two sleeping sorority women, Lisa Levy and Margaret

Bowman, and assaulted Karen Chandler and Kathy Kleiner. After leaving the Chi Omega house, Bundy broke into another house and brutally beat Cheryl Thomas, another Florida State University student.

On February 9, 1978, in Lake City, Florida, Bundy abducted, raped, and murdered Kimberly Leach, age 12. On February 12, he stole a Volkswagen Beetle and drove west from Tallahassee through the Florida panhandle. On February 15, 1978, he was stopped by a police officer in Pensacola, Florida. When the license plate came up as a stolen vehicle, Bundy was arrested. The use of an alias was unsuccessful for Bundy, as his fingerprints correctly identified him. Bundy was held in Tallahassee until his trial for the Florida State University murders began in June 1979 in Miami.

Bundy was convicted of the murders of the Chi Omega Sorority women and received the death penalty. He was also charged, convicted, and sentenced to death for the murder of junior high school–age Kimberly Leach. In both of his trials, Bundy refused court-appointed defense counsel and presented his own defense. During the Kimberly Leach trial, Bundy married Carole Ann Boone.

Bundy filed appeal after appeal from 1980 until 1989, and all were dismissed by appellate jurisdictions. Prior to his execution, Bundy attempted to gain time, or perhaps commutation of his death sentence to life imprisonment, by offering to provide additional information regarding the murders. He provided vivid descriptions of the murders, the dump sites, and his postmortem behavior with the corpses. Bundy admitted to decapitating many of his victims and keeping their heads. He would discard the heads after they became putrefied from decomposition. Bundy also discussed his sexual activities with the corpses.

After three stays of execution, Ted Bundy was executed in the electric chair on January 24, 1989.

EVALUATION

While on death row, Ted Bundy provided interviews to a number of persons, including Robert Ressler, one of the original founders of the Federal Bureau of Investigation's Behavioral Science Unit. Ressler interviewed Bundy in the course of evaluating all of the serial murderers incarcerated in the United States. Bundy also provided an interview to evangelist Dr. James Dobson the night before his execution, and to author Ann Rule, who he had met at the suicide crisis help line in Seattle, Washington. These interviews provided significant additional insight into the etiology and characteristics of Bundy's pathologies.

Bundy indicated that he was addicted to pornography, and that his first exposure to it occurred at an early age when he found his grandfather's hidden collection. As Bundy aged, his pornographic interests fixated on violent sexuality. This statement clearly demonstrates that Bundy was afflicted with the paraphilia of sexual sadism. Bundy was recurrently, intensely sexually aroused by the violent sexual activity he observed in pornography. True to form as in all forms of addiction, Bundy eventually found the pornography to be insufficient to produce his sexual arousal and subsequent sexual gratification. Consequently, he stepped outside of his world of pornographic fantasy to look for flesh. In one of his interviews, Bundy indicated that the initial murders were difficult, but as the number of victims mounted, he was at ease in the abduction, rape, and murder.

Bundy's choice of victims may also demonstrate his interest in revenge. Some have speculated that Bundy killed women that looked like his first love, Stephanie Brooks, as a revenge for her rejection of him. Yet in all cases of human sexuality, the person has a preferred fantasy love group of a certain age and gender. It is more likely that women in their late teens and twenties, with long dark hair parted in the middle, were Bundy's preferred fantasy love group, and that this preference influenced Bundy's involvement with Stephanie Brooks as well as his subsequent choice of victims.

Further demonstration of Bundy's specific interest in young, attractive women with long brown hair comes from his decapitation of his victims. Law enforcement personnel, following terminology created by the FBI, would indicate that Bundy kept his victims' heads as "trophies"; however, clinicians and this author dispute this hypothesis. Bundy kept these victims' heads in memory of them, not as "trophies" from his successful conquests. As with to his return to the dumpsites to engage in sexual activity with the corpses, Bundy was reliving his relationship with them.

It was later in Bundy's spree that his behavior turned to prolonging his memory of his victims. Bundy dumped four bodies, and the skulls of other victims, at the dumpsite on Taylor Mountain. Bundy would return to this dumpsite, lie with the bodies, and engage in sexual activity with them until they reached a stage of decomposition that drove him away. Similar behavior presents in necrophilia, which is defined as recurrent, intense sexual arousal over dead bodies. Yet Bundy's behavior also throws into question the validity of diagnoses of sexual sadism and necrophilia.

With the exception of Bundy's interest in pornography that portrayed explicit violent sexuality, there does not seem to be evidence to demonstrate that he was recurrently, intensely sexually aroused by the delivery of pain and humiliation. Rather, he was recurrently, intensely sexually aroused over his specific fantasy age and gender group. The available evidence does not suggest torture of Bundy's victims prior to death, but rather postmortem mutilation for the purpose of preserving the skulls to assist him in recalling the events of his relationship with the victim.

Similarly, one must question the validity of a diagnosis of necrophilia. This author suggests that Bundy was not recurrently, intensely sexually aroused over dead bodies. He was, instead, recurrently, intensely sexually aroused by the age, gender, and appearance of his fantasy love group, in life and death. If Bundy was afflicted with necrophilia, he would have been sexually aroused by the corpses of random persons not representative of a specific fantasy love group.

Therefore, one must question whether Bundy was truly a necrophiliac and also afflicted with sexual sadism, or whether he was instead addicted to violent sexuality. This author contends that the diagnosis of psychopathy, or psychopathic personality disorder, is accurate. While awaiting execution, Bundy filed an appeal based upon his incompetence due to mental disease. Bundy was examined and evaluated by court-appointed clinicians and determined to be free from mental defect. One clinician diagnosed Bundy as manic depressive, and found that the murders were precipitated by depressive episodes. Bundy's behavior clearly demonstrates the clinical characteristics requisite for a diagnosis of psychopathy.

Bundy's personality disorder reflected an absence or deficiency of conscience. At no time did his behavior show evidence to support the contention that he felt any empathy for his victims or remorse for the injuries and death he inflicted upon them. However, Bundy did demonstrate his egocentricity and his capacity to do whatever he desired in meeting his own intrinsic psychological needs. He also demonstrated his ability to manipulate others with premeditation and ease. He was intelligent and articulate, and would use these attributes to exploit others for his personal pleasure. He was a pathological liar. Finally, he accepted no responsibility for his behavior, but rather excused it as a product of a society that failed to control the proliferation of pornography.

While it is reasonable to identify the etiology of Bundy's psychopathy and his violent sexuality in his experiences with his grandfather and with pornography, this does not excuse his behavior. Ted Bundy was fully in control of his faculties, and in fact utilized these attributes to meet his desires—and was subsequently held accountable for his behavior.

Bibliography and Suggested Reading

American Psychiatric Association. (2000). *Diagnostic and Statistical Manual of Mental Disorders* (Rev. 4th ed.). Arlington, VA: Author.
Dobbert, D. L. (2004). *Halting the Sexual Predators among Us*. Westport, CT: Praeger.
Dobbert, D. L. (2007). *Understanding Personality Disorders*. Westport, CT: Praeger.

Federal Bureau of Investigation. *Ted Bundy: The FBI Files.* Quantico: Author.

Kendall, E. (1981). *The Phantom Prince: My Life with Ted Bundy.* Seattle: Madrona.

Larsen, R. (1980). *Bundy: The Deliberate Stranger.* New York: Prentice Hall.

Michaud, S., & Aynesworth, H. (1999). *The Only Living Witness.* New York: Authorlink.

Michaud, S., & Aynesworth, H. (2000). *Ted Bundy: Conversations with a Killer.* New York: Authorlink.

Nelson, P. (1994). *Defending the Devil: My Story as Ted Bundy's Last Lawyer.* New York: Morrow.

Rule, A. (2000). *The Stranger Beside Me.* New York: Signet.

16

John Norman Collins (1947–)

John Norman Collins was born on June 17, 1947, in Ontario, Canada, to Robert and Loraine Chapman. Robert and Loraine divorced in 1949 when John was two years old, and Loraine moved back to the United States and married Warren Collins. John became a naturalized U.S. citizen in 1953, and in 1956, Warren Collins adopted him. The family resided in Centerline, Michigan. John became extremely attached to Warren, and was devastated when his mother and Warren divorced.

John attended a Roman Catholic parochial elementary school, and while the parochial teaching staff held him in high regard, they registered concern about his insecurity and his sleeping with his mother until the age of 12. John was a talented athlete, and while attending Mt. Clemens High School, he held offensive and defensive starting positions on the varsity football team. He was also a pitcher on the varsity baseball team and received three varsity letters in basketball. In addition to his athletic achievements, John was also an honor student. Working alongside of his stepfather, John became a skilled motorcycle mechanic.

Following the completion of his high school education, John enrolled as a freshman at Central Michigan University in Mt. Pleasant, Michigan, in 1965. The primary reason for the selection of Central Michigan University was the close residential proximity to his older brother. John transferred to Eastern Michigan University in Ypsilanti, Michigan, in 1966 to major in Education. He joined the Theta Chi fraternity, and lived in the fraternity house until he was caught stealing money from the fraternity's entertainment account and was asked to leave.

John possessed an intense need to be the center of attention, and when not able to maintain that position, he would change his acquaintances. While using humor and laughter as a mechanism to maintain his popularity, he would also teach friends to ride his motorcycle. His good looks and athletic body attracted female attention as well. He kept himself in clean and fit condition. He was featured in *Tomorrow's Man* magazine because of his bulging biceps. There was no indication that John was abusing drugs or alcohol.

While John Norman Collins was only convicted of one murder and sentenced to life in prison, it is believed that he killed eight college-age women over the course of two years. The murders of these college-age women—in the Ann Arbor, Michigan, area, home to the University of Michigan, and in nearby Ypsilanti, home to Eastern Michigan University—drew national attention, and the unknown suspect was dubbed "the Co-Ed Killer." Collins's first alleged victim was Mona Fleszar, who disappeared on the evening of July 9, 1967. Fleszar was a student at Eastern Michigan University, and while walking home to her apartment, it was reported that she was followed by a vehicle whose occupant was attempting to pick her up and give her a ride.

On August 7, 1967, two boys playing near a cornfield heard a car door slam and a vehicle speeding off. Investigating the incident, the boys discovered a badly decomposed carcass. It was difficult to determine whether the carcass was human. Crime scene investigators and medical examiner personnel determined that carcass was, in fact, human, and dental records established that it was the body of Mona Fleszar. Fleszar had been badly beaten and stabbed repeatedly.

Nearly a year passed before the murder of another young woman. On June 5, 1968, Jean Schell disappeared. Witnesses reported that Schell was attempting to find a ride to Ann Arbor to see her boyfriend. The witnesses also indicated that she had hitched a ride in a convertible with three white males, but that the car was seen not driving in the direction of Ann Arbor. Others informed police that Schell was seen in the presence of John Norman Collins the night before her disappearance. On July 5, Schell's mutilated body was found on an Ann Arbor roadside. She had been sexually assaulted and then stabbed 25 times in the back, carotid artery, lungs, and head. Collins was identified as a suspect in Jean Schell's murder. However, no charges were brought forth.

On March 20, 1969, June Mixer disappeared. Mixer was in need of a ride to Muskegon, Michigan, and, as is common at all universities, she had posted a note on a bulletin board. Following a phone call response, Mixer called her boyfriend to tell him that she had found a ride. She never reached Muskegon. Shortly thereafter, her body was found in a nearby cemetery. Mixer was strangled with her own nylon stocking and shot twice in the head with a .22 caliber weapon. Interestingly, the victim's blood was caught in a towel, thus suggesting that the cemetery was a dump site, rather than the murder site. Mixer had apparently not been sexually assaulted, as a menstrual pad remained in place.

Two days following the disappearance of June Mixer, Maralynn Skelton, age 16, went missing. Skelton was hitchhiking from Flint, Michigan, to Ypsilanti to see her fiancée. She would not arrive at her destination. Her body was discovered on March 25, 1969, in an empty lot. This empty lot was in the same general area as the location where Jean Schell's body had been found. Skelton was found naked with a stick driven into her vagina. A cloth had been stuffed into her throat, obviously to silence the girl, and she had subsequently swallowed her tongue. She had been badly beaten about her head and body, with markings indicating a belt and buckle. While Skelton had not been sexually assaulted, her genital area was mutilated. A soiled tampon was found several feet from her battered body.

On April 15, 1969, Dora Basom, age 13, was walking home after spending the evening with her boyfriend. She did not arrive at home, and at 12:46 a.m., her mother called the police to inform them of her daughter's failure to return. On April 16, Basom's body was discovered next to a rural Ann Arbor road. She was gagged with her shirt and she was strangled with electrical wire. There were scrape marks on her breast which medical examiner personnel believed were inflicted with a beer can opener. The rural road was the dump site, and physical evidence, including Basom's sweater, was found in an abandoned farmhouse.

On June 8, 1969, Anne Kalom disappeared, and her body was found near a barn on June 9, 1969. Kalom had been raped, shot with a .22 caliber weapon, and stabbed twice. Collins's roommate informed the police that he had seen Anne Kalom with Collins on the night of her disappearance. The roommate testified that Kalom had been at his and Collins's apartment, and that she then ran out with Collins in pursuit. Collins informed his roommate that she ran away when she refused to have sex with him.

Collins remained at large. The murder for which he was convicted was committed on July 23, 1969. Eastern Michigan University freshman Karry Sue Bieneman agreed to a motorcycle ride with a stranger. She did not return to the dormitory. On July 26, 1969, Bieneman's body was found nude at the bottom of a hill, where it appeared her body had been dumped and rolled down the hill. Dental records and fingerprints were necessary to identify the badly mutilated and decomposing body. Bieneman died from multiple blows to her head. Her shorts were stuffed in her mouth. Bieneman was having her menstrual period; however, seminal fluid was found in her vagina. Further, short, clipped hair was found on her body and clothing. John Norman Collins was identified as the motorcycle driver, and he became a suspect in the case. Collins had been staying at his uncle's house while they were on vacation. His uncle was a law enforcement officer, and he found blood and clipped hair in his basement. The blood and clipped hair would match that found on the victim's panties.

On August 17, 1970, John Norman Collins was convicted of the first-degree murder of Karry Sue Bieneman. He was sentenced to life in prison.

EVALUATION

John Norman Collins demonstrates classical behavioral manifestations of psychopathy and sexual sadism. At no time did he express remorse or a sense of guilt for the murder(s) he performed. His conscience deficiency allowed him to continue to his repugnant behavior. He also manifested classic symptoms of narcissism, which is commonly a part of psychopathic personality disorder. Collins felt he was entitled to these women's favors, and when finished, he discarded them with no remorse. He was gregarious, attractive, and well liked. He used his charismatic features to manipulate others. When he was not the center of attention, he sought other acquaintances. When people rejected him for social or sexual favors, he forced himself upon them and, if necessary, murdered them. It certainly would not surprise this author to find dozens of young women who were forced into nonconsensual sex with Collins but were too fearful to report it.

Collins also exhibited the psychopathic symptom of needing ever-increasing levels of stimulation. If all of the Michigan murders are attributed to Collins, one can see increasing levels of violent behavior and a shortening of the time between events. This decreased amount of time between incidents also suggests that Collins felt superior to the law enforcement community and imagined he would never be caught. Collins believed that he was smarter than the professionals who were working to solve the cases. In addition to this sense of being "smarter" and the increasing number of victims, the failure of law enforcement to apprehended Collins allowed him to commit his acts with impunity, thus further reinforcing his sense of superiority and his belief that women existed to meet his pleasures.

Collins also demonstrated symptoms characteristic of the paraphilia sexual sadism. He practiced torturous behaviors in his rapes and murders. His murders are classic examples of lust homicide. He found intense sexual arousal in the delivery of pain and humiliation. This is demonstrated in his use of more force than was necessary to control and execute his victims. Collins enjoyed these behaviors as they were sexually arousing. It is particularly interesting to note that when his victim was on her menstrual period, he would attack the body with rage—demonstrating that he found the victim unclean and unable to perform sexual acts in the fashion he found gratifying, and felt that she was thus, in essence, rejecting him.

There is insufficient case history to identify, with some degree of certainty, the etiology of Collins's psychopathy and sexual sadism. The absence of a consistent male figure in his childhood, and his sleeping in his mother's bed until near puberty, suggest that he may have been nurtured into his psychopathy. A person who is pampered and overnurtured, and for whom natural development is prevented, develops a sense of importance and heightened egocentricity. During Collins's adolescence, he experienced great success athletically and academically, thus reinforcing his sense that he was better than others. His physical attractiveness was a magnet for young women, and he developed a sense of entitlement with them.

Bibliography and Suggested Readings

American Psychiatric Association. (2000). *Diagnostic and Statistical Manual of Mental Disorders* (Rev. 4th ed.). Arlington, VA: Author.

Dobbert, D. L. (2004). *Halting the Sexual Predators among Us*. Westport, CT: Praeger.

Dobbert, D. L. (2007). *Understanding Personality Disorders*. Westport, CT: Praeger.

Keyes, E. (1976). *The Michigan Murders*. New York: Pocket.

Lane, B., & Gregg, W. (1992). *The Encyclopedia of Serial Killers*. Terra Alta, WV: Headline.

ADDENDUM

There has been some controversy surrounding potential accessories to crimes, and some of these crimes have been attributed to others. While there has been insufficient evidence to charge others as accessories to the homicides believed to have been committed by Collins, Gary Earl Leiterman was charged and subsequently convicted of the murder of Jane L. Mixer on July 22, 2005, 37 years after her death. There is also controversy regarding the conviction of Leiterman as the DNA evidence was determined to be contaminated and consequently rendered inconclusive. Leiterman was sentenced to life imprisonment.

The murder of Eileen Adams, a high school student from Toledo, Ohio, was attributed to Collins. Abducted on December 19, 1967, her raped and murdered body was found on January 30, 1968, in Michigan. Robert Baxter Brown was a suspect in the case following a report filed by his wife. Following a "cold case" grant, Lucas County, Ohio law enforcement utilized DNA to confirm Brown's identification in the case. Warrants for his arrest were issued, but his whereabouts are still unknown.

17

Edmund Kemper (1948–)

The quiet tourist town of Santa Cruz, California, was shocked by multiple murders committed by three individuals in the 1970s. The Students for a Democratic Society counterculture movement appealed to the far-left students of the California State University System, and the campus of the University of California at Santa Cruz was no exception. The California "hippie free love generation" swarmed to the beautiful mountains, redwood forests, and superb surfing waters of Santa Cruz.

The Charles Manson "Family" committed the Helter Skelter murders in 1969. In 1970, John Linley Frazier, a devoted follower of Charles Manson, murdered five persons in Santa Cruz. In the early 1970s, Herbert Mullin, in a span of four months, murdered 13 people. Mullin was a paranoid schizophrenic who responded to auditory hallucinations that prompted him to murder people. Then, during 1972 and 1973, a string of murders of hitchhiking female students terrified the Santa Cruz community. Edmund Kemper was arrested, charged, and convicted of eight counts of capital murder for these crimes. Following the 1972 Supreme Court decision in *Furman v. Georgia* that capital punishment was unconstitutional due to cruel and unusual punishment, Kemper's death sentence was commuted to life imprisonment.

Edmund Kemper III was born on December 18, 1948, in Burbank, California, to Edmund Kemper Jr. and Clarnell Kemper. Edmund was the middle child, with a younger and an older sister. Clarnell divorced Edmund's father when Edmund was nine years old and relocated the family to Montana. Edmund demonstrated aggressive behavior at a young age, mutilating his sisters' dolls and practicing cruelty to animals. He tortured the family cat and beheaded it, placing the head on a pointed stick. When his mother replaced the cat, Edmund killed this cat and dissected it. Fearful that Edmund would assault his sisters, his mother would lock him in the basement of the family home. The divorce only added to Edmund's emotional impairment as he was shipped back and forth between his mother and his father and stepmother. When neither parent was able to control Edmund's behavior, he was shipped off at age 13 to live with his paternal grandparents at their North Folk, California, ranch. Edmund's behavior did not improve while residing with his grandparents, and arguments were a daily occurrence.

Edmund was very large in stature as a adolescent and subject to ridicule from his peers as well as family members. By the time of adolescence, he was 6 feet tall and socially inept, which was fuel for the fire of ridicule.

In August, 1964, 14-year-old Edmund argued with his grandmother and then shot her in the head with a .22 caliber rifle that he had received as a present from his grandfather. Hiding his grandmother in the bedroom, he heard his grandfather drive into the driveway. Edmund turned the rifle on his grandfather as he exited his vehicle and murdered him as well. Having no idea of what to do, Edmund called his mother and told her of his acts. His mother persuaded him to call the police, and upon arriving on the scene, law enforcement officers found Edmund calmly sitting on the front porch approach waiting for them to arrive. Later he would inform the investigating officers that he had killed his grandmother to find out what it felt like, and then killed his grandfather to keep him from seeing his murdered wife. Authorities would note that he was calm and not manifesting anxiety.

Edmund Kemper was not prosecuted for the murders, and was remanded to the Atascadero State Psychiatric Hospital, where he was diagnosed with paranoid schizophrenia. This diagnosis seems to have questionable credibility. Kemper's behaviors have demonstrated conduct disorder diagnostic criteria, while schizophrenia, particularly paranoid schizophrenia, is an anomaly for 14-year-old adolescents. Furthermore, there is no evidence that Kemper experienced hallucinations.

Kemper possessed a very high intelligence quotient, and consequently served as a clinical assistant to the clinical staff. Against the recommendations of the psychiatric staff of Atascadero, he was released at the age of 21 to the care and supervision of his mother, Clarnell. By the time of his release, Kemper was 6 feet 9 inches tall, and 300 pounds in weight. Pursuant to his conditions of release, he attended and graduated from the local community college. His career interest was law enforcement, but he exceeded the height parameters for attending the police academy. Disappointed that he was too tall for active duty law enforcement, Kemper began to hang around police officers at the county courthouse. His immense proportions and quiet demeanor prompted the nickname of "Big Ed" among area law enforcement officials, who enjoyed "hanging out" with him.

Kemper continued to live with his berating mother, moving in and out, depending upon the availability of money. Following a motorcycle accident, for which he received $15,000 for damages, Kemper purchased a yellow Ford sedan—the model, but not the color, of police patrol vehicles. As he traveled the highways of northern California, he came to notice the large number of college women hitchhiking. He began fantasizing about what he might do to them. Coupled with his fantasizing, he began to put a "kit" together that he would utilize when he abducted a hitchhiker. His physical size, which was a source of ridicule in earlier years, put his hitchhiker girls at ease. His "gentle Ben" appearance and gregarious personality did not alarm the girls. Edmund, "Big Ed," picked up many hitchhiking girls, perfecting his techniques before he attempted his first abduction and assault.

Hitchhiking female students began to disappear in May 1972. On May 7, two Fresno State College students, Mary Pesce and Anita Luchessa, did not appear to meet up with their friends at Stanford. It was not until August 15 that the head of Mary Pesce was found in the mountains. While no other body parts were discovered, Kemper would later confess to the abduction and grisly murder of these two students. Kemper put Luchessa in the trunk and handcuffed Pesce in the backseat. He tied a plastic bag over Pesce's head, yet she was able to bite through the bag and resist Kemper, at which time he stabbed her repeatedly until she was dead. He then turned his attention to Luchessa in the trunk, also stabbing her multiple times until she was dead. Kemper took the bodies back to his apartment, photographed them, and decapitated them. He dismembered the bodies and placed the body parts into plastic bags. He buried the body parts in different locations in the mountains surrounding Santa Cruz. Kemper told authorizes that he experienced a sexual rush while decapitating the girls.

Aiko Koo, a 15-year-old dance student, was abducted on by Kemper on September 14. He strangled, raped, and decapitated the girl. He discarded the body except for her head.

Economic circumstances forced Kemper to move back in with his mother, and she began berating him immediately. The single advantage for Kemper was that his mother worked at the University, and he was able to obtain a parking sticker for his car. In early 1973, Kemper picked up college student Cindy Schall and shot her in the head. He took the body back to his mother's house and secretly hid it in his bedroom. When his mother went to work he had sex with the corpse, drained the body of its blood, dismembered it, and threw the pieces, *sans* the head, off the cliffs into the Pacific Ocean. Kemper kept the head and utilized it to perform fellatio. When the head began to decompose, he buried it in his mother's backyard. The body parts began to float ashore in a couple of days, and Schall was identified as the victim. The Santa Cruz community was terrified at the possibility of another murderer abducting and killing college students.

Incredibly, on January 25, 1973, two local families were murdered in their homes and four boys camping were executed with gunshots. Authorities were confused by the sudden change in the victimology of the murders.

College students Rosalind Thorpe and Alice Liu were abducted by Kemper while hitchhiking on February 5, 1973.

On February 13, a woman reported a man being shot in his garden. Herbert Mullin, age 25, was arrested for the murder of this man in his garden. The investigation of Mullin resulted in his conviction on 10 charges of murder. Mullin's murders cleared up the shooting cases, but not the murders of the abducted, murdered, and dismembered students.

On March 4, 1973, the skulls and jawbones of Thorpe and Liu were discovered in a remote area. Both had been shot in the head.

On Easter weekend, 1973, Kemper murdered his mother. He came home to find his mother sleeping in her bed. Kemper used a claw hammer and beat her to death. He decapitated her and raped her lifeless corpse. In retribution for the years of verbal abuse, Kemper cut out her tongue and stuffed it down the garbage disposal, only to have the disposal plug up in rejection.

Later that day, Kemper invited his mother's friend over for a surprise dinner. He strangled, murdered, and decapitated his visitor. He stuffed both bodies into closets and left.

Kemper drove aimlessly around the West for four days, finally stopping in Pueblo, Colorado, to call the Santa Cruz police to confess to the murders. The Santa Cruz police assumed that "Big Ed" was amusing himself by calling in this murder confession, but agreed to investigate his claim by searching his mother's home. Officers found the two decapitated and decomposing bodies at the scene. The Santa Cruz Detectives called the Pueblo authorities and asked them to detain Kemper. Upon arrival in Pueblo, they found Kemper cooperative and anxious to confess. He waived his Miranda rights on two occasions and confessed to all of the murders.

Kemper was charged with eight counts of first-degree murder. His attorney entered a plea of not guilty by reason of insanity on his behalf. Kemper attempted suicide on two occasions while awaiting trial. Despite being diagnosed as mentally ill following his murder of his grandparents, Kemper was found competent at the time of the eight murders and at the time of the trial. In 1973, the State of California used the M'Naghten Rules as its standard to determine competency. Court-appointed psychiatrists determined that Kemper was free of mental defect and fully cognizant that his conduct was wrong and against the law. On November 8, 1973, Kemper was found guilty of the eight counts of premeditated murder and sentenced to life imprisonment.

EVALUATION

Following the psychiatric evaluations conducted during the murder trial, it is evident that Edmund Kemper was not mentally ill, was fully aware of the "wrongfulness" of his behavior, and was culpable for the murders. Kemper is afflicted with psychopathy, and his conduct readily demonstrates the diagnostic criteria.

Kemper exhibited a total lack of remorse for his behavior and no empathy for his victims. One may suggest that his decision to turn himself in to the Santa Cruz authorities demonstrates his remorse over his behavior, but this author contends that his decision to turn himself in and confess was strategic and manipulative. Kemper knew from his exposure to the criminal justice system that it was just a matter of time before he would be identified as the perpetrator of the murders of his mother and her best friend, and that identification as the killer of the female students would follow shortly thereafter. Kemper assumed that by turning himself in under the guise that he was fearful of and unable to control his own behavior, he could secure a "not guilty by reason of insanity" acquittal.

Kemper's experience and knowledge regarding the workings of the system of jurisprudence convinced him that he would prevail. He knew that he was not held culpable of the murders of his grandparents due to mental illness, and that he could suggest the notion that he had not been rehabilitated while in custody as a juvenile at Atascadero State Hospital and still suffered from psychosis. In reality, one has to question the validity of Kemper's diagnosis following the murders of his grandparents. Society has difficulty believing that a youth can commit murders of his grandparents in this manner, and as a result looks for mitigating variables. Clinicians certainly identified psychological variables that suggested the etiology of Kemper's adolescent behaviors, and, unwilling to support a conviction of Kemper on charges that he murdered his grandparents with malice and forethought, they offered a psychological excuse of psychosis.

Kemper, at an early age, manifested conduct disorder symptoms. Kemper exhibited aggression and cruelty by cutting off the heads and arms of his sisters' dolls, and by torturing and decapitating animals. Cruelty to animals is a foundational diagnostic criterion for conduct disorder. Further, mutilating his sisters' dolls demonstrates Kemper's lack of empathy for his sisters, another cornerstone criterion. Kemper is also of above-average intelligence and egocentric. Finally, Kemper's reason for killing his grandmother—"to see what it felt like to kill her"—supports the hypothesis that he was afflicted with conduct disorder of preadolescent onset. A diagnosis of psychopathy (antisocial personality disorder) cannot be ascribed without a finding that the patient, before age 15, was or would have been diagnosed with conduct disorder.

Kemper was also afflicted with sexual sadism. He indicated that he experienced a sexual rush when he decapitated his victims. This author contends that Kemper was a sexual sadist and experienced recurrent, intense sexual arousal over his acts of mutilating and decapitating the body. While Kemper did manifest the behaviors associated with necrophilia, this author contends that he was not intensely sexually aroused by random corpses, but rather was sexually aroused by sexual conduct with his selected victims. He kept the heads of some of his victims to perform fellatio on himself in memory of the specific victim. He also performed sexual acts on his mother's dead body as retribution.

The etiology of Kemper's pathology is rather straightforward. Beginning at a young age and continuing through the day of his mother's death, he was subject to emotional abuse. He was teased and criticized for gender issues by his mother, father, siblings, and grandparents. Lacking in nurture, Kemper found psychological safety in himself, thus precipitating the development of egocentricity. He felt no empathy for the plight of others, and manipulated them for his own psychological well-being. His lack of self-confidence was systematically created through his mother's abusive harassment. His murder and mutilation of her demonstrates his capacity for retribution.

Bibliography and Suggested Readings

American Psychiatric Association. (2000). *Diagnostic and Statistical Manual of Mental Disorders* (Rev. 4th ed.). Arlington, VA: Author.

Cheney, M. (1976). *The Co-ed Killer.* New York: Walker.

Damio, W. (1974). *The Urge to Kill.* New York: Pinnacle.

Dobbert, D. L. (2004). *Halting the Sexual Predators among Us.* Westport, CT: Praeger.

Dobbert, D. L. (2007). *Understanding Personality Disorders.* Westport, CT: Praeger.

Douglas, J. (1995). *Mindhunter.* New York: Scribner.

Everitt, D. (1993). *Human Monsters.* New York: Contemporary.

Frasier, D. (1996). *Murder Cases of the Twentieth Century.* Jefferson, N.C: McFarland.

Leyton, E. (2005). *Hunting Humans: The Rise of the Modern Multiple Murderer.* Toronto: McClelland& Stewart.

Ressler, R. (1992). *Whoever Fights Monsters.* New York: St. Martin's Press.

Santa Cruz Press. (1973, April 25; October 15; November 9). *Kemper.* Santa Cruz, CA: Author.

Schechter, H., & Eviritt, D. (1996). *The A to Z Encyclopedia of Serial Killers.* New York: Pocket.

Schechter, H. (2004). *The Serial Killers Files: The Who, What, Where, How, and Why of the World's Most Terrifying Murderers.* New York: Random.

Vronsky, P. (2004). *Serial Killers: The Method and Madness of Monsters.* New York: Penguin.

18

The Hillside Stranglers:
Angelo Buono (1934–2002)
and Kenneth Bianchi (1951–)

Los Angeles was in the grip of terror in the fall of 1977. Ten women were found naked, raped, and murdered on the hillsides of Los Angeles. The murders stopped as abruptly as they began in early 1978, and not until January 1979 was any disposition brought to these cases. Two women were murdered in Bellingham, Washington, in January 1979. Kenneth Bianchi was arrested for these two murders, and during the investigation it became evident that the murders bore similarities to the Los Angeles "Hillside murders." The investigation turned up a second suspect in the Hillside murders: Angelo Buono, Kenneth Bianchi's cousin. The pathologies of these two serial killers require examination.

ANGELO BUONO

Angelo Buono was born in Rochester, New York, on October 5, 1934. At the age of five, his mother moved him and his sister to Glendale, California. Buono was a troubled youth who demonstrated hostility toward his mother, his sister, and school officials. He was arrested on a charge of auto theft and was incarcerated in a state juvenile facility. Buono married in 1955, sired a son in 1956, and divorced his wife in the same year. Buono then married Mary Castillo in 1956 and had five children with her. Buono was a violent, dangerous man who expected complete sexual submission from his wife. Beatings were routine. His sexual sadism became so severe that Castillo divorced him in 1964. As in his first divorce, he refused to pay child support. Buono married again in 1965, but his wife accused him of sexually molesting her 14-year-old daughter, and she left.

Buono started a successful automobile upholstery business that was known for its quality work in the restoration of classic cars. As his business became successful, Buono was also successful in attracting young women. His cousin Kenny Bianchi, 12 years younger, left Rochester, New York, in 1975, and moved to Glendale to live with Buono. Bianchi was starstruck over his cousin's lifestyle, and enthusiastically agreed to Buono's business proposition to use Buono's harem of young girls as prostitutes. Bianchi was good-looking and a smooth talker, and he had no problem identifying young girls. By using intimidation and inspiring fear, Buono and Bianchi were able to force the girls to prostitute for them.

Buono's auto upholstery customers were a good source of clients for the prostitution ring, and he would make arrangements for minor-age girls to spend time with his clients. The girls were held in check with the threat of violence, and the customers with the fear of being reported for having sex with minors. Buono relied on his impersonation of a police officer to find runaway girls on the streets of Los Angeles. After picking up a girl under the disguise of law enforcement officers, he and Bianchi would beat her and force her to prostitute under the threat of death. On one occasion they stopped a girl by flashing their fake police badges and looked at her driver's license before abducting her. Next to her driver's license in her wallet was a photograph of her sitting with her father, the famous Hollywood gangster star Peter Lorre. Recognizing her father, they chose to release her and find a different girl to harass.

Buono and Bianchi purchased a list of customers from a known prostitute. The list was bogus, and, unable to find the "seller," they murdered her friend, Yolanda Washington. Yolanda was the first of the 12 women that Buono and Bianchi would murder.

KENNETH BIANCHI

Kenneth Bianchi was also born in Rochester, New York, on May 22, 1951, 12 years later than his cousin Buono. Bianchi's mother was an alcoholic prostitute who placed him for adoption. He was adopted by Nicholas and Francis Bianchi the same year. His preadolescent and adolescent behavior demonstrated the diagnostic criteria for conduct disorder, the juvenile version of the adult diagnosis of antisocial personality disorder, or psychopathy. Bianchi was a pathological liar, was manipulative, and possessed a violent temper. Psychological interventions were unsuccessful in modifying his behavior. Shortly after his high school graduation, at the age of 17, Bianchi married his high school sweetheart. He was too immature to handle marriage, and the union ended in less than a year. Bianchi viewed women dichotomously, as either good or bad. He was angry and disappointed when his wife left him and filed for an annulment.

Bianchi attended community college and studied psychology and public safety with the intention of finding employment as a police officer. Unable to secure employment as a police officer, he took a position as a security guard. Bianchi used this employment as an opportunity to steal. To avoid being caught for the thefts, he changed jobs and then stayed one step ahead of prosecution by moving to Glendale, California, to live with his cousin, Angelo Buono.

Unable to secure a position with the Los Angeles and Glendale police departments, Bianchi obtained a job at a title company, and then rented his own apartment. A tall, handsome man, he had little difficulty in finding women for companionship. Bianchi began to date Kelli Boyd, who worked for the same company. In May, 1977, they moved in together when she announced that she was pregnant with his child. During this period of time, he also set up a counseling service by creating fraudulent credentials and the alias of Steve Walker.

Bianchi, bored with his job, malingered illness and called in sick to work. Kelli Boyd was working hard to support them. Not ill, Bianchi spent his days drinking and playing cards with Buono, and running their prostitution ring. Friction between Bianchi and Kelli Boyd increased, and Boyd took their child and moved back to her home town of Bellingham, Washington.

THE HILLSIDE MURDERS

Following the murder of Yolanda Washington on October 17, 1977, Buono and Bianchi would murder nine more girls and women by February 16, 1978. Their reign of terror traumatized the citizens of Los Angeles. On October 31, the body of Judith Miller, age 15, was found bound and naked in a residential neighborhood. Miller had been raped, sodomized, and strangled. It was apparent that the location was a secondary crime scene. Miller had been murdered elsewhere and her body dumped at this location.

On November 6, the body of Lissa Kastin, age 21, was found. She was naked, bound, and had been raped and strangled. Authorities immediately saw the similarities to the Washington and Miller murders. They also surmised that there was more than one killer, as the body had been thrown over a guardrail.

By the time of Thanksgiving, the body count stood at seven, and two of the victims were 12-year-old Delores Cepeda and 14-year-old Sonja Johnson, abducted together on November 13. Their bodies were discovered on the side of a dump. They had been missing for a week. On November 23, the body of 28-year-old Jane King was found. King's decomposed body had lain there for two weeks before being located. Kristina Weckler, age 20, was found on November 20, 1977. She, like the others, had been bound, raped, strangled, and dumped alongside of the road.

On November 29, the body of Lauren Wagner, age 18, was found, naked, bound, raped, strangled, and dumped. Her car was found across the street from her house and a neighbor witnessed her abduction, but failed to call the police. The witness provided a description of the two men that had abducted her.

The body of Kimberly Martin was found in mid-December. Martin, a call girl, was reported missing after seeing her last client on December 9. The location of the clandestine meeting was a vacant apartment, and the call arranging the meeting was made from a public pay phone.

The last body found in the Los Angeles area was discovered on February 16, 1978. Cindy Hudspeth, age 20, was found in the trunk of her car, which had been pushed off a cliff. Hudspeth had been raped and strangled. She was a beautiful young woman who was working to save money for college. Hudspeth lived across the street from Kristina Weckler, whose body had been found on November 20, 1977. The residential proximity of these two victims bolstered the detectives' belief that the killer(s) lived in the same area.

Then, suddenly, the murders stopped.

BELLINGHAM, WASHINGTON MURDERS

Nearly a year after the last murder in Los Angeles, two women were reported missing in Bellingham, Washington. Karen Mandic, age 22, and Diane Wilder, age 27, had not returned from a house-sitting assignment arranged by a local security company. A police search of the girls' residence turned up the name of the security company and the name of the security guard, Kenneth Bianchi. Police contacted the security company, who in turn contacted Bianchi. Bianchi informed his employer that he knew nothing about the assignment. With the help of the local media, Mandic's car was located in a wooded area. The raped and strangled bodies of Mandic and Wilder were found in the car. Bianchi was arrested.

Physical evidence from the girls' bodies, the car, and the house where they were house-sitting conclusively tied Bianchi to the murders. The Bellingham chief of police was familiar with the unsolved Hillside Strangler murders from Los Angeles, and contacted the task force with the information about his murders. A subsequent search warrant of Bianchi's home turned up items of jewelry from two of the Hillside victims, and Bianchi's fingerprint matched a print found at the dump site of another victim. The Bellingham police and the Los Angeles task force were certain that they had at least one of the Hillside Stranglers in custody.

Bianchi was charged in the murders of Mandic and Wilder and remanded to the county jail awaiting trial. He pled not guilty, and informed his defense counsel that he had amnesia and could not recall the events of that evening. Bianchi malingered suicide gestures, and he was visited by a psychiatric social worker. Weaving his charm and pleasant personality though the interview, he provoked the social worker to wonder aloud how a pleasant man like Bianchi could ever have committed a heinous double murder, unless he was suffering from a mental defect such as multiple personality disorder. This set the stage for the next round of Bianchi's manipulation and malingering.

On a motion of defense counsel, Bianchi was evaluated by a clinician who was an alleged expert on amnesia and multiple personality disorder. In recognition of the amnesia, the clinician informed Bianchi that he would be using hypnosis to discover what transpired the night of the abduction and murders. Bianchi, realizing his opportunity for continued manipulation and malingering, agreed to the hypnosis. In the hypnotic state, Bianchi confessed to the murders; however, he indicated that they were committed by his evil alter ego, Steve. This clinician, who was on the verge of setting a record for the number of multiple personality disorder cases he had found, was completely manipulated by Bianchi.

This bizarre turn of events was beyond the detectives' ability to comprehend. They found that there was absolute, conclusive evidence that Bianchi had committed the Bellingham murders, as well as least some of the Hillside murders, with forethought and premeditation. Bianchi was exhibiting no symptoms of mental illness other than his alleged second personality. Continuing on with his manipulation and malingering, Bianchi, while under hypnosis and in the personality of Steve, confessed that he and his cousin, Angelo Buono, committed the Hillside murders. With this information in hand, Buono was arrested and charged with the Hillside murders. However, if Bianchi was successful in his plea of "not guilty due to insanity," his testimony accusing Buono would be dismissed.

The prosecution arranged for an internationally recognized psychiatrist to evaluate Bianchi. This psychiatrist suggested to Bianchi, in the nonhypnotic state, that a typical multiple personality had at least three personalities, and that as Bianchi only had two, he was probably malingering. The psychiatrist put Bianchi in a hypnotic state, and, interestingly, Bianchi produced a third personality, convinced that he was preparing himself for an insanity defense. The psychiatrist testified that Bianchi was faking his hypnotic states and was not afflicted with multiple personality disorder, but rather displayed psychopathy and was culpable of the charges. The detectives discovered that

Bianchi had previously used fake psychology credentials under the "Steve" alias, and located a copy of *The Three Faces of Eve* at his home.

Kenneth Bianchi agreed to change his plea to guilty under a plea bargain, in which he would testify against Angelo Buono in exchange for life imprisonment instead of execution. Bianchi was sentenced to life imprisonment in Washington State. Angelo Buono was convicted on nine counts of murder and sentenced to life imprisonment. Buono died of natural causes in his prison cell on September 21, 2002, at the age of 67.

EVALUATION

Angelo Buono was clearly afflicted with psychopathy. He was cruel, egocentric, and conscience-deficient. He demonstrated absolutely no empathy for his victims or remorse for his behaviors. He also demonstrated sexual sadism, not only in the murder of the Hillside victims, but also with his wives in his marriages. Buono relished in the torture, rape, and murder of his victims. He was recurrently, intensely sexually aroused over the delivery of pain and humiliation to his victims.

Kenneth Bianchi, likewise, was afflicted with psychopathy. However, while he manifested the symptoms of the disorder, he also exhibited the personable, gregarious, articulate, and manipulative symptoms of the disorder. He was nearly successful in achieving acquittal based upon his manipulation and malingering. However, he still demonstrated a lack of empathy for his victims and no remorse. Further, he displayed absolute egocentricity, opting to testify against Buono in order to reduce his own sentence. He also delighted in the delivery of pain and humiliation.

In the cases of both men, their psychopathy allowed them to commit their crimes in the fashion in which they did without guilt, anxiety, or remorse, and it was their sexual sadism that drove them to the exact method.

Buono came about his psychopathy and sexual sadism naturally over his psychological development. While Bianchi demonstrated conduct disorder behaviors in his adolescent development, he also exhibited regret in the loss of his relationships. However, after Bianchi met his cousin and enjoyed the pleasures Buono made available, he developed a taste and hunger for sadism in the absence of conscience. It is as if Bianchi developed deeper and more repugnant levels of depravity through association with Buono.

Bibliography and Suggested Readings

American Psychiatric Association. (2000). *Diagnostic and Statistical Manual of Mental Disorders* (Rev. 4th ed.). Arlington, VA: Author.

Dobbert, D. L. (2004). *Halting the Sexual Predators among Us.* Westport, CT: Praeger.

Dobbert, D. L. (2007). *Understanding Personality Disorders.* Westport, CT: Praeger.

Meloy, J. R. (1998). *The Psychopathic Mind: Origins, Dynamics, and Treatment.* UK: Oxford.

O'Brien, D. (1985). *The Hillside Stranglers.* New York: Carroll and Graf.

Schwartz, T. (2004). *The Hillside Strangler.* UK: Lightning Source.

Wilson, C., & Seaman, D. (1997). *The Serial Killers: A Study in the Psychology of Violence.* London, UK: Virgin.

19

Bobby Joe Long (1953–)

Bobby Joe Long currently sits on death row in Florida, awaiting execution by lethal injection. In addition to his death sentence, Long was also sentenced to numerous additional life sentences. He will never be a free man again. Long's criminal career began with an insatiable need for nonconsensual forced rape, and ended with the murder of at least nine women.

Robert Joe Long was born on October 14, 1953, in Kenova, West Virginia, to Joe and Louella Long. The Longs' marriage was short-lived due to Joe's excessive drinking and his physical abuse of Loella. Loella took Bobby Joe and moved to Florida in 1955. They would move back and forth between West Virginia and Florida. In 1966, Loella and Bobby Joe moved to Hialeah, Florida, where Loella worked as a waitress at a lounge. While living in Hialeah, Bobby Joe met Cindy Guthrie, who would become his first sexual partner and then his wife. Prior to meeting Guthrie, he slept with his mother every night, with the exception of those nights when his mother would bring home a man.

Bobby Joe Long enlisted in the armed forces in 1972, and following basic training was assigned to the Homestead Air Force base in Homestead, Florida. In 1974, Long and Cindy Guthrie were married at the base chapel. Long suffered a serious motorcycle accident shortly after their marriage, resulting in severe head trauma. This head trauma would later be used as a defense in Long's murder trial. It was alleged that this head trauma was the precipitating factor in the development of Long's insatiable sex drive.

Long was discharged from armed forces five months after the motorcycle accident, and there was much dispute pertaining to his discharge status, which would have a significant impact on his medical care and employment. Following legal appeal, Long's discharge status was changed to general. Long had difficulty in finding and keeping gainful employment with the exception of low-paying jobs. Long packed up his wife and infant son and moved throughout southern Florida looking for employment. Following the birth of their second child in 1975, the Longs moved again. In the course of one and a half years, the Longs lived in Homestead, Plantation, Fort Lauderdale, Miramar, and Hollywood, all communities in southeast Florida. Long had also traveled to West Virginia in search of employment, to no avail. Long enrolled in an X-ray technician certificate program at Broward Community College in 1977, and in 1979, after completion of his course of study, secured full-time employment as a hospital X-ray technician in North Miami Beach. Long's unemployment and nomadic lifestyle took its toll on the marriage, and Cindy filed for divorce in June 1980.

Bobby Joe Long left southeast Florida and moved to the Tampa Bay area of Florida looking for work. He moved from one menial job to another until he found work as a hospital X-ray technician in the Ybor City district of Tampa in January, 1981. Long was already behind on two months of child support payments by March 1981, and in August 1981, he quit his job. It was later determined that Long quit his job and fled to West Virginia because he was attempting to avoid prosecution for obscene contact with a minor child, specifically the 12-year-old daughter of a Tampa-area physician. However, Long was arrested and charged with exhibiting obscene literature to a minor child. He was sentenced to two days' incarceration and assessed fines and costs of $65.

By 1983, Long was in arrears on his child support payments again and he was facing jail time for failure to pay child support and for failure to appear on contempt charges. However, without significant employment, he caught up on his overdue child support payments and paid an additional $4,000 in hospital bills. Long had returned to a previous lifestyle to pay the child support.

As early as 1970, Long had begun to steal from the homes of persons who had placed classified ads to sell bedroom furniture, home appliances, or their houses. But Long did not use his access to these homes solely for the theft of items. He would locate the classified ad and then approach the home during the daylight hours, when head-of-household husbands would be at work and their wives would be home alone. If a woman answered the door, he would invite himself in to look at the appliance, or, in the case of a house for sale, ask to tour the house. Once satisfied that the woman was alone he would brandish a knife or gun, force the woman into the bedroom, and bind and rape her. He would then steal items before he left.

Between 1980 and 1983, in the Ocala, Miami, and Fort Lauderdale communities of Florida, Long used this method to commit as many as 50 rapes. The media referred to this unknown rapist as the "Classified Ad Rapist." Later, Long would confess to these rapes, and, with delight, would indicate that he started this activity in 1975, and that he found it sexually arousing just thinking about it.

On March 6, 1984, Long approached a home in North Port Richey that was advertised as for sale. Long told the woman at the door that he had read their classified ad and would like to tour the house. Once inside, he raped the woman at gunpoint and robbed the house of jewelry. Long would later be charged with and convicted of this home invasion and rape with a weapon. He would be sentenced to 99 years for this offense.

Apparently this form of nonconsensual rape was insufficient in meeting Long's intrinsic psychosexual needs, and he committed his first lust homicide in May 1984. With this first murder, Bobby Joe Long found a new avenue to sexual arousal and sexual gratification.

In May 1974, Ngeun Thi Long's decomposing body was found in a field near Tampa, Florida. Ngeun Thi Long, age 20, an exotic dancer, was found bound, raped, and strangled with a ligature. Her hips had been broken and her naked body had been posed with her legs at 90 degree angles from her body. She had been last seen working a lounge in Tampa.

On May 27, 1984, the body of Michelle Simms, age 22, was found in Hillsborough County, Florida. Simms, a known Tampa prostitute, had been bound, raped, stabbed, strangled, and struck in the head with a heavy object. Her bloodstained clothes were found hanging from a nearby tree branch. Similar to the Ngeun Thi Long murder, Simms had been strangled with a ligature that was different from the rope used to bind her, and a piece of red thread was found on her body similar to one found near Ngeun Thi Long.

On June 8, 1984, Bobby Joe Long abducted Elizabeth Loudenback, age 22, as she walked from the mobile home she shared with mother, stepfather, sister, and brother. At knifepoint, Long forced Loudenback to remove her clothes. He bound her hands behind her back, forced her down face first on the reclined front seat of his car, and raped her. Apparently, Long decided not to kill Loudenback and told her to dress herself. However, Loudenback's crying disturbed Long, and he dragged her out of the car, strangled her with a ligature, and then discarded the body. Her body was not discovered until June 24. Red carpet fibers were found on her clothes. Long committed an error in judgment when he stole an ATM card from her wallet and withdrew cash.

Nearly four months would elapse before Long would murder again. On October 7, 1984, the body of Chanel Williams, an 18-year-old prostitute, was found on a cattle ranch in Hillsborough County. She had been dead for week. Apparently, Williams had accepted a ride from Long, who beat her and ordered her to undress. He bound her wrists behind her back, forced her down face first on his front seat, and raped her from behind, as with the other victims. However, Williams struggled as Long attempted to strangle her, and he shot her in the head to dispatch her. The FBI lab results confirmed that the red fiber found on Williams's clothing matched the fiber found on the previous victims.

One week later, the body of Karen Dinsfriend, a 28-year-old known prostitute and drug addict, was found partially naked with her hands bound behind her back. Dinsfriend had been beaten, raped, and strangled with a ligature. The same red fiber was found on her body as well as semen matching that found with the other victims.

The next body was found on October 31 in Hillsborough County. The victim was later identified as Kimberly Hoops, a 22-year-old prostitute of the Tampa area. Hoops had been strangled with her own choker.

Bobby Joe Long erred on November 3, 1984, when he abducted 17-year-old Lisa McVey. While riding her bicycle home from work, she was knocked to the ground by someone hiding in the bushes along the side of the road. Long had seen her riding her bike and he passed her, pulled over up the road, and waited for her to ride by. He grabbed her, tied her up at gun point, and blindfolded her. Long forced her perform fellatio on him as he was driving. He then took her back to his apartment where he would keep her captive for 26 hours, raping and sodomizing her. Despite her terror, she was able to persuade Long to let her live. She also memorized information that she could visualize from underneath her blindfold—specifics regarding the inside of Long's vehicle and his apartment. Additionally, she left her hair barrette behind on the floor of Long's apartment as proof that she had been there. Incredibly, Long released her. Lisa McVey told the police everything she could remember about the terror-filled hours. Her information was critical in the identification of Long's red Dodge Magnum.

On November 4, 1984, before Long was identified and apprehended, Virginia Johnson, an 18-year-old Tampa prostitute, was found in Pasco County, a short distance from Hillsborough County. Johnson's body had been dismembered and parts scattered; however, it was determined that she died of strangulation with a ligature. On November 12, 1984, the body of Kim Swann was found. Swann, age 21, was bound, beaten, raped, and strangled with a ligature. It appeared that she had been dead for a few days. Swann was an exotic dancer at the Sly Fox Lounge, the same club where Ngeun Thi Long, Long's first victim, had worked. The same red fiber was found on Swann's body.

On November 15, Tampa detectives noticed a red Dodge Magnum cruising the prostitute strip of Tampa. Matching the vehicle description provided by Lisa McVey, the Detectives pulled over Bobby Joe Long. The interior of Long's vehicle also matched McVey's description, and Long's address was in an area where the suspect was thought to reside. Long was released, but the task force, upon reviewing the detective's vehicle stop report, decided that Long was a viable suspect and set up surveillance. Long's criminal record and a bank deposit were sufficient to obtain an arrest warrant and search warrants for his apartment and vehicle. In searching Long's apartment, officers located Lisa McVey's barrette exactly where she said she had dropped it, as well as photographs of Long raping women.

With physical evidence in hand, task force detectives interrogated Long. Long confessed to all of the Tampa Bay murders and a series of unsolved rapes.

Indicted on eight counts of murder and numerous counts of kidnapping and rape, Long was held without the availability of bail. Defense attorneys for Long argued that he was not culpable by reason of mental defect. They presented witnesses testifying that Long suffered from brain trauma from the 1974 motorcycle accident. They would also indicate that because he possessed an extra Y chromosome he was predisposed to, and unable to control, his behavior. The prosecution countered with clinical testimony indicating that Long was free of mental defect but was afflicted with a psychopathic personality disorder, and, most significantly, that he was fully aware of his actions and of their wrongfulness.

The jury found that Long had been competent at the time of the offenses and the trial, and that he was thus culpable. Long was found guilty of the charges and initially sentenced to two death penalties and numerous life sentences. While some of these sentences have been modified on appeal, Bobby Joe Long continues to sit on death row in Florida awaiting his execution by lethal injection.

EVALUATION

The psychiatrists that testified for the prosecution of Bobby Joe Long were accurate in their assessment that Long is afflicted with antisocial personality disorder, also known as psychopathy. Long exhibits all of the diagnostic criteria for this diagnosis:

- Long has an extensive criminal record
- Long is a pathological liar, and uses deceit to fulfill his pleasures at the expense of others
- Long's aggressive, assaultive behavior is readily apparent in his murder of at least eight women and his rape of 50–150 girls and women

- Long's work record demonstrates his irresponsibility and inconsistency in work behavior

Finally, Long has absolutely no remorse for his behaviors and exhibits no empathy for his victims. He is deficient of conscience, and because of this deficiency, he experiences no guilt for his behavior, and therefore no anxiety—thus allowing him to commit heinous crimes with impunity and disregard for others.

Obviously an inquiry into etiology is significant. Defense counsel indicated that Long's extra Y chromosome predisposed him to his aggressive, violent behavior. While research does indicate that there is higher probability of men with an extra Y chromosome developing antisocial personalities and mental illness, there is no direct correlation. If there were a direct correlation, then all men with an extra Y chromosome would be afflicted with either anti-social personality disorder or mental illness. The reality is that only a higher-than-normal percentage of such men are so afflicted, while the greatest majority are not. Bobby Joe Long was in full possession of his thought processes, as evident in his premeditated behavior. Furthermore, by his own admission, he was fully aware of what he doing and of the wrongfulness of his behavior.

This author suggests that Long developed his psychopathy through his mother's nurturing of him. He was able to sleep with his mother until he was 14 years old, with the exception of those nights when she brought home a lover. The act of sleeping with his mother into adolescence demonstrated to Long that his needs were of greater importance than those of others, particularly his mother. Furthermore, it is logical to assume that Long began to sleep with his mother because she brought him to her bed, either to counter her loneliness or to calm him as a child when he was fearful. Whatever the reason, this sleeping arrangement fostered a sense of entitlement in Bobby Joe Long—a sense that his needs were of paramount significance. He developed an egocentricity that would allow to him to do to others what he wished, without concern for their feelings or wellbeing.

Long's psychopathy permitted him to commit a great number of crimes against others, but it was his sexual sadism that motivated him to commit his specific sexual crimes. By his own admission, Long felt a sense of power and domination when he produced fear in others. He loved to flash a knife or a gun at his victims to see the fear it would instill. He was recurrently, intensely sexually aroused by this ability to produce fear and then pain. He loved to hear victims beg him not to hurt them. He loved forcing them through the humiliation of removing their clothes in his presence. He loved binding them, and he loved raping them from behind and sodomizing them, rather than offering them minimal dignity; rape from behind and sodomy are similar to sex with animals rather than humans. Finally, leaving his victims naked in seductive poses was not a provocative gesture to those who would find the corpses, but rather a final humiliation to the women.

Bibliography and Suggested Readings

American Psychiatric Association. (2000). *The Diagnostic and Statistical Manual of Mental Disorders* (Rev. 4th ed.). Arlington, VA: Author.

Dobbert, D. L. (2004). *Halting the Sexual Predators among Us.* Westport, CT: Praeger.

Dobbert, D. L. (2007). *Understanding Personality Disorders.* Westport, CT: Praeger.

Flowers, A. (1995). *Bound to Die: The Shocking True Story of Bobby Joe Long, America's Most Savage Serial Killer.* New York: Pinnacle.

Ward, B. (1995). *Bobby Joe: In the Mind of a Monster.* Boca Raton, FL: Cool Hand Communications.

Wellman, J. McVey, L., & Replogle, S. (1997). *Smoldering Embers: The True Story of a Serial Murderer and Three Courageous Women.* Far Hills, NJ: New Horizon.

20

Dayton Leroy Rogers (1953–)

The exact number of lust homicides that Dayton Leroy Rogers committed may never be known. However, the tortured, mutilated, and murdered bodies of seven women found in the Molalla, Oregon, forest in 1987 have been attributed to him. His silence on death row may preclude the possibility of locating and identifying other probable victims.

Dayton Leroy Rogers was born on September 30, 1953, to Ortis and Jasperelle Rogers. The family was blended, and Dayton was surrounded by siblings and stepsiblings. Ortis was a cruel and rigid disciplinarian, and Dayton received his fair share of serious beatings from his father. Ortis also demonstrated his belief that his wife was there to meet his every sexual desire without complaint. He believed that his sexual desire was a physiological need, not a rational demonstration of love and affection. His forceful sexual activity with Jasperelle would leave an impression on Dayton. Dayton found great pleasure in sneaking around to watch his sisters undress and bathe. He masturbated as he watched them.

The family moved frequently, and Dayton, although he possessed the capacity to succeed in formal education, became bored and dropped out of school at the age of 16. In 1972, at age 18, he married 16-year-old Julie, who was abusing drugs and alcohol. However, Rogers was always on the lookout for additional sexual partners. In 1972, at the age of 18, he was arrested for assaulting a 15-year-old girl with a knife. Rogers had picked up the hitchhiker, taken her to a remote location, and had sex with her. He picked her up a few days later, and, as they were holding hands and kissing, he plunged a knife into her side. He indicated to her that he didn't think she loved him and was afraid she would turn him in for having sex with a minor. She persuaded him otherwise and asked him to take her to a hospital. He complied, but upon arrival at the hospital, the girl told the police that he had stabbed her. Rogers was arrested and charged with assault with a deadly weapon. He pled guilty for a reduced sentence of four years' probation.

Within six months, Rogers was arrested again for assault with a bottle on two 15-year-old girls that he and his wife had taken in to live with them. He had begun to drink heavily and to request sexual favors from the girls. In disgust, Julie had walked out on him. She had returned after he told her that he would kill her and her roommates if she did not come home. Following the assault of the two girls, Rogers was arrested and charged. The court ordered a psychiatric evaluation, and he was subsequently diagnosed as a sociopath and was determined to have a mental defect. Rogers, surprisingly, was found not culpable for the assaultive behavior. He was remanded to the Oregon State Hospital, where he would remain until his release on December 12, 1974.

Julie filed for divorce while Rogers was incarcerated at the Oregon State Hospital. Three months after being released, Rogers found and married the innocent, attractive, and naive Sherry. Despite a very healthy sex life with Sherry, Rogers's insatiable sex drive could not be met, and he began to prowl the streets. In 1976, he picked up two high school girls who were skipping school. On the promise of marijuana and beer they accompanied him out of town. After smoking marijuana and drinking beer he pulled a knife and threatened the girls. He bound them with wire and raped one of them. Rogers was arrested and convicted of coercion rather than kidnapping and statutory rape. His prior acquittal due to mental defect was registered as a mitigating circumstance. He was sentenced to a maximum of 5 years' imprisonment. Rogers served a total of 27 months and was released from parole in January, 1983.

Rogers opened a small engine repair shop, and all appeared to be in order for him, Sherry, and their 18-month-old son. There were no arrests during the period from 1983 to the summer of 1987; however, Rogers was continuing his late night prowling of the "red light" district of Portland, Oregon. Rogers presented himself as a solid young business owner during the day, but he would solicit the prostitutes of Portland at night. Telling Sherry that he had repair work that needed to be completed, he would stay at his shop late at night and even all night long. He would wait at his shop working on projects until he knew Sherry had gone to bed and would not be calling, and then would sneak off to prowl the streets, fortified with his favorite mixture of vodka and small bottles of fresh orange juice. Rogers was well known among the prostitutes as "Steve the gambler" from Nevada.

On July 7, 1987, in the middle of the day, Rogers picked up Heather Brown, age 31, a known prostitute. He suggested that he buy some beer and that they engage in sex. They stopped on the way out of town to buy cigarettes for Brown and beer for Rogers. When the conversation turned to sex, Rogers said that he wanted to tie her up and have sex with her. Brown refused and told him to drive her back to Portland. Instead, Rogers turned into a dirt road in the Molalla forest and accelerated, despite Brown's demands to stop and let her out. She finally escaped by jumping from the truck moving along at 60 miles an hour. She bounced along the dirt road, landing in the middle of the road. Before Rogers could turn around and recapture her, a logging truck came by and picked her up. She told the trucker of her situation and made arrangements to be taken to the hospital, and then reported the incident to the police. The Clackamas County Sheriff's Department initiated an investigation.

On the evening of August 6, 1987, Rogers set out to find a prostitute. Fortified with vodka and orange juice, he told Sherry that he would be working very late that night. Shortly after midnight, Rogers left his shop and headed to the streets of Portland. He found Jennifer Smith, who recognized Rogers as a previous customer and immediately accepted his request. Rogers told her to undress and then bound her with her shoelaces. He then attacked Smith with a knife. She rolled out of Rogers's truck as he continued his assault on her. Her screams brought the attention of neighbors, who rushed to the parking lot. The first to arrive saw a man bent over the screaming Smith and assumed he was raping her, until he saw a gaping wound where Rogers had cut her throat. Rogers ran from the scene as the neighbors arrived. One attempted to resuscitate Smith to no avail, and she died en route to the hospital. Rogers returned to the scene of the crime to retrieve his truck, and jumped into the truck to escape. One of the neighbors followed him out of the parking lot and was able to write down his license plate number. Another neighbor vividly remembered the face of the assailant.

When the police arrived on the scene, the witnesses described Rogers and gave them a description of the truck and its license plate number. A fast check with motor vehicle registration identified the name of the owner of the truck, Dayton Leroy Rogers, and his home address. Upon arrival at Rogers's home the police were informed that he was not home and commonly worked through the night. The officers proceeded to Rogers's shop, where they confronted him. He told the officers that they could search the shop and his truck, which he informed them he had not driven that night. The hot engine proved otherwise, and Rogers told them that he had cut himself and went to the hospital for emergency care. Rogers was arrested and booked at the Clackamas County Jail.

The evidence against Rogers was overwhelming. Jennifer Smith's blood was found all over the cab of Rogers's truck, her fingerprint was found on the passenger-side outside door handle, and numerous knife cuts were found on the truck's interior. The investigating officers created a photo lineup and showed it to the witnesses from the crime scene, who, without hesitation, picked out Rogers. The same photo lineup was shown to prostitutes working the same area as Jennifer Smith, and they also identified Rogers as a frequent customer known as "Steve the gambler." They also informed the police that "Steve" had a penchant for wanting bondage and kinky sex that often got out of hand and became painful, including biting and cutting them. The medical examiner's autopsy of Jennifer Smith concluded that she was the victim of a wrongful death, with 11 stab wounds to the body and also indications that she had been bound with her shoelaces. The grand jury bound Rogers over on the charge of the aggravated murder of Jennifer Smith. Rogers pled not guilty and was held in jail without bound.

While Rogers was sitting in jail awaiting trial, a hunter located a body in the Molalla Forest. The hunter reported the decomposing body and the crime scene team responded. The body was a murder victim. Over the course of the next five days a total of seven bodies would be found in close proximity to the first one. Each of the bodies revealed evidence of mutilation and stabbing. Some of their feet had been removed. When orange juice containers of the same brand were found at the body dump location, it became apparent that Rogers had also committed these murders. Upon this recognition, the evidence mounted. All of the women, with one exception, were known prostitutes and drug abusers.

Rogers' trial for the murder of Jennifer Smith began in February, 1988. Following the testimony of many women who had escaped with their lives, the jury found Rogers guilty of aggravated murder and sentenced him to life imprisonment.

EVALUATION

Dayton Leroy Rogers has demonstrated no remorse for his behavior. He showed no empathy for his victims, and his conduct exceeded that necessary to subdue them. Rogers is conscience-deficient and manifests all criteria for a diagnosis of psychopathy. His psychopathy allowed him to be free of guilt for his actions, but it was his sexual sadism that motivated his torturous behavior.

Even the absence of murdering his victims, Rogers demonstrated his recurrent, intense sexual arousal when delivering pain and humiliation to them. Rogers's wife probably would not participate in his sadistic rituals of bondage and pain, and therefore he searched out victims among the prostitutes. Rogers' gregarious personality put his victims at ease, and they were unsuspecting of his sadistic desires until after they had agreed to his bondage. Rogers' desire to give pain increased significantly over time. He would find that his current levels of sadism would no longer achieve sexual arousal, and consequently he would have to increase the level of his sadism, until lust homicide was the only remaining act that would produce his sexual arousal and gratification.

The etiology of Rogers' pathology is directly related to his father's cruel abuse of him and his siblings and his father's insatiable need for sexual activity with his wife. His father's behaviors of being entitled to sex created the model that Rogers adopted and developed. Being the subject of cruel abuse forced Rogers to rely only upon himself, and thus to develop a pathological level of egocentricity that precluded consideration of others.

Comorbid psychopathy and sexual sadism were the motivating forces driving Rogers's homicidal behavior.

Bibliography and Suggested Readings

American Psychiatric Association. (2000). *Diagnostic and Statistical Manual of Mental Disorders* (Rev. 4th ed.). Arlington, VA: Author.

Baumeister, R. (1997). *Evil: Inside Human Violence and Cruelty.* New York: Barnes and Noble.

Dobbert, D. L. (2004). *Halting the Sexual Predators among Us.* Westport, CT: Praeger.

Dobbert, D. L. (2007). *Understanding Personality Disorders.* Westport, CT: Praeger.

Douglas, J., & Olshaker, M. (1996). *Mindhunter: Inside the FBI's Elite Crime Unit.* New York: Pocket.

Holmes, R., & Holmes, S. (2002). *Profiling Violent Crimes.* Thousand Oaks, CA: Sage.

Toch, H. (1992). *Violent Men: An Inquiry into the Psychology of Violence.* Hyattsville, MD: American Psychological Association.

21

Aileen "Lee" Wuornos (1956–2002)

Aileen Wuornos is the only female serial killer to be discussed in this book, partially because the concept of a female serial killer is almost an oxymoron. There are very few female serial killers, and Wuornos is the only contemporary one. It is significant that her case be examined, because despite the fact that all of her murders were associated with sexual activity, she did not murder because she was sexually aroused as is the case with most of the serial killers discussed in this book. Her pathology is different, and it was this pathology that was the precipitating force behind her murders. She is a very interesting clinical case with many circumstances that demonstrate the etiology of her pathology. Further, many women endure similar experiences in life, and while they may not become serial murderers, they are certainly emotionally impaired and manifest different disturbing and pathological behaviors. Studying Wuornos's life provides the opportunity to contemplate potential disturbances in others, which can be identified and therapeutically treated prior to the occurrence of violence directed at others or themselves.

Aileen Wuornos was born on February 29, 1956, in Rochester, Michigan, to teenage parents, Leo Pittman and Diane Pratt, who divorced before she was born. Leo was a convicted child molester who would commit suicide in prison in 1969. Diane abandoned Aileen and her older brother, Keith, when Aileen was five months old. Diane left the children with a babysitter and never returned. Aileen and Keith were adopted by their maternal grandparents, Lauri and Britta Wuornos. Aileen's grandfather, now her legal father, was an abusive alcoholic. Her early years were tumultuous. At an early age, Aileen and Keith were playing with lighter fluid and the ensuing fire left Aileen with facial scars that inspired ridicule from other school-age children. It was not until adolescence that Aileen discovered that she and her brother were abandoned by their mother and that her parents were really her grandparents. This exacerbated her rebellion against her abusive, alcoholic grandfather. At a crucial time in her psychological development, she found that her mother had abandoned her and that her abusive father was actually her grandfather, and was also experiencing difficulty with peers. Her emotional impairment manifested itself in substance abuse, incorrigibility, and promiscuity. Her sexual activity included activity with her brother Keith, and it is suspect whether her grandfather was sexually molesting her as well. Aileen became pregnant at 14 years old, was placed in a home for unwed mothers, delivered a baby boy on March 23, 1971, and placed him for adoption. Aileen claimed to have been raped while under the influence of alcohol, but her grandparents refused to believe her. Britta Wuornos died of liver failure on July 7, 1971, leaving Aileen and Keith in the care of their abusive grandfather.

The children's biological mother, Diane Wuornos, came back into their lives and offered them a home. Aileen refused due to her mother's abandonment of them. Aileen quit school and began a journey of hitchhiking across the country, supporting herself through robbery and prostitution. Aileen married a 70-year-old man in Florida in 1976, only to be divorced two months later for assaulting him with his cane. Aileen returned to Michigan. Her brother Keith died of throat cancer on July 17, 1976, at 21 years of age, and she received $10,000 as the beneficiary of his life insurance policy. The money disappeared as quickly as it came, and Aileen returned to prostitution to support herself. She would move from one relationship with a man to another, none of which continued. During this period in her life she attempted suicide by shooting herself in the stomach, only to fail at this endeavor as well.

Aileen Wuornos was successful in developing an extensive criminal record from Key West to Daytona Beach, Florida. During the period from 1981 through 1986, using a number of aliases, Wuornos committed uttering and publishing (writing bad checks), theft, assault, driving without a valid license, and armed robbery. The armed robbery occurred in Edgewater, Florida, in 1981. Wuornos was convicted and served 14 months in jail. She was subsequently arrested for uttering and publishing in Key West in May 1984.

A key turning point in Wuornos's life occurred when she met Tyria Moore at a gay and lesbian bar in Daytona, Florida in 1986. This relationship would continue for five years, flourishing in the early years, but became strained when money was short and Wuornos's behavior became more erratic and her alcohol consumption increased. Moore was content to stay with Wuornos as long as Wuornos was bringing home enough money to support them as a couple. Wuornos worked her prostitution through the truck stops and rest areas along Florida's Interstate highways. However, now she carried a .22 caliber pistol for protection fro m abusive customers. Wuornos began her spree of murders in 1989.

The first murder occurred on November 30, 1989, when Wuornos hitched a ride with Richard Mallory, age 51, from Clearwater, Florida. Mallory was known for his erratic behavior and alcohol abuse, and therefore no one was suspicious when Mallory did not open his electronics store the next day. Mallory's abandoned car was found in Ormond Beach that day. His body was not discovered until December 13, at a Volusia County junk yard. The cause of death was three .22 caliber bullet wounds.

Richard Humphreys went missing in May 1990, but his body would not be recovered and identified until September. Mr. Humphries died of six bullet wounds from a .22 caliber weapon. David Spears, age 43, left work in Sarasota, Florida, to visit his ex-wife in Orlando. He never arrived and his body was found in Citrus County with six bullet wounds. Charles Carskaddons, age 40, disappeared en route to Tampa. His body was found on June 6, 1990, with-nine bullet wounds, 30 miles south of Spears's body. On June 7, missionary Peter Siems disappeared en route to visit relatives. While his body has never been located, his wrecked car was found abandoned on July 4. Witnesses described two women abandoning the car. These two women would later be identified as Aileen Wuornos and Tyria Moore. Wuornos's palm print would be found on the door handle of the vehicle.

On July 30, 1990, Eugene Burress did not return from his daily deliveries. His vehicle was located, but it was not until August 4 that his body was found. Burress died of two gunshot wounds. Wuornos's last victim was Walter Antonio. His body was discovered with four bullet wounds. Law enforcement officials released sketches and descriptions of Wuornos and Moore. Despite being identified through fingerprints and motel receipts, they continued to elude law enforcement. Finally, on January 9, 1991, Wuornos was arrested by two undercover police officers at a biker bar in Daytona Beach, Florida. Wuornos was held on an outstanding warrant on one of her aliases. Law enforcement officers tracked down Tyria Moore in Pennsylvania. Moore agreed to testify against Wuornos in exchange for immunity. On January 16, Aileen Wuornos confessed to six of the killings, but claimed they were in self defense. Wuornos informed law enforcement that these men had attempted to assault and rape her.

Following numerous trials and appeals, Aileen Wuornos was convicted of 6 murders and sentenced to 6 death sentences. After 12 years of appeals and sitting on death row, Wuornos was executed by lethal injection on October 9, 2002.

EVALUATION

During the course of Aileen Wuornos's trial, sentencing, and appeals, she was examined by clinicians on numerous occasions to determine whether she was mentally ill and incompetent. On one occasion, defense counsel moved that she was suffering from schizophrenia and thus incompetent. Wuornos was found to be competent to stand trial and assist in her own defense, and was diagnosed with borderline personality disorder.

The American Psychiatric Association describes the primary diagnostic criteria of borderline personality disorder as an inability to maintain stable relationships, an irrational fear of abandonment, and poor self-image. The behavioral manifestations of these criteria include a sense of loneliness, despair, impulsivity, rapidly attaching oneself to new relationships, angry outbursts, and suicide. Aileen Wuornos demonstrated all of these behaviors, and thus her diagnosis appears to be accurate. While male serial killers over-whelmingly manifest the diagnostic criteria for sexual sadism, one can con-clude that Wuornos was not afflicted with this paraphilia. The American Psychiatric Association informs that the sexual paraphilias are male-exclusive, with exception of sexual masochism. While there are some women who are afflicted with sexual sadism, their numbers are few and statistically insignifi-cant. A diagnosis of sexual sadism requires that the afflicted person be recur-rently, intensely sexually aroused over delivering pain and/or humiliation to others. It is ludicrous to assume that Aileen Wuornos was sexually aroused during prostitution. Prostitution was her source of income.

The etiology of Wuornos's borderline personality disorder is easily iden-tified by comparing the diagnostic criteria with her life experiences. From the day she was born, Aileen Wuornos began to experience real, not imag-ined, abandonment. Her father left before she was born and her mother abandoned her and Keith when Aileen was five months old. Not knowing until adolescence that her maternal grandparents were not her biological parents was also damaging. Aileen was living with a man she believed was her father, who was abusive. While Aileen's grandmother attempted to nur-ture, she was also the recipient of the grandfather's abuse and could do lit-tle to prevent his abuse of Aileen. Then Aileen's grandmother died. Then her brother died. There was no imagination of abandonment. Aileen Wuornos was abandoned.

The sense of abandonment, the cruel abuse, and the ridicule she endured from her facial disfigurement from the fire created Wuornos's poor self-image.

In attempts to find self-worth and acceptance, Wuornos reached out to males at an early age for love and tenderness. She transferred boys' sexual interest in her to feelings of love and acceptance, but as the relationships were only sexual and short-lived, the sense of abandonment was reinforced when they ended, and each such occurrence brought a lowering of self-worth.

Obviously Wuornos was not practicing birth control, and she became pregnant at age 14. It is not uncommon for young women who experience borderline personality disorder symptoms to subconsciously desire a baby. The baby will be totally dependent and give unconditional love to the mother. The baby also becomes a "possession" that is hers and hers alone. One cannot ascertain whether Wuornos desired the pregnancy or was raped while intoxicated as she told her grandparents. Regardless, her grandparents did not believe her, demonstrating continuing abandonment at a time when Wuornos was in dire need of support and acceptance. The baby was given up for adoption. As a minor child herself, Wuornos was not even given the opportunity to consider keeping her child. One has to wonder how Wuornos's life would have been different if she had kept the baby and received the requisite support from her grandparents. On the other hand, if she had received support from her grandparents, she may not have needed to keep the baby. The support would have been evidence of acceptance.

Wuornos's life is a continuing demonstration of borderline personality disorder. She experienced loneliness and poor self-worth, and she self-medicated with alcohol and drugs to temporarily eliminate these feelings. The drug and alcohol abuse reduced her inhibition sufficiently to allow for promiscuous sexual conduct. Wuornos accepted the temporary physical lust, as it indicated that someone desired her and that she had worth. Her life was a revolving door of continuous failed relationships with men. It was not until she met Tyria Moore and developed a continuing lesbian relationship with her that she found love, affection, and acceptance. Further, Moore, who from description would probably be diagnosed with a dependent personality disorder, depended upon Wuornos for her existence. Moore liked being taken care of, and it was only when money was low that there were disturbances in their relationship.

Wuornos, fearful of losing Moore, recognized that she must make a living to support them. Wuornos's work experience was limited to cutting forged checks, theft, and prostitution. She also would have vividly remembered that forgery and theft are criminal acts that police will pursue, prosecutors will prosecute, and judges will punish with sentences of incarceration. On the other hand, prostitution is often considered a victimless crime and police will turn a blind eye to it as a criminal act. Furthermore, the demand exists. The decision was an easy one: continue to prostitute. Wuornos's disfigurement, hygiene, and general appearance prohibited her from commanding high prices like top-shelf call girls; however, there was constant demand from less affluent customers. Men are fully aware that a woman hitchhiking or looking for a ride at a truck stop or rest area is probably looking to arrange for more than a ride. Wuornos was not without customer demand. However, the aggregate income did not meet her alcohol dependency and Tyria Moore's demands. Consequently, the combination of theft and prostitution was the logical choice, but a dangerous choice.

Wuornos's first murder victim was Richard Mallory. Wuornos, to the very end, contended that the killing of Mallory was in self-defense. Although it was not submitted as evidence, Mallory had served 10 years in prison in another state for a violent rape. Following Mallory's murder, Wuornos was always armed with the .22 caliber pistol. The fear of assault, the need for additional cash, and leaving no witness to an armed robbery were driving forces in the Wuornos murders. Did Wuornos lack remorse for her murder victims? The numbers of gunshot wounds indicate that more shots were used than was necessary to kill the victims. Thus one must conclude that revenge toward men and rage were motivational forces, not sexual arousal.

Wuornos was able to elude apprehension due to her constant movement, her use of aliases, and the political structure of law enforcement in Florida at the time of her murders. County Sheriffs are the dominant law enforcement officials in Florida counties. The Florida Highway Patrol is merely that, a highway patrol that is not involved in criminal investigation. The Florida Department of Law Enforcement (FDLE) provides law enforcement support services—crime scene analysis, criminal investigation, and crime laboratory services—to small rural county sheriff departments and city police departments that have inadequate manpower and budgets for these services. However, the County Sheriff must request FDLE services, and the FDLE cannot assume jurisdiction. County Sheriffs are elected officials, who, in order to win reelection, must demonstrate to their constituency that they can competently perform their jobs and protect their Counties. Abdicating jurisdiction to the FDLE is not considered a viable alternative; consequently, investigation in small rural Counties is limited. The terrorist attacks of September 11, 2001, created new and effective law enforcement collaborations and jurisdictional cooperation; however, Wuornos committed her murders prior to 9/11.

The tragedy of Aileen Wuornos is twofold. She left a trail of murdered victims, but she was also victimized throughout her life. This does excuse her behavior. She was competent and made choices. However, it is evident that her life experiences precipitated the development of the borderline personality disorder that was the driving force behind her murders.

Bibliography and Suggested Reading

American Psychiatric Association. (2000). *Diagnostic and Statistical Manual of Mental Disorders* (Rev. 4th ed.). Arlington, VA: Author.

Arietta, R. (2001, July 7). Tearful Wuornos Ruled Competent by Judge. *Ocala Banner.*

Chesler, P. (1993). Sexual Violence against Women and a Woman's Right to Self Defense: The Case of Aileen Wuornos. *Criminal Practice Law Report 1*(9).

Dobbert, D. L. (2004). *Halting the Sexual Predators among Us.* Westport, CT: Praeger.

Dobbert, D. L. (2007). *Understanding Personality Disorders.* Westport, CT: Praeger.

Kelleher, M., & Kelleher, C. (2000). *Aileen Wuornos: Sexual Predator.* Chicago: Greenhaven.

Kennedy, D., & Robert, N. (1992). *On a Killing Day: The Bizarre Story of Convicted Murderer Aileen "Lee" Wuornos.* Santa Monica: Bonus.

Reynolds, M. (2003). *Dead Ends: The Pursuit, Conviction, and Execution of Serial Killer Aileen Wuornos, the Damsel of Death.* New York: St. Martin's.

Wuornos, A., & Berr-Dee, C. (2004). *Monster: My True Story.* London: Blake.

22

Joel Rifkin (1959–)

Joel Rifkin is considered the most prolific serial killer from New York. Rifkin confessed to the murder of 18 women between 1989 and 1993.

Joel Rifkin was born on January 20, 1959, to an unwed mother who placed him for adoption. He was adopted by Bernard and Jeanne Rifkin. Bernard was a structural engineer, and the couple lived comfortably in New City, New York. Following a second adoption, of a baby girl, the family moved to an exclusive neighborhood in East Meadow, Long Island. Joel and his sister Jan were raised and attended school in this well-off neighborhood with other children of privilege.

Bernard and Jeanne deeply loved and cared for Joel, and provided shelter from an abusive peer-group environment. They were active parents, serving on the parent-teacher association and the district school board. Joel, despite an above-average intelligence, did poorly in school, much to his parents' disappointment and embarrassment. Joel was unsuccessful in school because he was unsuccessful in life. Introverted and shy, he was the brunt of teasing and bullying throughout his elementary and secondary education. Growing up in an exclusive neighborhood in an era when athletes and "beautiful" people were admired and held the positions of popularity, Joel was an outcast. He was the classic "nerd," acting and dressing in a fashion that made him stand out as different from the mainstream students. He was everyone's target.

Bernard's disappointment and embarrassment over Joel resulted in conflict. Jeanne would share her gardening hobby with Joel, but was never fully cognizant of the torture he was receiving at the hands of his peers. At his parents' encouragement, Joel joined the high school track team; it was hoped that, despite not achieving academically or socially, he might find a modicum of self-worth through his participation in a noncontact sport. Unfortunately, the football players of the fall semester were the track stars of the spring sport, and Joel's humiliation only increased. He was subject to even more ridicule because he was not capable of competing with the athletic stars.

Joel quit the track team and served on the staff of the high school yearbook. The bullying would follow him, but he was committed to completing his responsibility, and finished the year. However, he was not invited to the party celebrating the completion of the yearbook, and this rejection was overwhelming. Despite the tremendous ridicule, Joel Rifkin graduated from East Meadow High School.

Rifkin's social life and dating were also negative experiences. The privileged girls of his high school followed the lead of the high school boys, and subjected him to ridicule and rejection. Even when he attempted to date, his privileged peers would find out and mercilessly tease him. Physically inferior and greatly outnumbered, Rifkin developed hermit-like behaviors to insulate himself from his cruel peers. He would later reveal his fantasies of inflicting rape and sexual sadism on these girls.

College brought little relief, despite Rifkin's attendance at a community college where he was not subject to the ridicule of his high school peers, who enrolled in distinguished colleges and universities. Rifkin, following his mother's interest in gardening, studied horticulture. His choice of curriculum once again fell outside of the perceived mainstream college experience, and he found little self-worth in this course of study. Rifkin moved from one college to another, gaining a few credits, between 1977 and 1978. Burdened with poor self-worth and depression, he bounced back and forth between menial jobs. He was never able to make sufficient income to keep an apartment, and he moved in and out of his parents' home.

What little money Rifkin was able to make, he spent on prostitutes. This newfound sexual experience became central to his thoughts and leisure life; however, his experiences with prostitutes were not entirely positive. Prostitutes would take his money and run off without providing the sexual service he had contracted. Some of the prostitutes and their pimps robbed him. He had little recourse. He certainly could not take his complaint to law enforcement, and he was physically unable to forcibly retrieve his stolen funds.

Bernard Rifkin became afflicted with prostate cancer, and committed suicide in February 1987. The death of his father deepened Joel Rifkin's depression, and his obsession with prostitutes also increased. He was able to ignore the fact that he was purchasing their affection, and fantasized at the physical pleasure he experienced with them. Rifkin was arrested in August of that year for soliciting prostitution from an uncover officer. His frustration increased, as he had been robbed by prostitutes and their pimps, and was now arrested for soliciting.

At his mother's encouragement, Rifkin enrolled in a horticulture program at a technical college in 1988, and experienced academic success resulting in his receiving an internship at the Planting Fields Arboretum in Oyster Bay, New York. His self-worth spiked with the honor, and at this high point in his life he met an attractive female intern. Rifkin fantasized about a relationship with her, and when it did not occur, he was traumatized, his self-worth dropped, and his depression increased. However, his response to his circumstances was different this time. Rather than internalizing his anger and frustration as he had always done in the past when rejected, he struck out, directing his anger at women. He channeled this anger and frustration at prostitutes. His anger toward prostitutes was both a response to the robberies he had experienced from them, and a transfer of his anger at the rejection and humiliation he had experienced from mainstream girls and women throughout his life. Prostitutes were available and accessible to Rifkin for him to release his anger and frustration.

Rifkin committed the first of his 18 murders in March 1989. What started out as his normal cruising to find a suitable prostitute to meet his needs ended up as his first lust homicide. Rifkin located a hard-core drug addict and prostitute on the street in the Village of Manhattan. After picking her up, he took her back to his mother's Long Island home. Following uneventful and unfulfilling sex, the woman asked Rifkin to take her out to look for drugs. Rifkin's pent-up fury was unleashed on this unsuspecting prostitute. He beat her and then strangled her to death in the living room of the house. As if in a post-seizure response, Rifkin went to sleep for several hours. Upon awaking, he assessed the situation and made preparations to hide his brutal murder. He thoroughly cleaned the living room of evidence, and took the prostitute's lifeless body to the basement, where, with surgical care, he dismembered the body. The dismemberment served not to fulfill Rifkin's sexual desires, but rather to hide the murder. Rifkin cut off his victim's fingers and pulled her teeth to make identification more difficult. He stuffed her decapitated head into a paint can and put the remaining body parts in plastic trash bags. He disposed of the head in the woods of a golf course in New Jersey, and threw the body parts in the East River. He did not expect the body to be found or identified.

However, the paint can containing the woman's head was found shortly thereafter by a golfer searching for his golf ball following an errant shot. The prostitute would never be identified. Her condition as positive for HIV was reported by the media. This information was a temporary deterrent for Rifkin; he did commit another murder for a year.

In late 1990, while Rifkin's mother was out of town, he picked up prostitute Julie Blackbird and drove her to his mother's house. After spending the night with Blackbird, Rifkin beat her unconscious and then strangled her to death. Determined not to have his victim discovered on this occasion, he dismembered the body and put the parts in buckets filled with concrete, which he then dropped into the East River and the Brooklyn canal.

In April 1991, Rifkin rented space and opened his own landscape company. He used his business revenue to support his addiction to prostitutes. He also used the rented space to dump murdered prostitutes' body parts. On July 31, 1991, he picked up 31-year-old addict and prostitute, Barbara Jacobs. He took her back to his mother's home, beat her unconscious, and then strangled her as he did Julie Blackbird. Not interested in spending the time to dismember the body, he packaged it up in a box, placed in the back of his mother's pickup truck, and disposed of it in the river. The body was found several hours later.

Unbelievably, the coroner ruled the death accidental due to a drug overdose. Apparently, drug-addicted prostitutes do not receive the same level of investigation as others; otherwise, the strangulation marks would have been discovered. Indeed, the number of addicts and prostitutes that are found dead in the New York metropolitan area is so high that law enforcement officials and medical examiners do not have the time or interest to carefully establish true causes of death. The addicts and prostitutes are a forgotten community within the large metropolitan area.

Rifkin picked up addict and prostitute Mary DeLucca, age 22, on September 1, 1991. He strangled DeLucca at a motel and then purchased a freight trunk to dispose of the body. He dumped the body out of the trunk at a rest area in upstate New York. The body was not discovered until October 1, and due to the advanced state of decomposition could not be identified. DeLucca was identified following Rifkin's confession.

Rifkin struck again in September 1991, strangling 31-year-old prostitute Yun Lee. He used the same freight trunk that he had used in disposing of DeLucca's body. He stuffed Lee's body in the trunk and dropped it into the East River, where it would be discovered before DeLucca's body. Rifkin strangled his sixth victim in his car, while she was performing fellatio, shortly before Christmas, 1991. He took the body to his rented landscape space. Rifkin stole a 55-gallon drum, wedged the body into the drum, and rolled it into the East River. This means of disposal delighted Rifkin, and, obviously premeditating future murders, he purchased additional barrels.

On December 26, Rifkin picked up prostitute and cocaine addict Lorraine Orvieto, age 28. He strangled her in his car as she performed fellatio on him, just as he had done to his previous victim a few days prior to Christmas. Rifkin stuffed Orvieto's body in a drum and deposited it in the Coney Island Creek, not to be found until July 11, 1992.

On January 2, 1992, one week after he murdered Lorraine Orvieto, Rifkin picked up prostitute Mary Holloman, age 39. Following the pattern that he had with the two previous prostitutes, he strangled Holloman as she performed fellatio. He stuffed Holloman into a barrel, and, using different rivers to keep law enforcement from recognizing the similarity in the crimes, dropped the barrel into Newton Creek.

Later, in the spring of 1992, with his business closed, Rifkin started taking university classes again. However, this activity was secondary to his lust for killing prostitutes. He picked up 25-year-old addict and prostitute Iris Sanchez in mid-May, 1992. He strangled Sanchez and dumped her body at an illegal dump site off the island. Sanchez would not be discovered until June 1993 following Rifkin's confession. Continuing on his spree, Rifkin picked up addict and prostitute Anna Lopez, age 33, on May 25, 1992. He strangled Lopez in his car and dumped her body, with less ceremony or planning than usual, next to an interstate highway. Lopez's body was found the next day by a motorist.

While demonstrating little concern for detection in his disposal of Lopez, Rifkin exercised great care in disposing of his next victim, 21-year-old Violet O'Neill. He returned to his mother's home to strangle O'Neill. He then dismembered her body, and disposed of the torso in the Hudson River, while he discarded the limbs in a suitcase.

On October 2, 1992, Rifkin picked up a prostitute that he had previously solicited, 31-year-old Mary Catherine Williams. He strangled Williams in his mother's car and dumped her body in Westchester County, where it was found on December 21, 1992. Rifkin's next victim, Jenny Soto, was picked up and strangled on November 16, 1992. Rifkin dumped Soto's body in the Harlem River, where it was discovered the next day.

Rifkin would not strike again until February 27, 1993, when he picked up 28-year-old addict and prostitute Leah Evans. Rifkin strangled Evans, and, in a gesture not given to his other victims, buried her in a shallow grave. Evans was discovered by hikers on May 9, 1993. Rifkin's next victim was Lauren Marquez, age 28. An addict and prostitute, she was picked up by Rifkin on April 2, 1993. Rifkin broke her neck while attempting to strangle her, and dumped her body in the woods in Suffolk County. Her body was not discovered until after Rifkin's confession.

Rifkin's final victim was Tiffany Bresciani. A heroin addict who prostituted to support her habit, Bresciani was picked up by Rifkin on June 24, 1993. He strangled her, bound her body in a tarp, and put her in the trunk of his mother's car. As Rifkin returned to his mother's home, his mother appeared and demanded her car back in order to run errands. Rifkin's mother took her car, ran her errands, and returned home without knowing the body was in the trunk. As if this near-detection by his mother was a traumatic experience, Rifkin removed the body from the trunk and moved it with a wheelbarrow to the backyard, where he left it untouched for the next three days. Oblivious to the decomposing body in the backyard, Rifkin worked on his pickup truck. On June 27, 1993, he placed the tarp-covered body in the bed of the truck, and drove off without license plates on the truck to dump the body. Rifkin was stopped by two law enforcement officers for failing to have license plates on the truck. The body was found, and Rifkin was arrested on site.

There is controversy whether Rifkin was denied the right of counsel. Regardless, he confessed to all 17 murders before his mother retained counsel. On June 29, 1993, Rifkin entered a plea of not guilty for the murder of Tiffany Bresciani. Defense counsel attempted a variety of motions to have Rifkin's confessions excluded. If the confessions could be excluded and not allowed into evidence, then all of the physical evidence, including the bodies, would also be inadmissible as illegally obtained "fruit of the poison tree." It was not until March 1994 that the presiding judge dismissed the defense motions. Rifkin's trial was scheduled for April 11, 1994.

The trial began as scheduled, and the defense entered a plea of not guilty by reason of insanity. Following a number of psychiatric evaluations, it was determined that Rifkin was sane and had knowingly committed the crimes. Despite the testimony of clinical witnesses for the defense that Rifkin was a paranoid schizophrenic, the jury concurred with the prosecution witnesses' diagnosis that Rifkin was afflicted with psychopathy and fully aware of his conduct. Rifkin was found guilty of the Brescani murder. He was also found guilty of the other murders in other jurisdictions, and his total sentence is imprisonment for 203 years to life.

EVALUATION

Joel Rifkin's diagnosis is relatively straightforward. As acknowledged in the court-ordered psychiatric evaluations, Rifkin is afflicted with psychopathy and sexual sadism. His behaviors clearly demonstrate the criteria for both diagnoses.

Rifkin exhibited no empathy for his victims or remorse for his behaviors. He is conscience-deficient, and it is this deficiency that allowed him to plan and commit his murders. Rifkin would plan in order to improve his murderous actions between each successive murder. Initially, he was concerned about detection, and carefully planned elaborate mechanism to dispose of the bodies. Over time, he came to realize that no one seriously investigates the death of a drug addict who prostitutes to support her habit. The media would provide news coverage of the discovery of a body, but the police and medical examiners would dismiss the death as a natural case of drug overdose rather than a wrongful death. Following this recognition, Rifkin stopped dismembering the bodies, as a dismembered body was an obvious sign of a wrongful death instead of a drug overdose.

In that all of Rifkin's murder victims were prostitutes that he contracted for sex, he derived pleasure from the sex received. He began by murdering the prostitutes after sex, and later found that he took greater pleasure in killing them while they were performing fellatio on him. Rifkin was recurrently, intensely sexually aroused over the delivery of pain to his victims. In the end, he derived pleasure in watching them die while he strangled them. With the early victims, Rifkin would beat them unconscious and then strangle them. He modified his approach when he was no longer sexually aroused by strangling the unconscious body.

While the comorbid diagnoses of psychopathy and sexual sadism are relatively straightforward, the etiology of Rifkin's pathology is somewhat unique and complex. Rifkin grew up in a hostile peer environment. He was the subject of ridicule from his male and female peers. He experienced this torture on a daily basis, and only through his mother's love, affection, and nurture was he able to endure the daily harassment. His mother offered unconditional acceptance of her son. She did not judge him for his eccentric mannerisms, but rather served as his shelter from his peers. This dependent relationship with his mother continued up to the day Rifkin was arrested for the murders. At the age of 34, Rifkin was still living with his mother, and she was rejecting him.

Rifkin developed deep resentment for his peers, and he knew from his high school experiences that he could retaliate against the males. He could not, however, retaliate against the girls who laughed at him and refused to date him. Most commonly, rejected introverted persons who experience torment such as Rifkin experienced turn the anger and aggression inward, and commit suicide. Rifkin chose to direct his anger and aggression at the perceived source of his torture, women. He also recognized that he could not specifically direct his actions at those specific persons who humiliated and ridiculed him. Therefore, he displaced his anger and aggression toward a class of women he could access and control: drug addicts who were prostituting to support their habits. This group of women also offered the additional perk of sex.

Bibliography and Suggested Readings

American Psychiatric Association. (2000). *Diagnostic and Statistical Manual of Mental Disorders* (Rev. 4th ed.). Arlington, VA: Author.

Clues Emerging in Slayings of N.Y. Prostitutes. (1993, July 1). *USA Today.*

Dobbert, D. L. (2004). *Halting the Sexual Predators among Us.* Westport, CT: Praeger.

Dobbert, D. L. (2007). *Understanding Personality Disorders.* Westport, CT: Praeger.

Eftimiades, M. (1993). *Garden of Graves.* New York: St. Martin's.

Kasindorf, J. R. (1993, August 9). The Bad Seed: Serial Killer Joel Rifkin's World. *New York, 26,* 38–45.

Mladinich, R. (2001). *From the Mouth of the Monster: The Joel Rifkin Story.* New York: Pocket.

Pulitzer, L., & Swirsky, J. (1994). *Crossing the Line.* New York: Berkley.

The Quiet Man. (1993, December 6). *People Weekly.*

23

Jeffrey Dahmer (1960–1994)

During the summer of 1991, people throughout the world watched with disbelief, disgust, and morbid fascination as the story of Jeffrey Dahmer unfolded in Milwaukee, Wisconsin. Authorities, wearing hazmat suits, removed human remains from Dahmer's apartment. They found full skeletons in his closet; a 55-gallon drum, used to hold decomposing body parts, in his bedroom; decomposing bodies hanging in his shower; hands and genitals in a lobster pot; skulls with decomposing flesh in the freezer; skulls scraped free of flesh in a filing cabinet; and a penis preserved in formaldehyde. This grisly crime scene brought international media attention to Jeffrey Dahmer.

Jeffrey Dahmer was born on May 21, 1960, to Lionel and Joyce Dahmer, in West Allis, Wisconsin. Jeffrey was the Dahmers' first born child. With Jeffrey still in infancy, Lionel, a chemist, moved the family to Iowa, where he was working on his PhD at Iowa State University. While residing in Iowa, Lionel found a pile of small animal bones under the house. Jeffrey was delighted with the new treasure and played with the bones. Lionel and Joyce had a volatile marriage, and the implications of this violence were observed in Jeffrey's early behavior. Early home movies of Jeffrey depict hyperactivity, incorrigibility, and displaced aggression in the form of violently beating trees with sticks. Following completion of his graduate work, Lionel found employment as a chemist in Akron, Ohio. Coinciding with the family's move, Jeffrey's younger brother was born. Jeffrey, a mere six years old, demonstrated significant sibling rivalry and disdain over the attention his brother was receiving. He manifested a change in behavior, shifting from being an exuberant active child to one that was shy, insecure, and fearful. The parental discord, the attention his younger brother received, and the move to a unfamiliar neighborhood precipitated this change in personality and disposition.

In 1968, when Jeffrey was eight years old, Lionel and Joyce moved the family again to a home on an acre of land in Bath, Ohio. Jeffrey began to exhibit bizarre behavior following this move. Lionel purchased a chemistry set for Jeffrey while on a sales trip. Jeffrey would spend countless hours with the chemistry set, experimenting with insects, small animals, and amphibians that he caught in the forest and pond of his home, and animals that been struck by vehicles on the road nearby. Jeffrey would use different chemicals to burn off the animals' skins. He would cut off the heads of animals, place the heads on pointed sticks, and position the sticks among a ring of fire in the woods. Jeffrey would also preserve animal body parts in formaldehyde, and he had a small cemetery in the woods on the property where he would bury the animal remains. He began to manifest these abnormal behaviors in elementary school, prompting his teachers to register concern. However, there were no attempts at intervention. Jeffrey also showed interest in human anatomy, and would persuade neighborhood children to remove their clothes so he could observe them and listen to their heartbeats.

During his high school years, Jeffrey maintained average grades, and played in the high school band and on the intramural tennis team. He was described as a "loner" with no close friends; however, he was commonly the center of attention as the "class clown." Although on the surface he appeared well-adjusted, Jeffrey was in turmoil. School records indicate that he was disciplined for faking a seizure in class, as well as for making animal sounds and disrupting the class. Jeffrey also had a serious drinking problem as a high school student, with others reporting that he was frequently drunk and even drank scotch from a paper cup in class. He appeared in the yearbook photograph of the National Honor Society although he was not a member.

Lionel and Joyce continued to fight through their marriage, and finally were divorced when Jeffrey was 18 years old. Both Lionel and Joyce fought for custody of Jeffrey's 12-year-old brother. Joyce received custody of Jeffrey's brother and then immediately moved out of state, living Jeffrey in the marital home alone, without food or money. This obvious rejection by both Lionel and Joyce had a significant impact on Jeffrey. Jeffrey was deeply involved in autoerotic behavior, in addition to his continuing experiments on roadkill animals. On one occasion, while searching for roadkill, he observed a jogger running up the road toward him. Jeffrey hid in the foliage on the side of the road with a club in hand. While he did not assault the jogger, he was sexually aroused at the thought of knocking the person unconscious and having sex with the still body.

On June 18, 1978, while living alone in the marital home, Jeffrey committed his first murder. He met hitchhiker Steven Hicks, 18 years old, and invited him back to his home. He and Hicks became drunk and engaged in sex. When Hicks attempted to leave, Jeffrey struck him with a barbell, killing him. Jeffrey dragged Hicks's lifeless body to the basement, where he dismembered the body, put the body parts in plastic bags, and buried them in his back yard.

Lionel remarried, and Shari, his new wife, registered concern over Jeffrey's alcoholism. They persuaded Jeffrey to enroll at Ohio State University in fall, 1978. Jeffrey stayed only for the fall semester, and was continuously drunk. Lionel gave Jeffrey an ultimatum, insisting that he either work or enlist in service. Jeffrey enlisted in the U.S. Army in early 1979. He served with the Army in Germany for two years, but was discharged short of his enlistment period as unsuitable for military service. Jeffrey was reportedly drunk most of the time and often belligerent. His alcoholism and self-imposed isolation deepened during his enlistment.

Following discharge from the Army, Jeffrey was arrested in October 1981 for drunken and disorderly conduct in West Allis, Wisconsin, where his father had moved him to live with his grandmother. Jeffrey began to exhibit strong homosexual tendencies. During this six-year period, he stole a department store mannequin, cruised the streets looking for young gay men, and contemplated exhuming a body from the graveyard. In 1986, he was arrested for exposing himself and masturbating in front of two 12-year-old boys, and was sentenced to probation. He continued to live with his grandmother and continued his behavior. It is believed that Jeffrey began his murder spree while he was residing with his grandmother. He would cruise the gay bars to find gay lovers, bring them back to his grandmother's house, drink heavily, and engage in sexual activity. It is suspected that he would also murder some of these young men after he was sexually gratified. In November 1987, Jeffrey awoke in a hotel room with a dead man, Steven Toumi, at his side. He bought a suitcase, dismembered the body, and took it back to his grandmother's basement. In early 1988, Jeffrey claimed his next victim, 14-year-old Jamie Doxtator. Lionel and his wife Shari visited Jeffrey at his grandmother's home, and were struck by the foul smell coming from her basement. Lionel excused the smell as part of Jeffrey's ongoing hobby of dissecting small animals and disposing of their decomposing remains. In the summer of 1988, Jeffrey's grandmother asked him to move out because of the smell and loud noise from Jeffrey and his male friends. It is believed that Jeffrey Dahmer murdered four young men while living with his grandmother.

Dahmer moved into an apartment in Milwaukee in September 1988. Shortly after moving into his apartment, he was charged with and convicted of sexually assaulting a 13-year-old Laotian boy. Dahmer offered the boy money to be photographed naked, drugged the boy, fondled him, and then released him. The boy's parents noticed their son's obvious drug-induced stupor, and took him to the hospital for examination. Dahmer was subsequently arrested at his job at Ambrosia Chocolate and convicted of sexual assault. He moved back in with his grandmother awaiting his sentencing on this charge. While on bond awaiting sentencing, he offered money to 24-year-old Anthony Sears, an African American model, to pose nude. Dahmer drugged and murdered Sears and had sex with the corpse. He then dismembered Sears's body, and boiled and preserved the skull. Dahmer would later confess that he kept victims' skulls to masturbate in front of them while remembering his sexual activity with these victims.

Dahmer was sentenced to five years of probation, incarcerated for the first year at the Milwaukee House of Corrections. Following his release after serving 10 months of the one-year sentence, he moved into an apartment in Milwaukee. On May 30, 1991, 14-year-old Konerak Sinthasomphone was found, naked, wandering the streets. Neighbors observed him running around naked and called 911. When the police arrived they found a tall man arguing with the women who had called 911. The man, Jeffrey Dahmer, told the police that Sinthasomphone was his 19-year-old gay lover, and had left after they had an argument. Sinthasomphone was drugged and incoherent. The police, believing Dahmer's story and intent upon releasing Sinthasomphone back into his care, were confronted by the neighbors who had called them. The police nonetheless took Sinthasomphone back to Dahmer's apartment, and, despite encountering a strange odor, left him with Dahmer, not interested in intervening in a gay couple's dispute. Later that night, Dahmer strangled Sinthasomphone, and had sex with and then dismembered the body, preserving the skull in memory of him. Following Dahmer's arrest, the police officers who left Sinthasomphone with him were fired from the department. However, they were reinstated with back pay after an appeal, and both were named officers of the year by the Fraternal Order of Police.

Jeffrey Dahmer would commit four more murders before he was apprehended two and a half months later:

- Matt Turner, age 20, June 30, 1991
- Jeremiah Weinberger, age 23, July 5, 1991
- Oliver Lacey, age 23, July 12, 1991
- Joseph Bradehoft, age 25, July 19, 1991

On July 22, 1991, Dahmer's murder spree came to an end. Two officers patrolling the Marquette University district of Milwaukee came upon a black man, Tracy Edwards, running down the street with handcuffs hanging from one wrist. The officers stopped the man, expecting him to be fugitive from an arrest, only to hear a story about a man attempting to handcuff him at an apartment. The officers took the man back to the apartment and were greeted by a tall, friendly, blond man. One officer remained with Dahmer and Edwards, while the other searched the apartment. In contrast to the malfeasance of the other Milwaukee officers on May 30, this officer noticed photographs of murdered victims and human remains. He hollered for his partner to cuff Dahmer, and, after a brief struggle, Dahmer was in police custody.

District Attorney Michael McCann charged Dahmer with 17 counts (later reduced to 15) of open murder in January 1992. In the face of solid evidence that he perpetrated the murders, Dahmer entered a plea of not guilty by reason of insanity. The jury was selected and seated by January 29, 1992. During the course of the trial, Dahmer's 160-page confession was read into evidence, thousands of photographs and evidentiary items were submitted to the court, and the psychiatrists for both the defense and prosecution debated Dahmer's sanity. Unwilling to continue with the trial, and against the instructions of his defense counsel, Dahmer changed his plea to guilty on July 13, 1992. The jury found him sane and guilty on all 15 counts of murder. He was sentenced to 15 consecutive life sentences, or 957 years.

Dahmer was remanded to the Wisconsin Department of Corrections and imprisoned at the Columbia Correctional Institution, Wisconsin's supermaximum security facility in Portage, Wisconsin. Initially placed in general population, Dahmer was moved to protective custody following an assault by an inmate. As protective custody is virtually a "lockdown" with no outside-the-cell privileges, Dahmer asked the Warden to place him on a work detail when the other prisoners were locked down. The Warden agreed, and on November 29, 1994, Jeffrey Dahmer was beaten to death by inmate Christopher Scarver. The decision to allow Dahmer out of protective custody for a work detail is perplexing, but not as strange as the subsequent decision to have Dahmer participate on a work detail with two other men—Jesse Anderson, who had murdered his wife and blamed it on African Americans, and Christopher Scarver, a schizophrenic.

EVALUATION

Jeffrey Dahmer attempted a plea of not guilty reason by reason of insanity. However, the jury found him sane and guilty of 15 murders. Lay persons obviously will question the sanity of a man who abducted, tortured, and killed at least 15 men while demonstrating no remorse for his behaviors or empathy for his victims and their families. However, it is exactly this lack of feeling that demonstrates that Dahmer was afflicted with psychopathy. Dahmer, as an adult, was intelligent and articulate; he was very manipulative and a pathological liar; and his conscience deficit allowed him to engage in whatever behaviors he needed to adopt to meet his intrinsic psychological needs. His egocentricity worked together with his conscience deficit in allowing him to perpetrate the horrors he inflicted on his victims with no remorse, empathy, guilt, or anxiety. He found his needs paramount to the needs, wants, and desires of his victims; his mantra was "if it feels good, do it." Finally, Dahmer was free of hallucinations and delusions associated with mental illness. He was completely aware of his behavior, and of the nature of right and wrong. His actions were thoroughly premeditated. He carefully planned out and implemented his actions, from abduction through assault, murder, and disposal of the body. He was also fully cognizant of his actions in preserving body parts of his victims, in memory of them and his sexual relationship with them. Dahmer clearly exhibited all of the requisite clinical criteria for a diagnosis of psychopathy.

Dahmer was also afflicted with the paraphilia of sexual sadism. He experienced recurrent, intense sexual arousal in his homosexual activity with his lovers. His sadism is demonstrated through his egocentric need to achieve his own sexual gratification. His arousal increased as he strangled the life out of his victims. If Dahmer had killed his victims merely to prevent them from identifying him, he would have murdered them in a less personal, intimate manner. Shooting with a gun lacks intimacy; murder with a knife brings a killer somewhat closer to a victim; and murder with a garrote allows the use of a tool, rather than the murderer's own hands, to stop the breathing of a victim. By contrast, strangling a victim with one's own hands while looking into his eyes is intimate and personal—and, in the case of Jeffrey Dahmer, sexually arousing.

Dahmer confessed that he had attempted chemical lobotomies, drilling holes in the skulls of his still-living victims and pouring acids onto the exposed brains. This was not because he was sexually aroused by the activity of drilling the holes, or by pouring the acid to produce pain and incapacitate his victims; rather, he was sexually aroused by the thought of being able to create his own sex slave or zombie who would stay with him forever. Because of Dahmer's attempts at chemical lobotomies, it is reasonable to contemplate that if a man had stayed with him as a consensual lover, meeting his intrinsic psychosexual needs, Dahmer may not have moved from victim to victim. Dahmer was obsessed over rejection and abandonment.

Dahmer also practiced mutilation, cannibalism, and necrophilia with the corpses of his victims. His preservation and display of body parts was not undertaken for the acquisition of trophies, as is popularly suggested. Rather, these body parts were kept and preserved in order that Dahmer could revisit his relationship with the lover and become sexually aroused and, subsequently, sexually gratified. Likewise, Dahmer ate body parts because he believed that it was the most intimate way he could keep his lover close to and part of him. This may appear as delusional, but for Dahmer it was not. He would revisit his relationship with a victim as he consumed that victim's body part. It was not a trophy—a physical demonstration of his conquest—but rather the most valued expression of his love for that victim.

What, then, was the etiology of Jeffrey Dahmer's psychopathy and sexual sadism? This author contends that Dahmer's pathology was directly related to the rejection he experienced in his formative years. Jeffrey Dahmer appears to have been a relatively normal preschool child despite the hostility he witnessed between his parents. His behavior began to spiral downward, and his personality and disposition began to change, following the birth of his younger brother when he was six years old. Jeffrey's father, Lionel, was busy with his career, and when home was fighting with his wife, Joyce. Joyce, after experiencing a difficult pregnancy and birthing with Jeffrey, had difficulty demonstrating love and affection to her child or her husband. Moreover, Lionel blamed Joyce's use of medications during her pregnacy as the source of Jeffrey's problems. At the time of the custody dispute for Jeffrey's younger brother, both Lionel and Joyce cited the other as an extremely neglectful parent.

At an early age, Jeffrey Dahmer exhibited poor self-worth because he believed he was a burden to his parents, a source of their violent arguments, and secondary to his younger sibling. His developing introversion and lack of confidence exacerbated his inability to find close companions among his peers, unless he was performing for them through bizarre behaviors. Dahmer became a recluse, and withdrew into his lifelong interest in animal anatomy and in "how things worked." Eventually, he found warm entrails pleasurable to touch and sexually arousing. This sexual arousal led to subsequent sexual gratification in autoerotic behavior. Dahmer transferred his autoerotic behavior into a gay sexual preference because the act of masturbating was comfortable and a common activity with men. Autoerotic behavior, and eventually homosexual behavior, was simple and could easily be shared with other men without complication. If Dahmer cruised in the right neighborhoods and frequented gay bars and lounges, he had no trouble identifying young men who had similar interests and proclivities.

Jeffrey Dahmer was looking for intimate companionship without rejection and abandonment. His motives are understandable, but his actions to achieve his goals were unacceptable.

Bibliography and Suggested Reading

American Psychiatric Association. (2000). *Diagnostic and Statistical Manual of Mental Disorders* (Rev. 4th ed.). Arlington, VA: Author.

Baumann, E. (1991). *Step into My Parlor: The Chilling Story of Jeffrey Dahmer.* Los Angeles: Bonus.

Dahmer, L. (1994). *A Father's Story.* New York: Morrow.

Davis, D. (1991). *The Jeffrey Dahmer Story: An American Nightmare.* New York: St. Martin's.

Davis, D. (1995). *The Milwaukee Murders: Nightmare in Apartment 213—A True Story.* New York: St. Martin's.

Dobbert, D. L. (2004). *Halting the Sexual Predators among Us.* Westport, CT: Praeger.

Dobbert, D. L. (2007). *Understanding Personality Disorders.* Westport, CT: Praeger.

The Little Flat of Horrors. (1991, August 5). *Time.*

Martingale, M. (1993). *Cannibal Killers.* New York: St. Martin's.

Masters, B. (1993). *The Shrine of Jeffrey Dahmer.* London: Hodder and Stoughton.

Pincus, J. (2001). *Base Instincts: What makes Killers Kill?* New York: Norton.

Schwartz, A. (1992). *The Man who could not Kill Enough.* New York: Kensington.

24

Richard Ramírez (1960–)

Richard Ramírez, nicknamed "the Night Stalker," terrorized southern California in the mid-1980s. On August 31, 1985, at the age of 25, Ramírez was arrested and charged with 13 murders, 5 attempted murders, 6 rapes, 2 kidnappings, 5 robberies, 14 burglaries, and a number of other counts of criminal sexual conduct. On September 2, 1989, Ramírez was convicted of 13 charges of first-degree murder and 30 other felonies. He was sentenced to execution for 19 capital offenses, and to six years' imprisonment each for the remaining felonies. His crimes were heinous, and they lacked the characteristic similarity in victimology common to most serial killers. Richard Ramírez was an equal-opportunity murderer, and his victims covered all age groups and both genders.

Richard was the youngest of five children born to Julian and Mercedes Ramírez. The eldest four children were born in Juarez, Mexico. Juarez, a border town, received fallout from the nuclear tests conducted in New Mexico in the early 1950s, and a disproportionate number of birth defects were reported in the Juarez and El Paso areas. Rubin, the eldest of the Ramírez children, was diagnosed as mentally retarded and displayed behavioral problems. Joseph, the next oldest child, was diagnosed with Collier's disease, which causes bones to grow at abnormal angles. Robert, the third child, was diagnosed with learning disabilities and placed in special education classrooms. After the birth of Ruth, the fourth and only female Ramírez child, the Ramírez family moved from Juarez to El Paso. Julian found work at the rail yard, and Mercedes was employed at a boot manufacturing company, where she was exposed to toxic chemicals used in the tanning process. Mercedes was pregnant with a fifth child, and her physician advised her to quit her employment or risk losing the baby. Mercedes left her job, and on February 29, Richard Ramírez was born with no apparent physical defects. His sister Ruth loved Richard as her own personal doll.

Richard was described as a hyperactive youngster who could never sit still and was in constant motion, commonly drawing him into conflict with other family members. At an early age, Richard was knocked unconscious by a swing at the park. His gash was treated and the attending physician did not believe there were any further health issues. In elementary school, Richard developed a seizure disorder. However, medical personnel did not prescribe medication for his condition, and indicated that he would grow out of it. Richard's family described his post-seizure behavior as long periods of staring with no talking or movement. Richard was a good student and a talented athlete, but following a seizure, a coach informed him that he could no longer play on the football team. This removal from the team devastated Richard, and he began to lose interest in school. Two of the Ramírez sons, Ruben and Robert, manifested the same violent temper as their father, Julian. Julian would deliver vicious beatings to Rubin and Robert. Rubin and Robert abused drugs, were behaviorally disordered in school, and committed breaking and entering. Neither finished high school, and both left home to escape their father's rage. Joseph and Ruth both married and left, thus leaving Richard alone at home as the only target of Julian's angry and violent outbursts. Richard would escape his father's beatings and sleep in the cemetery. He also accompanied Ruth's husband as he stalked the neighborhoods at night, peeking into the windows of people's houses.

Richard developed a close relationship with his cousin Miguel, a decorated Vietnam War veteran. He spent countless hours with Miguel, learning the tactics of a veteran soldier: stalking, camouflage, and killing and eviscerating animals. Miguel also talked to Richard about his sexual escapades during the war, and showed him explicit photos—including a series in which he first was engaged in sexual activity with a woman and next was holding her severed head. Miguel's wife was very angry with his behavior following his return from his tour of duty, and the couple would have violent arguments. During one argument in Richard's presence, Miguel became extremely angry, grabbed a gun, and murdered his wife. Miguel was found incompetent for trial and placed in a mental hospital. This incident had a significant influence on Richard. Having lost all interest in school, on a steady diet of marijuana, and driven by fear of his father's violent episodes, Richard moved to Los Angeles to live with his oldest brother, Rubin. Rubin was now a heroin addict and stole cars to support his habit.

Richard then returned to El Paso, began experimenting with other drugs, and became involved with the worship of Satan. He found employment at a hotel, and, with access to a master key, began to rob the rooms. He would also sneak into the rooms of women and watch them disrobe. On one evening he entered a woman's room, bound her, and attempted to rape her. Her husband came back to the room and Richard was arrested. Due to his age, the judge was lenient and the consequence minimal.

At the age of 18, Richard moved back to Los Angeles with the intent of supporting himself through the sale of marijuana. His lifestyle in Los Angeles was not the "high society" existence he believed he would achieve, but rather involved a disturbing relationship with the drug culture of the inner city. Richard continued to practice his worship of Satan. His drug of choice became cocaine, and he supported his habit through burglaries. It was during one of these burglaries that Richard committed his first murder. On June 28, 1984, he entered the home of 79-year-old Jennie Vincow, slashed her throat, and stabbed her repeatedly. Richard Ramírez's reign of terror had begun.

The next confirmed murder did not take place until March 1985, which in itself is an anomaly. Ramírez's brutal murder of Jennie Vincow, his serious drug habit, and his later recurrent sexual arousal over killing suggests that there were other murders in the interim, but none have been directly attributed to Ramírez. In March 1985, Ramírez attacked Maria Hernandez as she pulled her car into her apartment's parking garage. He fired a .22 caliber bullet at Hernandez, but the bullet, unknown to him, was deflected by her car keys. Hernandez faked death, and Ramírez proceeded to enter her apartment, where he found her roommate Dayle Okazaki hiding. Ramírez killed Okazaki with a close-quarter shot to the forehead.

Ramírez then drove to Monterey Park, where he attempted to pull Tsai-Lian Yu from her car. He shot Yu twice in the side and she died of her wounds. Witnesses described the assailant as tall and dark, possibly Hispanic. The murders were not recognized as connected, because they occurred in different locations and the victims were of different ethnic groups. Eight days later, Ramírez would strike again, entering the Whittier suburban home of Vincent and Maxine Zazzara. Vincent was sleeping on the couch and Maxine in the bedroom. Richard shot Vincent in the head and then proceeded to bind Maxine. Maxine struggled to acquire her husband's shotgun from under the bed, only to find it empty. Ramírez shot her three times, attempted to cut out her heart, cut out her eyes, and mutilated her pubic area. He left his shoeprint behind, and it was this piece of evidence that would eventually tie the murders together.

On April 15, Ramírez's mayhem continued as he broke into the home of William and Lillian Doi of Monterey Park. He shot William Doi in the face and beat him until he was unconscious. Ramírez then restrained 63-year-old Lillian Doi with thumb cuffs and raped her. Ramírez's possession of the thumb cuffs indicates that he intended to restrain a victim when he entered the house. William Doi died of his injuries en route to the hospital. Lillian Doi would recover from her injuries and provide law enforcement with a description of Ramírez.

On May 29, 1985, Ramírez broke into the home of Mabel Bell and her sister, Nettie Lang. He murdered Bell with a hammer, then raped and murdered Lang. Using red lipstick, he drew a pentagram on Bell's thigh and on the wall. Ramírez then drove to Burbank, where, on May 30, he entered the home of 41-year-old Ruth Wilson and her 12-year-old son. Ramírez sodomized Ruth while her son was locked in a closet, and then left without further injuring Ruth or her son. Ruth was able to describe her attacker.

The Los Angeles area was terrorized by these random heinous crimes. Ramírez moved his trail of death to Arcadia, where he would murder 28-year-old Patty Higgins and 75-year-old Louise Cannon. On July 5, Ramírez beat 16-year-old Whitney Bennett with a tire iron. Miraculously, Whitney would survive the vicious beating. Ramírez's shoe print was found at the scene.

On July 7, Ramírez returned to Monterey Park, where he murdered 61-year-old Joyce Nelson. Later that night, Ramírez broke into the home of 63-year-old Sophie Dickman. He bound her and attempted to rape her. He was unable to achieve sexual arousal and he left, sparing her life.

On July 20, Ramírez moved his mayhem to Glendale. Armed with a machete, Ramírez broke into the home of Max and Lela Kneiding, both 66 years of age. He shot them both and then mutilated their bodies with the machete. Moving to the community of Northridge, Ramírez entered the home of Christopher Peterson, age 38, and his wife Virginia, age 27. Christopher and Virginia were both shot in the head; however, Christopher remained capable of fighting, and Ramírez fled the scene. Both Christopher and Virginia survived the ordeal. Two days later, in the community of Diamond Bar, Ramírez broke into the home of Elyas and Sakina Abowath, murdering Elyas as he slept and then repeatedly raping Sakinah. Following Sakinah's description of the intruder, the police linked six of the murders, and the press dubbed the unknown serial killer "the Night Stalker."

Ramírez traveled to San Francisco to evade the authorities in the Los Angeles area. He entered the home of Peter and Barbara Pan. In typical form, he shot Peter Pan, age 66, and then attempted to rape Barbara Pan, age 64. Mrs. Pan was shot by Ramírez as she attempted to fight her attacker. Ramírez drew a pentagram on the wall, thus concerning the San Francisco police that the Los Angeles "Night Stalker" had moved to their locality. The Los Angeles police shared evidence with the San Francisco authorities. Unfortunately, in her haste to protect the community, San Francisco Mayor Dianne Feinstein provided too much detail to the press; information pertaining to Ramírez's weapons and the shoe print became public knowledge, and Ramírez discarded his incriminating possessions. A hotel manager called the San Francisco police and informed them that a man matching the killer's description had stayed at his hotel. Upon investigation, the police found a pentagram drawn on the bathroom door. The police received additional evidence from a man who indicated that he had purchased some jewelry from a man matching the description. The jewelry belonged to the Pans.

Richard Ramírez left San Francisco for Los Angeles and stopped in Mission Viejo, where he broke into the home of William Carns and his fiancée, Carol Smith. Ramírez shot Carns and then repeatedly sexually assaulted the bound Smith. As Ramírez left Carns's home, a witness wrote down the description and partial license plate number of the stolen vehicle Ramírez was driving. Ramírez abandoned the car, but the crime scene investigators were able to find one fingerprint that did not match the owner's. The print matched a print from the Pans' home and one from the San Francisco hotel. The state crime lab put a name to the fingerprint: "the Night Stalker" was Richard Ramírez.

The Los Angeles police flooded the media with sketches of Ramírez, and on August 31 he was observed by citizens, who pursued and subdued him until the police could take him into custody. Ramírez was convicted on September 20, and sentenced to death on November 7, 1989. The California Supreme Court upheld the conviction and death sentence on August 7, 2006. Ramírez sits on death row at San Quentin awaiting his execution.

EVALUATION

On the surface, Ramírez's psychopathy, comorbid with sexual sadism, is obvious. However, a careful examination of his behavior demonstrates his passion for lust homicide. His lack of conscience is evident, as well as his lack of remorse and empathy for his victims. The randomness of his victims defies analysis, as does the heinous nature of his brutality. Sexual sadists generally have preferred age and gender groups, and their sexual arousal is enhanced by their specific fantasy group. Consequently, the prediction of future behavior is possible. This was not the case with Richard Ramírez.

Ramírez appears to have been sexually aroused by the brutality of his attacks, not by his victim's age. During his murderous spree, he sexually assaulted women as young as 16 and as old as 75. He would mutilate the corpses and sexually assault the dead women. This author contends that Ramírez was not a necrophiliac, but that his assault on a victim's corpse was instead a continuation of his assault on the living person. He did not kill to keep from being identified, or he would have not spared the lives of any of his victims. He may have been more sexually aroused by murder than by rape.

The etiology of Ramírez's pathology is multifaceted. He was severely abused by his father, a serious substance abuser, and was a professed worshiper of Satan. Ramírez's cousin Miguel played a significant role in his psychological development. Ramírez admired his cousin for his military service, and was influenced by Miguel's demonstration of pleasure in his sexual activity with and murder of the young woman in Vietnam.

Bibliography and Suggested Readings

American Psychiatric Association. (2000). *Diagnostic and Statistical Manual of Mental Disorders* (Rev. 4th ed.). Arlington, VA: Author.

Carlo, P. (1996). *The Night Stalker: The Life and Crimes of Richard Ramírez.* New York: Kensington.

Dobbert, D. L. (2004). *Halting the Sexual Predators among Us.* Westport, CT: Praeger.

Dobbert, D. L. (2007). *Understanding Personality Disorders.* Westport, CT: Praeger.

Holmes, R. M., & Holmes, S. T. (1998). *Serial Murder.* Thousand Oaks: Sage.

Lane, B., & Greg, W. (1992). *The Encyclopedia of Serial Killers.* New York: Berkley.

Lester, D. (1995). *Serial Killers: The Insatiable Passion.* Philadelphia: Charles Press.

Linedecker, C. L. (1991). *Night Stalker: A Shocking Story of Satanism, Sex, and Serial Murders.* New York: St. Martin's.

Marshall Cavendish. (1991). The Night Stalker. *Murder Casebook 7*(101). London: Author.

Miller, T. (1989, November 7). The Night Stalker Verdict. *USA Today.*

Newton, M. (1990). *Hunting Humans.* Washington: Loompanics Unlimited.

Newton, M. (1992). *Serial Slaughter.* Washington: Loompanics Unlimited.

Newton, M. (1999). *The Encyclopedia of Serial Killers.* New York: Checkmark.

Norris, J. (1989) *Serial Killers.* New York: Doubleday.

Seltzer, M. (1998). *Serial Killers: Death and Life in America's Wound Culture.* New York: Routledge.

25

Lessons for Future Prevention

This comparative analysis of the pathologies of 22 serial killers provides the opportunity to draw some conclusions about patterns and similarities among them.

While most law enforcement investigators indicate that serial killers do not have similar patterns of behavior, this analysis has demonstrated the contrary. 18 of the 22 killers have exhibited behaviors that are symptomatic of the diagnostic criteria of antisocial personality disorder, referred to as psychopathy in this study. Further, it has been demonstrated that all of the serial killers evaluated in this study were afflicted with one or more sexual paraphilias or disorders.

The diagnostic criteria for psychopathy, as delineated in chapter two, are explicit. Each criterion has behavioral manifestations that are readily observable. Further, each of these behavioral manifestations has precursor behaviors that are readily observable. In order for a person to be diagnosed with psychopathy, they must demonstrate their failure to conform to social norms. Failure to conform to social norms falls on a continuum, from minimum conformity at one end to law violations on the other end. Law violations also fall on a continuum, from minor violations on one end to serial murder at the other end. Consequently, one may assess the level of severity of nonconformity through observation of the manifested behavior and of the person's response to his or her behavior. A man may demonstrate infidelity with empathy for his spouse at one end of the nonconformity continuum, or infidelity with multiple mistresses, no empathy for the victims, and no remorse for his behavior when detected at the other end of the continuum. Similarly, a person may demonstrate no remorse for filing a false tax return on one end of the law violation continuum, or may commit murder with no remorse at the opposite end. In both examples, the level of severity of the manifested behavior can be ascertained, and by continuing to observe, one can determine whether the nonconformity and law violations increase in severity.

It is not necessary to wait for severe violations of law to register concern about individuals' developing pathology. Persons afflicted with psychopathy do not wake up one morning with a plan to commit murder. Rather, they grow into it from less severe behaviors. Unless a person is experiencing a psychotic break, their behavior has motivation. The motivation that drives all behavior is the acquisition of pleasure or the reduction of discomfort. Each person has a set of pleasures that meet their intrinsic psychological needs, and is motivated to acquire them. In acquiring these pleasures that meet their intrinsic psychological needs, each person evaluates the rewards and punishments associated with acquiring these pleasures. The man who chooses infidelity has determined that the pleasures derived through his intimate relationship with another outweigh the consequences he may have to face if detected. The pleasure he derives is worth the risk, and, accordingly, he carefully plans to reduce the possibility of detection and the ensuing consequences.

The decision is easier if the person is conscience–deficient, as is the case in psychopathy. In the absence of conscience, a person experiences no anxiety, guilt, or remorse over his behavior. He possesses no empathy for the impact of his behavior on his wife, children, or mistress—and these are persons he allegedly loves. His egocentricity empowers his sense of entitlement. His needs, wants, and desires are of paramount importance, and the needs, wants, and desires of others are insignificant and irrelevant. Thus such a person's pathology allows him to do whatever he wants.

An interesting aspect of psychopathy is that the behaviors that are desirable and that manifest pleasure change over time. Behaviors that were previously pleasurable no longer provide the same level of gratification, and thus greater levels of stimulation are required to achieve this level of gratification. Similarly, for a heroin addict, the volume of heroin required to achieve the desired state increases with time. The heroin addict analogy is appropriate because the addict not only needs additional heroin to achieve the desired state, but also finds it necessary to reduce the discomfort of withdrawal. The man practicing infidelity will tire of his partner and require more excitement, which may come in the form of a new mistress.

A man afflicted with psychopathy intent upon arranging an intimate relationship with another woman will exhibit early behaviors that forecast his intent. A spouse can therefore predict her husband's infidelity by recognizing these precursor behaviors. The husband will demonstrate less interest than is normal in his home and family, and increased interest in other women, which manifests as flirtatious behaviors with others' wives and with office personnel. The husband that flirts with others' wives in the presence of his wife is demonstrating a lack of respect for his wife. He does not care if his wife is embarrassed or insulted by his conduct, and will dismiss her concerns as the "absurd jealousy of a hysterical, irrational woman." Confronting him may result in an aggressive outburst or a manipulative retreat; each is an effective mechanism to keep his wife at bay. This husband is demonstrating a lack of empathy for his wife's feelings and no remorse over his behavior. His intrinsic psychological needs have been met by his flirting with the other woman, and his wife's needs, wants, and desires are insignificant and irrelevant, and, thus, dismissed.

The alert wife recognizes these precursor behaviors and responds accordingly, preparing herself for the potential of more serious nonconformist behavior from her husband. The wife who presents a fresh set of consequences for her husband may be successful in deterring his behavior. If the wife contacts an attorney and makes provisional plans for a legal separation, she has raised the bar of consequences and puts the ball back in her husband's court. Now he must reevaluate the pleasure principle. He does not modify his behavior because he experiences remorse for hurting his wife's feelings. He modifies his behavior because he finds its potential consequence of divorce, alimony, and child support discomforting, and he would rather change his infidelity behavior than face this consequence.

Psychopathy is a personality disorder that is chronic and lifelong. Consequently, this husband will still need to meet his intrinsic psychological needs and evaluate alternative behaviors. It is the foolish wife who believes that his behavior has changed. He has only modified it to reduce the potential of detection. The narcissism inherent in psychopathy dictates that, in his mind, the husband is smarter than anyone else, and just needs to think and act accordingly.

This example of infidelity is transferable to other less serious and more serious manifestations of psychopathy. There will always be precursor behaviors. A sense of entitlement permits the psychopath to begin stealing by falsifying IRS documents. This behavior, *sans* consequences, will worsen, because it is pleasurable to have additional spendable income and there is no consequence for the behavior.

Psychopathy becomes more serious if the afflicted individual is predisposed to the use of aggression and violence to acquire his desired results. Such behavior is commonly learned, sometimes through observation. The adolescent who observes his father punch his mother when she berates him for coming home drunk learns that this behavior achieves his father's desire to shut up his mother. He also observes that there is no consequence for the behavior. Consequently, he himself uses this behavior to achieve his desired results with his girlfriend. The young woman who is a victim of dating violence needs to recognize that this behavior is a precursor behavior for domestic violence in a marital union.

Psychopathy is extremely dangerous when it coexists with sexual pathology. A man afflicted with psychopathy, predisposed to aggressive behavior, and obsessed with sex develops a pathological relationship with his own sexuality. This man becomes recurrently, intensely sexually aroused by the delivery of humiliation and pain to his partner or victim. His intrinsic psychological needs are being met through the forcing of sexual activity. When the young woman has determined that she wishes to halt the advancing sexual encounter, the psychopathic male forces her into sex without consent. His needs are paramount. Hers are irrelevant and insignificant.

In the absence of consequences, the psychopathic male's sexual desires are fueled, and the extremity of his sexual encounters must increase to meet his growing need for greater excitement. Few will ever be the victim of abduction, rape, and lust homicide; however, many will experience the aggressive nature of a person afflicted with psychopathy and a sexual pathology. Recognition of the precursor behaviors is requisite for the development of safe intimate relationships.

This study has demonstrated that psychopathy allows a person to do whatsoever they please, and that, in the case of lust homicide, sexual pathology is the motivating force that determines the modus operandi that meets the individual's intrinsic psychological needs. A person who commits lust homicide has left a trail of precursor behaviors behind him. Careful examination of the nature and method of the criminal behavior assists in understanding the intrinsic psychological needs of the perpetrator. By understanding these intrinsic psychological needs, one can predict the future behavior the person will exhibit.

As demonstrated, serial killers commit lust homicide. Before they commit their first lust homicide, they have committed less serious precursor behaviors that met their intrinsic psychological needs, and this pathology was observable and definable. By recognizing the behavioral patterns delineated in this study and comparing them to evidence from crimes, informed decisions regarding investigation, apprehension, plea bargaining, and sentencing can be made. The potential to decrease the incidence of sexual assault and lust homicide exists.

Index

About the Series

In this series, experts delve into a broad range of psychological perspectives that can be applied to the criminal justice system. The forensic psychology illuminated here includes approaches to law and legislative issues, public policies, police and detective systems and policies, and court issues including competency and temporary insanity. Forensic psychology can be applied in its various forms to areas ranging from determining treatment for mentally ill offenders, to analyzing a criminal's mind or intent, to consulting with attorneys on jury selection.

ABOUT THE SERIES EDITOR AND ADVISERS

Series Editor DUANE L. DOBBERT is a 39-year veteran of the criminal justice profession. A Professor of Criminal Forensic Studies at Florida Gulf Coast University, and an Adjunct Professor in the School of Human Services at Capella University, he is a Fellow of the American College of Forensic Examiners and a Diplomate of the American Board of Psychological Specialties. Dr. Dobbert is also a Juvenile Court Administrator with the National Council of Juvenile and Family Court Judges, and a certified Social Worker. As President of Forensic Consulting and Training, he has consulted in more than 300 criminal justice jurisdictions across the United States. He developed and presented training programs pertaining to the nature and identification of sexual predators to law enforcement officers, educators, mental health counselors, and attorneys. Dr. Dobbert has also authored a program and trained thousands in that program, School Bus Drivers: The First Line of Defense against Sexual Predators. He is also an active member of Child Abduction Response Teams in Florida and Indiana. Dobbert's books produced by Praeger Publishers include *Understanding Personality Disorders and Halting the Sexual Predators among Us: Preventing Attack, Rape, and Lust Homicide.*

Adviser DANIEL BRUCE KENNEDY is a Professor in the Department of Criminal Justice and Security Administration at the University of Detroit, Mercy, and Principal Consultant to Forensic Criminology Associates, Inc. in Troy, Michigan. He is a Certified Sociological Practitioner, Licensed Social Worker, Certified Protection Professional, and Certified Police Academy Instructor. In previous roles, Dr. Kennedy was Head of Research and Development at the Wayne State University Criminal Justice Institute, and Director of the Criminal Justice Program at the College of the Virgin Islands, St. Thomas.

He has also served as a Visiting Lecturer at the FBI Academy at Quantico. Kennedy has been a consultant on crime- and security-related issues for media including CNN, the Associated Press, 20/20, and the Detroit News. He serves as Chair of the Ethics Committee for the Academy of Behavioral Profiling, and Co-Chair of the Jail Suicide Task Force for the American Association of Suicidology. His work has been widely published in journals including *Crime and Delinquency, Professional Psychology, Journal of Police Science and Administration Police Quarterly, American Jails, Journal of Criminal Justice,* and others. He began his career as a civilian crime analyst with the Detroit Police Department in 1966.

Adviser GARY F. MEUNIER is President of Diagnostics, Inc., a private organization dedicated to providing expert psychodiagnostic and psychiatric assessments in forensic and industrial settings. He is a Fellow of the American College of Forensic Examiners and a Diplomate in forensic personality assessment of the American Board of Psychological Specialties. He has published widely in the area of forensic assessment and has qualified as an expert witness in local, state, and federal courts. Dr. Meunier is currently Emeritus Professor of Psychology at Ball State University, having served 37 years in various faculty and administrative positions, and he has also served on the faculties of Oklahoma State University (Department of Psychology) and the Indiana University Medical School (Department of Psychiatry). Dr. Meunier has been Managing Partner of a large private mental health center, Staff Psychologist at two state mental hospitals, and Intake Psychologist at a state women's prison. He has created and directed mental health programs in jails and secure adolescent treatment facilities. Dr. Meunier has provided training and consulting services to many different forensic organizations throughout his career and continues to do so today. He has been granted honorary life membership in the Indiana Sheriff's Association and has also received specific honors for his work at suicide prevention in jails and prisons from the American Correctional Association.

Adviser PAMELA K. S. PATRICK is a Clinical Psychologist and Registered Nurse, and Academic Director for Colloquia at Capella University. Having worked 15 years as a Clinical and Consulting Psychologist, she also served as Executive Director, Dean, and on the Faculty at the School of Human Services, Capella University. She has also served as Clinical Director for Child and Adolescent Services at Atlantic Shores Hospital, as Director of Psychological Services at Halifax Medical Center, as Director of Psychological Services at North Mississippi Medial Center, and as Assistant Chief for Nursing Services at the Veterans Administration at Bay Pines.

About the Author

Duane L. Dobbert is Series Editor for the Praeger Series in Forensic Psychology, a Full Professor of Criminal Forensic Studies at Florida Gulf Coast University, a Fellow of the American College of Forensic Examiners, and a Diplomate of the American Board of Psychological Specialties. He has been a Forensic Behavioral Analyst over 39 years and has served as consultant for law enforcement departments throughout the United States, Europe, and Asia. He authored *Forensic Psychology* (1996), *Halting the Sexual Predators among Us* (Praeger, 2004), and *Understanding Personality Disorders* (Praeger, 2007).

Lightning Source UK Ltd.
Milton Keynes UK
UKOW06n1912170216

268588UK00016B/319/P